SAT®
Writing Workbook

Fifth Edition

RELATED KAPLAN TITLES FOR COLLEGE-BOUND STUDENTS

AP Biology
AP Calculus AB & BC
AP Chemistry
AP English Language & Composition
AP English Literature & Composition
AP Environmental Science
AP European History
AP Human Geography
AP Macroeconomics/Microeconomics
AP Physics B & C
AP Psychology
AP Statistics
AP U.S. Government & Politics
AP U.S. History
AP World History

ACT Strategies, Practice, and Personalized Feedback with 8 Practice Tests
ACT 6 Practice Tests with 12 Video Tutorials
ACT English and Reading Workbook
ACT Math and Science Workbook
ACT Strategies for Super Busy Students

SAT Strategies, Practice, and Review
SAT Premier
12 Practice Tests for the SAT
SAT 2400
SAT Math Workbook
SAT Writing Workbook
SAT Strategies for Super Busy Students

Frankenstein: A Kaplan SAT Score-Raising Classic
The Tales of Edgar Allan Poe: A Kaplan SAT Score-Raising Classic
Dr. Jekyll and Mr. Hyde: A Kaplan SAT Score-Raising Classic
The Scarlet Letter: A Kaplan SAT Score-Raising Classic
The War of the Worlds: A Kaplan SAT Score-Raising Classic
Wuthering Heights: A Kaplan SAT Score-Raising Classic
SAT Subject Test: Biology E/M

SAT Subject Test: Chemistry
SAT Subject Test: Literature
SAT Subject Test: Mathematics Level 1
SAT Subject Test: Mathematics Level 2
SAT Subject Test: Physics
SAT Subject Test: Spanish
SAT Subject Test: U.S. History
SAT Subject Test: World History

SAT®
Writing Workbook
Fifth Edition

By the Staff of Kaplan Test Prep and Admissions

KAPLAN

PUBLISHING

New York

SAT® is a registered trademark of the College Board, which neither sponsors nor endorses this product.

This publication is designed to provide accurate and authoritative information in regard to the subject matter covered. It is sold with the understanding that the publisher is not engaged in rendering legal, accounting, or other professional service. If legal advice or other expert assistance is required, the services of a competent professional should be sought.

© 2014 Kaplan, Inc.

Published by Kaplan Publishing, a division of Kaplan, Inc.

395 Hudson Street

New York, NY 10014

Printed in the United States of America

July 20114

10 9 8 7 6 5 4 3 2 1

ISBN-13: 978-1-61865-563-9

Kaplan Publishing books are available at special quantity discounts to use for sales promotions, employee premiums, or educational purposes. For more information or to purchase books, please call the Simon & Schuster special sales department at 866-506-1949.

Contents

AVAILABLE ONLINE

FOR ANY TEST CHANGES OR LATE-BREAKING DEVELOPMENTS

kaptest.com/publishing

The material in this book is up-to-date at the time of publication. However, the College Board may have instituted changes in the test after this book was published. Be sure to read the materials you receive when you register for the test. If there are any important late-breaking developments—or any changes or corrections to the Kaplan test prep materials in this book—we will post that information online at **kaptest.com/publishing.**

FEEDBACK AND COMMENTS

kaplansurveys.com/books

We'd love to hear your comments and suggestions about this book. We invite you to fill out our online survey form at kaplansurveys.com/books. Your feedback is extremely helpful as we continue to develop high-quality resources to meet your needs.

For customer service, please contact us at **booksupport@kaplan.com.**

How to Use This Book

Welcome to the SAT Writing section and Kaplan's program for getting you your highest Writing score possible. No hype, no frills—everything in this book will help you get results. Here's how:

- We show you how to write the kind of essay that SAT graders give their highest score. It's not just about being able to write well; it's also about being organized.
- We give you strategies for tackling all of the Writing section's multiple-choice questions.
- We provide many opportunities for you to practice, practice, practice. We also offer strategies and easy-to-remember tips to help you on test day!

Kaplan has been helping students improve their scores on standardized tests for more than 60 years. Plus, we are a *huge* company. No other test-prep company has our long history and our resources.

So how will this help you score higher? We know the SAT like the backs of our many hands. Our strategies have been raising students' SAT Writing scores for years.

Proper preparation is the key to improving your score on the Writing section. This is why we *strongly suggest* you use this book.

TAKE A PRACTICE TEST

Take one of our Practice Tests *before* you work your way through this book. That will give you a benchmark score, so you can see how much you improve after working through this book. It doesn't take long to take a Practice Test—under an hour—and it's well worth it.

MEET THE WRITING SECTION

Find out what you need to know about the Writing section—what kinds of questions are on it, how it's scored, and the best way for you to approach it. This gets your brain in SAT Writing mode.

ACE THE ESSAY

We start you off with the essay section—the section most students are most afraid of. We show you that writing a high-scoring essay is more like building a birdhouse than writing like Shakespeare. Take it one popsicle stick at a time.

MASTER THE MULTIPLE-CHOICE

After that, we dissect the Writing section's multiple-choice questions on Identifying Sentence Errors, Improving Sentences, and Improving Paragraphs. Using Kaplan's techniques, you will score higher on these sections even if you don't learn every single thing there is to know about grammar or correct sentence construction. It's all in your approach.

TEST AGAIN

It's time to put it all to use and take another Practice Test. How much better was your score?

EVALUATE YOUR STRENGTHS AND WEAKNESSES

Read through the answers and explanations for the questions you got wrong on both of your Practice Tests. Go back to the book and review any sections you still feel shaky on.

TEST ONE LAST TIME

Take your third Practice Test. Score it. And you're done. Your score will be better. You will feel better. And you will be more confident on test day!

SAT Writing Essentials

Chapter One: **Strategy Overview**

Here is a breakdown of the entire SAT, from start to finish.

FORMAT AND TIME

The SAT is 3 hours and 45 minutes long.

The Math Section

There are two kinds of questions on the Math section: **Regular Math** questions, which are straightforward multiple-choice questions with five answer choices, and **Grid-ins**, which require you to write your response in a little grid. Grid-ins test the same math concepts as Regular Math questions—they're just a different kind of question.

Math questions will be arranged in order of difficulty. The first few questions in a set will be fairly easy, the middle few questions a little harder, and the last few the most difficult. Keep this in mind as you work.

The Critical Reading Section

The Critical Reading section contains three types of questions:

Sentence Completion questions test your ability to see how the parts of a sentence relate to each other. They are basic fill-in-the-blank questions. About half the time you'll have to fill in one blank, and half the time you'll have to fill in two. Both types test vocabulary and reasoning skills.

Sentence Completion questions will also be arranged in order of difficulty. The first few questions in a set will be fairly easy, the middle few questions a little harder, and the last few the most difficult. Keep this in mind as you work.

Short Reading Comprehension questions test your ability to understand a short piece of writing. You are given a short passage of around 100 words and are asked a couple of questions about the text.

Long Reading Comprehension questions test your ability to understand a longer piece of writing. The passages here are a few paragraphs long. You'll be asked about such things as the main idea, contextual references, and vocabulary. There will be several reading passages in total; of those, one will be a set of two related readings, which you'll be asked to compare and contrast.

Reading Comprehension questions are *not* arranged in order of difficulty. The passages are all time-consuming to read, so you need to keep moving at a good pace. If you find yourself spending too much time on a Reading Comp question, skip it and come back to it later. The next question may be a lot easier.

Most Reading Comprehension questions test how well you understand the passage, some make you draw conclusions, and some test your vocabulary.

The Writing Section

The Writing section is broken into two parts: an essay (that you compose) and multiple-choice questions. The essay tests your ability to organize and communicate ideas clearly in response to a given topic (a prompt). The multiple-choice questions test your grasp of grammar, usage, and vocabulary.

The essay assignment comes first. In fact, it is the very first section on the test. You'll have 25 minutes for that. As for the multiple-choice questions that come in later sections, those will test whether you can recognize—and in most cases fix—errors in the grammar, diction, and structure of sentences and paragraphs.

Experimental Section

Each test will have an extra 25-minute Math, Critical Reading, or Writing section that is not included in calculating your personal score. This section is used to evaluate new test questions and to calibrate the test. The experimental section is not labeled and may appear at any point in the test. Approach every section as if it counts toward your score, even if you suspect that it is the experimental section.

GENERAL SAT STRATEGIES

Now that you know some basics about how the test is set up, you can approach each section with a plan. Kaplan has an eight-step method for handling all SAT questions:

1. Think about the question first.
2. Pace yourself.
3. Know when a question is supposed to be easy or hard.
4. Move around within a section.
5. Be a good guesser.
6. Be a good gridder.
7. Manage your time (so it doesn't manage you!).
8. Two-minute warning: locate quick points.

Note: These steps work for the multiple-choice questions in the Writing section. But there is a different approach we suggest you take with the essay.

1. Think About the Question First

Before you look at the answer choices, consider the question. The people who write the SAT put distractors among the answer choices. Distractors are answer choices that look right, but aren't. If you jump into the answer choices without thinking about what you're looking for, you're much more likely to fall in a test writer's trap. So always think for a second or two about the question—before you look at the answers.

2. Pace Yourself

The SAT gives you a lot of questions to answer in a short period of time. To get through a whole section, you can't spend too much time on any one question. Keep moving through the test at a good speed. If you run into a hard question, circle it in your test booklet, skip it, and come back to it later if you have time.

3. Know When a Question Is Supposed to Be Easy or Hard

Some sections will have their multiple-choice questions arranged in order of difficulty. In other words, the questions get harder as you move through the problem set. Here's a breakdown:

		Arranged Easiest to Hardest?
Math	Regular Math	Yes
	Grid-ins	Yes
Critical Reading	Sentence Completions	Yes
	Short Reading Comprehension	No
	Long Reading Comprehension	No
Writing	Essay	N/A
	Usage	No
	Sentence Correction	No
	Paragraph Corrections	No

As you can see, all question sets in Math are arranged in order of difficulty, as are Sentence Completions in Critical Reading. As you work through a section that is organized this way, *be aware of where you are in a set*. When working on the easy questions, you can generally trust your first impulse—the obvious answer is likely to be right. As you get to the end of the set, you need to be more suspicious of "obvious" answers, because the answer should not come easily. If it does, look at the question again because the obvious answer is likely to be wrong. It may be one of those distractors—a wrong answer choice meant to trick you.

Hard SAT questions are usually tough for two reasons:

- Their answers are not immediately obvious.
- The questions do not ask for information in a straightforward way.

Here's an easy question:

> Known for their devotion, dogs were often used as symbols
> of ------- in Medieval and Renaissance painting.
>
> (A) breakfast
> (B) tidal waves
> (C) fidelity
> (D) campfires
> (E) toothpaste

The correct answer, *fidelity*, (C), probably lunged right out at you. This question would likely be at the beginning of a problem set. Easy questions are purposely designed with obvious answer choices.

Here is virtually the same question, made hard:

> Known for their -------, dogs were often used as symbols of
> ------- in Medieval and Renaissance painting.
>
> (A) dispassion . . bawdiness
> (B) fidelity . . aloofness
> (C) monogamy . . parsimony
> (D) parity . . diplomacy
> (E) loyalty . . faithfulness

This question would likely be at the end of a problem set. This time the answer is harder to find. For one thing, the answer choices are far more difficult. In addition, the sentence contains two blanks.

The answer is (E). Did you fall for (B) because the first word is *fidelity*? Choice (B) is a good example of a distracter.

4. Move Around Within a Section

On a test at school, you probably spend more time on the hard questions than you do on the easy ones, since hard questions may be worth more points. *Do not do this on the SAT.*

Easy problems are worth as many points as the tough ones, so do the easy problems first. Work through the ones you can. But don't rush through them just to get to the hard ones. Remember, all the questions are worth the same number of points. When you run into a question that looks tough, circle it in your test booklet and skip it for the time being. (Make sure you skip it on your answer grid, too.)

Then, if you have time, go back to it *after* you have answered the easier ones. Sometimes, after you have answered some easier questions, troublesome questions can get easier, too.

5. Be a Good Guesser

You may have heard there's a penalty for guessing on the SAT. That's not quite accurate. There's no penalty for guessing—there's a penalty for a *wrong answer*. That's not the same thing. Here's how it works:

If you get a multiple-choice answer wrong, you *will* lose a fraction of a point. If you get a Grid-in answer wrong, no points are taken away.

If you are guessing on a multiple-choice question, it is best to use your deductive reasoning to eliminate the answers you know are incorrect and make an educated guess based on the remaining choices. This will increase your chances of getting it right.

Take a look at this question:

> After spending countless hours helping the poor and home-less in their community, the basketball players were as rec-ognized for their acts of ------- as they were for their slam dunks.
>
> (A) breakfast
> (B) sincerity
> (C) charity
> (D) contribution
> (E) animosity

Chances are, you recognized that choice (A), *breakfast*, was wrong. You then looked at the next answer choice, and then the next one, and so on, eliminating wrong answers to find the correct answer. This process is usually the best way to work through multiple-choice questions. If you still don't know the right answer but can eliminate one or more wrong answers, you should *guess*. (The correct answer is (C). Although some of the other choices are close, really what is being recognized is the basketball players' acts of *charity*.)

6. Be a Good Gridder

Don't make mistakes filling out your answer grid. When time is short, it's easy to get confused skipping around a section and going back and forth between test booklet and grid. If you misgrid a *single* question, that will throw off your entire grid. Even if you discover the mistake, you'll waste valuable time fixing it. You can lose many points this way, so make sure you keep track of your grid.

To avoid mistakes on the answer grid:

- In your test booklet, circle the answers you choose. By circling your answers, you'll have an easier time checking your grid against your book later.

- Grid five or more answers at once. Don't transfer your answers to the grid after every question. Transfer your answers after every five questions, or, in the Reading Comprehension questions, at the end of each passage. That way, you won't keep breaking your concentration to mark the grid. you'll save time and improve accuracy.

Note: There is one *exception* to this rule: When time is running out at the end of a section, start gridding one by one so you don't get caught at the end with ungridded answers.

- Circle the questions you skip. Put a big circle in your test book around the numbers of any questions you skip, so they'll be easy to locate when you go back later. Also, if you realize later that you accidentally skipped a box on the grid, you can more easily check your grid against your book to see where you went wrong.
- Write in your booklet. Take notes, circle hard questions, underline things, etc. Proctors collect booklets at the end of each testing session, but the booklets are not examined or reused.

7. Manage Your Time (So It Doesn't Manage You!)

Track your time by recording your start and stop times for subsections. If you have ten minutes to complete a section and 25 questions to answer within that time frame, periodically make sure you're on pace to complete every question.

8. Two-Minute Warning: Locate Quick Points

When you start to run out of time, locate and answer any of the quick points that remain. For example, some Improving Paragraphs questions can be done at the last minute, even if you haven't read the passage.

CHAPTER 1 SUMMARY

The Writing section has two parts: a written essay and multiple-choice questions on Identifying Sentence Errors, Improving Sentences, and Improving Paragraphs.

The Math section tests math up through algebra II. And the Critical Reading section has three kinds of questions: Sentence Completion, Reading Comprehension, and Long Reading Comprehension.

No matter what multiple-choice question you're working on, be sure to apply the following Kaplan strategies:

1. Think about the question first.
2. Pace yourself.
3. Know when a question is supposed to be easy or hard.
4. Move around within a section.
5. Be a good guesser.
6. Be a good gridder.
7. Manage your time (so it doesn't manage you!).
8. Two-minute warning: locate quick points.

Chapter Two: **Introduction to SAT Writing**

The Writing multiple-choice questions measure your ability to recognize and produce acceptable *written* English. Standard written English is a bit more formal than spoken English. Things that you're used to saying in everyday conversation may well be considered wrong on the Writing section. Standard written English is the kind of English that you find in textbooks and that your professors expect on college papers.

You don't have to use or define grammatical terms on the SAT, so don't worry if your grasp of grammar terminology is shaky. You won't be tested directly on spelling or capitalization, either. Punctuation is tested only in connection with sentence structure.

The hour-long section is divided into two parts—an essay and multiple-choice questions. The essay will be the very first section on the SAT. You'll have 25 minutes to write it, and once those 25 minutes are up, you won't be able to return to the essay.

The test makers include an essay on the SAT so that prospective colleges can see how well you respond to an assigned topic. They do not expect the essay to be perfect. It is intended to be submitted as a good first draft. That means you can make a few minor mistakes and not have points deducted. The topic will be open-ended yet focused enough for you to be able to present clear examples and concrete information.

There will be two multiple-choice sections, one 25 minutes long and one 10 minutes long. These questions test your ability to identify mistakes in sentences and paragraphs with respect to three main areas of written English:

1. Basic grammar
2. Sentence structure
3. Choice of words and idiom

KAPLAN

THE ESSAY

Your task is to write a short, persuasive essay on an assigned topic. The most important word in that last sentence was *persuasive*. You need to write an essay that supports your point of view. You can write the best essay ever on the pros and cons of achieving world peace, but if you have not argued for seeing things from a particular point of view (pro *or* con—not both), you won't get a high score.

You don't need specific knowledge of a particular topic to complete the SAT essay. There's no real way to "study"; however, you can prepare and have your writing skills. The essay prompt will be so broad in scope that you'll be able to apply it to something that you know about and are interested in.

Colleges will be able, at no charge, to view and print essays written by individual students who request that a college receive their scores. We suspect that college admissions officials, being short on time, will probably not, as a rule, read an extra essay. But they may use it for comparison's sake with a student's application essay, or if a student's score indicates a major discrepancy with the rest of the student's application package. The essay may also be used to supplement or replace a college's current application essay or for college placement purposes, and the scores themselves may be used as an extra measure of a student's ability.

Essay Directions

You have 25 minutes to complete this section. The essay assignment will be to write a *persuasive* essay; that is, to write an essay that supports a point of view and then provides clear-cut examples that reinforce your position.

Your essay prompt will consist of a quotation of one or more sentences or a pair of quotes. Then you'll see the essay assignment, which asks you to comment on a topic related to the ideas raised in the quote(s).

The directions for the essay will look something like this. We have inserted our own topic just to illustrate the format.

Directions: Consider carefully the following statement and the assignment below it.

> "The weirder you're going to behave, the more normal you should look. It works in reverse, too. When I see a kid with three or four rings in his nose, I know there is absolutely nothing extraordinary about that person."
>
> —P. J. O'Rourke

Assignment: Does weird behavior indicate an ordinary or an extraordinary person? In an essay, support your position by discussing an example (or examples) from literature, science and technology, the arts, current events, or your own experience or observation.

The quotes or excerpts serve primarily as springboards, or food for thought. They are there to help jumpstart your creative juices and to give you some ideas about how to build your essay. That's helpful, especially when you're asked to write on demand. While you are free to refer directly to the quote(s) or excerpt in your essay, the assignment will not require you to do so. The main goal is to address the topic raised in the assignment. The "side" you take in your essay is irrelevant; there are no right and wrong positions when it comes to the answer you choose. So choose whichever position you feel more comfortable with, and that will enable you to develop your ideas and write the stronger essay.

Essay Scoring

The essay is scored holistically by two readers. *Holistically* means your essay gets a single score—a number—that indicates its overall quality. This number takes into account a bunch of essay characteristics described below.

The number assigned to your essay will range from a high of 6 to a low of 1. Your essay is read and scored by two people, so the scores they each assign to your essay will be added together to get a total score. This total score will range from a high of 12 to a low of 2. Your essay will account for one-third of the overall Writing score.

The following chart shows the main criteria that the readers use to score your essay:

The SAT Essay Scoring Chart

Score	Topic	Support	Organization	Language
6	effectively address-es the topic	insightful, relevant support	well organized and fully developed with supporting examples	displays consistent language facility, varied sentence structure, and range of vocabulary
5	effectively address-es the topic	developed, relevant support	generally organized and well developed with appropriate examples	displays language facility, with syntac-tic variety and a range of vocabulary
4	addresses the writ-ing topic	sufficient relevant support	organized and ade-quately developed with examples	displays adequate but inconsistent lan-guage facility
3	occasionally digress-es from the topic	insufficient detail to support ideas	inadequate organi-zation or develop-ment	many errors in grammar or diction; little variety
2	only partially addresses the topic	little or inappropri-ate detail to support ideas	poor organization, thin development	frequent errors in grammar and dic-tion; no variety
1	does not address the topic	little or inappropri-ate detail; ideas obscure	no organization, no development	severe grammar and diction errors obscure meaning

Here is what this means in plain English:

6: Outstanding Essay

Convincingly and insightfully fulfills the writing assignment; ideas are well developed, clearly pre-sented, and logically organized; superior command of vocabulary, grammar, style, and accepted conventions of writing; a few minor flaws may occur.

5: Solid Essay

Convincingly fulfills the writing assignment; ideas are adequately developed, clearly presented, and logically organized; strong command of vocabulary, grammar, style, and accepted conven-tions of writing; some minor flaws may occur.

4: Adequate Essay

Fulfills the writing assignment; ideas are adequately developed, presented, and organized; satisfactory command of vocabulary, grammar, style, and accepted conventions of writing; some flaws may occur.

3: Limited Essay

Doesn't adequately fulfill the writing assignment; ideas aren't adequately developed, clearly presented, or logically organized; unsatisfactory command of vocabulary, grammar, style, and accepted conventions of writing; contains many flaws.

2: Flawed Essay

Doesn't fulfill the writing assignment; ideas are vague, poorly presented, and not logically organized; poor command of vocabulary, grammar, style, and accepted conventions of writing; contains numerous serious flaws.

1: Deficient Essay

Doesn't fulfill the writing assignment; ideas are extremely vague, very poorly presented, and not logically organized; extremely poor command of vocabulary, grammar, style, and accepted conventions of writing; is so seriously flawed that basic meaning is obscured.

Sample Essays

Six sample essays follow. For each topic, we show a strong essay (5–6 range), an acceptable/mediocre essay (3–4 range), and a weak essay (1–2 range), along with sample grader comments. Use these essays to get a sense of the scoring process and also as a standard by which to judge your writing.

Tip: Despite what you might have been taught, writing in the first-person voice (using *I* or *we*) is perfectly acceptable for your SAT essay response, especially if you're using personal experiences to support a response.

Essay Topic 1

You will have 25 minutes to write your essay in your test booklet (two pages).

Directions: Consider carefully the following statement(s) and the assignment below it.

"Trouble is only opportunity in work clothes."

—Henry J. Kaiser

"The best way out is always through."

—Robert Frost

Assignment: Is it true that one can always find opportunity, even in trouble? In an essay, support your position by discussing an example (or examples) from literature, science and technology, the arts, current events, or your own experience or observation.

Grade 6 Essay

When my mother and father divorced, I felt like it was the end of the world. It seemed as if a cloud had settled over me, and that there was no such thing as a reliable relationship anymore. But as I've grown older, I've actually come to appreciate the breakup. My family went through some growing pains and we all had to re-evaluate ourselves and our family dynamics, but ultimately the divorce has served to bring my family closer together than we might have been had my parents not separated. Situations like mine demonstrate that opportunities can rise from problematic conditions.

My parents divorced when I was around 11 years old. I never thought I'd see my father again. However, he didn't just vanish from sight. He lived in the same neighborhood, and he'd see my brother and me pretty much every weekend. I had to adjust to not seeing my dad every day anymore, which was difficult, but with time things got easier. We would go to a movie or out to dinner on weekends, and I discovered sides of him I never knew before. My father seemed happier, and in return he lavished affection on me and my brother, something he'd never really done before. These experiences with my dad encouraged me to start focusing on the positive aspects of the divorce, and the good that can come from it.

As I got older, I found my older brother was quickly becoming my best friend and advisor, something that wouldn't have happened to me had my father still been living at home. My brother helped me when I needed to know how to ask out girls or how to fight, and he even helped me with my calculus homework at night when my mother would be at school. If my dad had been there all the time, I wouldn't have had the same opportunity to really get to know and respect my brother in the same way. Now that I'm almost a "man," I see how I have become what I am by learning from my father's mistakes and from the resourceful advice of my brother. I'm sure it wasn't always easy for my brother to take on this mentoring role, but he rose to the challenge and was always there for me when I needed him.

My relationship with my mother is also extremely close, closer than it would have been had my father lived at home and persevered in the negative behavior that ultimately led to their divorce. My mom is a strong woman and she's always been honest and supportive, even in the worst of times. Following the divorce, she worked really hard to keep our family thriving, even under our new arrangement.

I'm not saying that the divorce was a wonderful event, but I believe that the bond between my mother, brother, and myself is much stronger since we learned valuable lessons about depending on one another rather than on some kind of Ward Cleaver father-husband figure. My relationship with my dad has also improved. There have been hard times without my father around, but in the end, the "trouble" of my parents' divorce actually opened a few doors for my family, and presented the opportunity for us to grow even closer to one another.

Grader's comments: This essay is very good. It addresses the topic statement in a thorough and imaginative way. Its ideas are extremely well organized, clearly stated, and amply supported by evidence. The essay addresses the ideas presented in the quotes, that taking advantage of inconspicuous opportunities often requires hard work. Finally, the essay displays an excellent command of the conventions of standard written English.

Grade 3 Essay

I remember the way my teacher's face looked when she entered the classroom and saw its condition. She sat down starting to cry. The sight of the vandalized room, with broken glass and books everywhere, was too much for her.

Me and the other students decided we had to get together and help her fix up the place. Who or why destroyed the room? This question didn't matter in the end. The class was motivated to figure out ways to fix and replace everything. Of course we cleaned up first. Glass and other dangerous things were disposed of. Then we replace all the posters and other educational material. We held town car-washes and bake sales to raise money for these things. I was really happy after a month of this kind of work we even had enough money to get new text-books.

By working through this misfortune we figured out how to work together. Also, our teacher got to know us as people, not just students. We showed her how we could take charge of a situation and make it better. When we finally got to take classes again in our old classroom I felt that we proved that saying listed above, "trouble is only opportunity in work clothes."

Grader's comments: While this essay reflects a basic understanding of the topic assignment, it doesn't address the topic in a convincing or direct way. Its ideas are neither well developed nor well organized. Its use of evidence to support those ideas is unsophisticated. Furthermore, the essay displays an unsatisfactory command of the conventions of standard written English.

Grade 1 Essay

I've had bad things happen to me and good things have come out of it. Sometimes when something terrible hapens you have to look for a sign that proves not everything is so bad.

In the book The Good Earth written by Pearl Buck their are many examples of this situation. The main character starts off really poor as a result of a terrible draught and no food. But then all sorts of terrible things hapen to him, however he meets a wonderful woman and gets the opportunity to become rich! So the main character proves that even when you think their is no hope their might be an opportunity you don't see. If a person thinks that things couldn't get any worse, he/she should take a look around and you will see that life has some nice surprises in store for you.

Grader's comments: This essay is extremely poor. It's very vague, repetitive, and almost completely devoid of developed evidence. It is also riddled with grammatical problems.

Essay Topic 2

You will have 25 minutes to write your essay in your test booklet (two pages).

Directions: Consider carefully the following statement(s) and the assignment below it.

> "The greater danger for most of us lies not in setting our aim too high and falling short, but in setting our aim too low and achieving our mark."
>
> —Michelangelo

Assignment: Do you believe, with Michelangelo, that it is better to risk failing in the attempt to do something too ambitious or to succeed at something you were already sure you could do? In an essay, support your position by discussing an example (or examples) from literature, science and technology, the arts, current events, or your own experience or observation.

Grade 6 Essay

I think Michelangelo was right, that it is much more dangerous to aim low and achieve our mark than to aim high and fall short. If we aim *too* low, we never challenge ourselves—we never find out what we are capable of. If we aim *too* high, we will make mistakes, but we may also achieve greatness.

Michelangelo might have made this statement with his fellow artist Leonardo da Vinci in mind. Leonardo always challenged himself to do things no one had ever done before. He failed as often as he succeeded, but his failures are as technically breathtaking and emotionally moving as his successes. Leonardo's famous mural *The Last Supper* is perhaps the most famous instance in which he aimed too high and fell short. He painted the picture of Jesus and his twelve apostles at their final meal on the wall of a dining room in a monestery. Leonardo had to prepare the wall with a coat of what we would call "primer" today, before he began to paint the picture. He invented a new kind of primer that turned out to be unstable. Very soon after the painting was finished it began to flake off the wall. Today, after a major restoration project, it appears as a ghost of what it must have been when it was finished. But it is a magnificent ghost.

The technique of the painting is impressive. Leonardo shows thirteen men all on one side of a long table and makes it look natural. The apostles are in four groups of three, two groups on each side of Jesus. Each of these groupings forms a sort of pyramid. No two apostles are posed alike; no two have the same facial expression. The design is full of variety and visual interest.

The image is tremendously moving. Leonardo shows each apostle reacting emotionally to Jesus' announcement that one of them will betray him. The facial expressions range from guilt to bewilderment to disbelief to anguish. Judas' snarl of amazement at the announcement of his guilty secret is especially striking. The serenity on the face of Jesus, knowing the torture and execution he faces, has probably made millions of viewers cry.

Leonardo tried to do something that had not been done before. In this way he fell short of achieving his original goal. But because he aimed high, he gave the world one of its great treasures, even in its present condition.

Grader's comments: This essay does a fine job of addressing the topic. It is well organized, stating an opinion and then backing it up with a specific example. Leonardo da Vinci is a perfect choice for discussion because of his connection to Michelangelo, the source of the quotation. The student did well to give only one example (the artwork discussed) with which she is very familiar; this allows her to analyze that example in detail and gives the essay a central focus. There are a few grammatical errors and the word *monastery* is misspelled, but these mistakes do not detract from the high quality of the writing.

Grade 4 Essay

Michelangelo may be right in one way, but he is wrong in another way. Trying to do more than we think we can do may build our character, but it's safer and more practical to stay within our limits and succeed.

Last year I took a course in advanced biolagy. The teacher warned me that I might not be ready for it. But I thought that if I did all the homework and was good about regular atenndance, I'd learn a lot and wouldn't have any trouble. But the teacher was right; the course was too hard for me and I got a very low grade. Now my transcript won't look so good to the colleges I'm applying to. I did learn a lot about biolagy and I loved the class. But it wasn't practical for me to fail when making good grades and getting into college was so important.

Another example is that my father recently applied for a job that was too much of a challenge for him. He set his aim high and fell short. My father is an architect but he had never worked on a concert hall before. He didn't know enough about the special sound requirements and things like that. When the hall opened for its first concerts, everyone agreed that it was a beautiful building. But the critics thought the orchestra sounded muffled in the audetorium and they are calling for the acoustics to be redone. My father's name has been mentioned as the person responsable for the bad acoustics. Now maybe clients won't hire him to design and build new projects. Ever since my mother died, we depend on my father's income to support the family. When he aimed too high, he fell short and that has bad consequenses for the whole family. It's just not practical to try to do more than you know you can do when important things are riding on the result of your failure or success.

Grader's comments: The essay responds thoughtfully and well to the topic. The student takes an unexpected point of view—disagreeing with the genius—and supports it with relevant, specific examples. The essay is well organized, making the main point in the opening paragraph and then describing specific supporting examples below.

The quality of the writing is poor, although some sentences are strong. The language is too casual ("my transcript won't look so good" or "things like that"), and there are many errors in spelling, grammar, and usage. Except for the architectural terms, which the student probably hears at home all the time, the vocabulary is basic.

Grade 2 Essay

If you aim *too high* and fall short, it's not a big deal. You just try again until you manage. That's what the coach at the stables always tells us. If the horse doesn't make the jump the first time you try, then you try again. Even if the horse throws you, you wear your helmet and you won't probably get badly hurt. You get right back on the horse and get him to take the jump again until he *obeys* you.

If you don't aim high at all you won't ever get any better at anything, You have to read a book you think you can't finish just to *prove* to yourself that you can do it. Tom Sawyer never thought he could paint the whole fence, he studied the situation and he figured out a way to get his friends to paint it for him. That was something he thought he couldn't *do*, but he did it.

Grader's comments: The essay addresses the topic and argues a clear point of view, but fails to support it well. It's also much too short. The example of working to perfect the athletic skill of jumping is a good one, but the writing is poor quality. The Tom Sawyer example is inappropriate because Tom didn't doubt that he could paint the fence; he just didn't want to make the effort. "You have to read a book...just to prove you can do it" is a poor example and not relevant to the rest of the paragraph. The vocabulary in the essay is elementary-level. There are grammatical errors, and phrases like "it's not a big deal" are too colloquial. The words *you* and *your* are repeated far too often for such a short essay.

MULTIPLE-CHOICE QUESTIONS

So you wrote the perfect essay. Congratulations! But you're not done yet. Now you have 35 minutes to answer multiple-choice questions about issues in other people's writing.

There are three types of multiple-choice questions:

1. Identifying Sentence Errors questions
2. Improving Sentences questions
3. Improving Paragraphs questions

The Identifying Sentence Errors and Improving Sentences are based on single unrelated sentences on a variety of topics. The Improving Paragraphs questions are based on two brief passages, with several questions per passage.

Note: It is likely that there will be almost twice as many Identifying Sentence Errors questions as Improving Sentences, and more Improving Sentences than Improving Paragraphs.

Multiple-Choice Directions

The official directions for the multiple-choice questions will be something like this:

Identifying Sentence Errors Questions

Directions: The following sentences test your knowledge of grammar, usage, diction (choice of words), and idiom.

- Some sentences are correct.
- No sentence contains more than one error.
- You will find that the error, if there is one, is underlined and lettered. Elements of the sentence that are not underlined will not be changed. In choosing answers, follow the requirements of standard written English.
- If there is an error, select the one underlined part that must be changed to make the sentence correct and fill in the corresponding oval on your answer sheet.
- If there is no error, fill in answer oval E.

These Identifying Sentence Errors sample questions are just like what you'll see on test day. Give them a try. The answers and explanations appear at the end of the chapter.

1. <u>Nearly</u> all scientists believe that the
   A
   current threat <u>to</u> the environment
   B
   <u>could be abated</u> if the general public
   C
   consumed more <u>wiser</u>. <u>No error</u>
   D   E

2. The Dean and the Curriculum

   Committee plan <u>increasing</u> the number
   A
   of credits <u>required</u> <u>for graduation</u>,
   B   C
   <u>beginning</u> with the incoming freshman
   D
   class. <u>No error</u>
   E

Here is the Kaplan Method for approaching Identifying Sentence Errors questions. We will go into more detail in chapter 6.

The Kaplan Four-Step Method for Identifying Sentence Errors

Step 1. Read the whole sentence, "listening" for the mistake.

Step 2. If you "heard" a mistake, choose it and you're done.

Step 3. If not, read each underlined choice and eliminate choices that contain no error.

Step 4. If you're sure the sentence contains no errors, choose (E).

Improving Sentences Questions

The directions for Improving Sentences questions will look like this. Read them now so you don't have to waste time on test day.

Directions: The following sentences test correctness and effectiveness of expression. In choosing answers, follow the requirements of standard written English; that is, pay attention to grammar, choice of words, sentence construction, and punctuation.

In each of the following sentences, part of the sentence or the entire sentence is underlined. Beneath each sentence you will find five ways of phrasing the underlined part. Choice A repeats the original; the other four are different.

Choose the answer that best expresses the meaning of the original sentence. If you think the original is better than any of the alternatives, choose it; otherwise, choose one of the others. Your choice should produce the most effective sentence—clear and precise, without awkwardness or ambiguity.

Here are a few examples. Give them a try. The answers and explanations appear at the end of the chapter.

3. <u>The workers searched for trapped survivors, digging as fast as they could in the rubble of the collapsed building.</u>

(A) The workers searched for trapped survivors, digging as fast as they could in the rubble of the collapsed building.

(B) Digging, the workers searched for trapped survivors, as fast as they could in the rubble of the collapsed building.

(C) Digging as fast as they could in the rubble of the collapsed building, trapped survivors were searched for by the workers.

(D) The workers, searching for trapped survivors, while digging as fast as they could in the rubble of the collapsed building.

(E) Digging as fast as they could in the rubble of the collapsed building, the workers searched for trapped survivors.

4. Doctors have been advising their patients to eat less fat, exercise more, <u>and reducing stress</u>.

    (A) and reducing stress

    (B) and stress is reduced

    (C) also reducing stress

    (D) and they should reduce stress

    (E) and reduce stress

Here is the Kaplan Method for approaching Improving Sentences questions. We will go into more detail in chapter 7.

The Kaplan Four-Step Method for Improving Sentences

Step 1. Read the sentence carefully, "listening" for a mistake.

Step 2. Identify the error(s).

Step 3. Make a prediction. Remember, your prediction may not be listed in the answer choices, but this is a good way to recognize what is wrong in the sentence.

Step 4. Check the choices for a match that doesn't introduce a new error.

Improving Paragraphs Questions

The directions below are basically what you'll see on test day. Read through them and try the sample Improving Paragraphs questions that follow. The answers appear at the end of the chapter.

Directions: The passage below is an early draft of an essay. Parts of the passage need to be rewritten. Read the passage and answer the questions that follow. Some questions are about individual sentences or parts of sentences; in these questions, you are asked to select the choice that will improve sentence structure and word choice. Other questions refer to parts of the essay or the entire essay and ask you to consider the organization and development of the essay. You should follow the conventions of standard written English in answering the questions. After you have chosen your answer, fill in the corresponding oval on your answer sheet.

Here are a few examples. Give them a try.

Questions 5–7 are based on the following essay.

(1) Our urban public schools need to be smaller. (2) In an environment where streets are crowded and sometimes unsafe, it's necessary that schools offer an intimate sense of community so that students can learn in a nurturing atmosphere.

(3) Some people argue that creating smaller schools will be expensive. (4) We don't have to spend lots of money to achieve this vision. (5) A school-building that already exists can be partitioned into two or three smaller schools. (6) And depleting funds by bying state-of-the-art equipment won't be necessary. (7) School boards can find other ways to get supplies. (8) A private business or bank can donate anything from money to computers. (9) And such donations would be beneficial for both parties involved. (10) The bank or business would gain valuable publicity by investing in the community, and the schools would get the products they need. (11) Parents can play a more active role in the school system, and then chaperone for school trips or volunteer to teach. (12) We need to change the way our schools are built because students need a sense of community in our large cities. (13) Such a reformation might be difficult, but if we work together and we would have invested our time and energy, we can improve the schools for good.

5. Which of the following options is the best way to edit the underlined portions of sentences 3 and 4 (reproduced below)?

    Some people argue that creating smaller schools <u>will be expensive. We don't have to spend</u> lots of money to achieve this vision.

    (A) is expensive, and we don't have to spend
    (B) will be expensive, so we don't have to spend
    (C) will be expensive, but we don't have to spend
    (D) are expensive, but we don't have to spend
    (E) are expensive, yet we will not be spending

6. In context, which version of the underlined section of sentence 11 (reproduced below) is the clearest?

   Parents can play a more active role <u>in the school system, and then chaperone for school trips or volunteer to teach</u>.

   (A) by chaperoning in the school system for school trips and volunteering to teach

   (B) in the school system, as a chaperone for school trips or volunteer to teach

   (C) in the school system, then chaperoning for school trips and volunteering to teach

   (D) in the school system by chaperoning for school trips or volunteering to teach

   (E) as chaperones for school trips or volunteers to teach in the school system

7. Which of the versions of the underlined section of sentence 13 (reproduced below) is best?

   Such a reformation might be difficult, <u>but if we work together and we would have invested</u> our time and energy, we can improve the schools for good.

   (A) (As it is now)

   (B) and if we work together and we invest

   (C) but if we work together and invest

   (D) furthermore, if we work together, also investing

   (E) although if we are working together and will be investing

Here is the Kaplan Method for approaching Improving Paragraphs questions. We'll go into more detail in chapter 8.

The Kaplan Five-Step Method for Improving Paragraphs

Step 1. Read the passage quickly for the overall idea and tone.

Step 2. Read the question.

Step 3. Reread the relevant portion and its context.

Step 4. Predict the correction.

Step 5. Check the choices for a match that doesn't introduce a new error.

Multiple-Choice Scoring

If you get a multiple-choice question right, you earn one point. If you get it wrong, you lose a fraction of a point. If you leave it blank, you neither earn nor lose anything.

Once your raw score has been tallied, it is converted into a scaled score. Your multiple-choice scaled score will account for two-thirds of your overall Writing score.

After your essay and multiple-choice raw scores have been converted into scaled scores, they are combined into a single scaled score that reflects the different weight given to each section. This new scaled score will then be converted into a final score.

CHAPTER 2 SUMMARY

The Writing section is one hour long and divided into three sections: the essay and two multiple-choice sections. Your essay counts for one-third of the overall Writing score, and the multiple-choice for two-thirds.

You'll be asked to write a persuasive essay. Use the sample essays and grader's comments to get a sense of what the readers will be looking for so that you can get closer to a fantastically persuasive essay and farther away from an unconvincing essay.

The multiple-choice questions test your grasp of English usage, sentence structure, and paragraph structure. You get one point for every question you get right and lose a fraction of a point for every question you get wrong.

For Identifying Sentence Errors questions, use the Kaplan Four-Step Method:

Step 1. Read the whole sentence, "listening" for the mistake.

Step 2. If you "heard" a mistake, choose it and you're done.

Step 3. If not, read each underlined choice and eliminate choices that contain no error.

Step 4. If you're sure the sentence contains no errors, choose (E).

For Improving Sentences, use the Kaplan Four-Step Method:

Step 1. Read the sentence carefully, "listening" for a mistake.

Step 2. Identify the error(s).

Step 3. Predict a correction.

Step 4. Check the choices for a match that doesn't introduce a new error.

For Improving Paragraphs, use the Kaplan Five-Step Method:

Step 1. Read the passage quickly for the overall idea and tone.

Step 2. Read the question.

Step 3. Reread relevant portion and its context.

Step 4. Predict the correction.

Step 5. Check the choices for a match that doesn't introduce a new error.

ANSWERS TO PRACTICE QUESTIONS

1. D

Wiser should be *wisely* because *wiser* is intended to describe how the general public consumed an action. The verb *consumed* needs the adverb *wisely*.

2. A

The gerund (*-ing*) form of the verb (*increasing*) is not idiomatic with the verb *plan*. *Plan* requires the infinitive form of the verb, in this case, *to increase*.

3. E

Digging as fast as they could in the rubble of the collapsed building is a long modifying phrase. It modifies the noun *workers*. Only choice (E) places the modifying phrase right next to the noun that it modifies. Choice (D) might have been tempting, but it doesn't have any verb, so it doesn't make a complete sentence.

4. E

This sentence requires parallel construction because it presents a list. Only choice (E) presents the last item in a manner parallel to the first two items.

5. C

This choice sets up the contrast between some people who argue that creating the schools will be expensive and the author's belief that creating smaller schools won't be expensive.

6. D

This choice is the only one that clearly shows how parents can work as volunteers or chaperones within the school system.

7. C

This choice is grammatically consistent with the rest of the paragraph. Notice that it's the shortest, simplest, and clearest choice.

The Essay

Chapter Three: **How to Write a High Scoring Essay**

There are some things that essay graders don't care about. That you managed not to spill your orange juice on your paper—doesn't count. That you were quite polite to your test proctor—doesn't count. That you have gotten A's on every essay you have ever written in your life—doesn't count either. Here's what does count.

LENGTH COUNTS

There is a clear pattern to how SAT essays are graded. Essays given high scores—scores ranging from 10–12 when both judges' scores are combined—are generally longer than essays with lower scores. In fact, essays in the 10–12 range are *always* at least three to five paragraphs long, and each of those paragraphs always contains more than two or three sentences.

So, you need to write an essay with three to five paragraphs. One or two paragraphs, no matter how well written, simply will not cut it. This means you need to fill up as many answer sheet lines as possible and create new paragraphs whenever appropriate. Each paragraph should contain several well-developed sentences. Plan to write at least a page and a half—that's around 350 words, depending on your handwriting. Also keep in mind that you'll have two pages to fill (46 lines, to be exact), and you *cannot* go over that length. Therefore, if your handwriting tends to fall on the larger side, you may want to make an effort to write smaller so that your complete essay is of adequate length and substance.

On the other hand, do not think that you'll earn yourself any points by filling up all the lines with large letters and not focusing on putting together a well-developed argument. That's not how it works. Something too short is bad, but don't forget: so is something rambling and wordy. A blank line is better than a lame sentence that is just fluff or that repeats something you wrote earlier in the essay.

CONTENT COUNTS

You don't need to be an expert in any subject to write your essay. You don't need specific knowledge of history, current events, or other specialized information. You may choose to include examples from history, famous books, or the nightly news, but you don't *have* to, so do not stay up late reading the encyclopedia or back issues of *Business Week*. Essay topics are so broad that you'll always be able to write about a subject with which you are familiar. Remember: The main thing the graders are looking for is a logical, well-written argument supported by relevant examples. An essay based on personal experience alone is perfectly acceptable and can earn you a perfect score.

Just make sure you do the following:

- Address the topic that you are given.
- Write persuasively.

The object is to convince your reader to see something from your point of view. Don't worry about what the reader thinks—write about what *you* think. You are *not* fair and balanced! (Well, you should be fair, but definitely not balanced.)

NEATNESS COUNTS

Your essay must be readable. If you edit what you've written, do it neatly. If you add a word, change a phrase, or cross out a sentence, do it carefully. It may sound silly, but neatness matters. It matters a lot.

Why? The graders have thousands of essays to read and grade. That means they don't spend much time judging your essay—just a couple of minutes on average! They aren't going to read an essay three or four times in order to decipher hard-to-read words or sentences. So if the handwriting in your essay is messy and hard to follow, graders may conclude that the content itself is, too. A good essay may not get the score it deserves because it is presented shabbily.

ESSAY WRITING FAQ

To address some of the basics about the SAT essay (and to offer you some additional tips and tricks), here are our answers to some frequently asked questions.

How Long Should the Essay Be?

As we said before, the length of an essay is no assurance of its quality. However, it's hard to develop an argument in depth, something the graders look for, in 200 words. Don't ramble, digress, or write off topic just to make your essay longer. Practice writing organized essays with developed examples, and you'll find yourself writing more naturally. Aim for 300–450 words as you practice.

Can I Get Extra Paper?

No. The test booklet has 46 lines for the essay. If your handwriting is large, it may be a challenge to fit in all your ideas. You won't get any additional sheets, so practice printing, writing smaller, whatever works.

How Many Examples Should I Use?

A good essay can have a single well-developed example; two or more examples can also make for a strong essay, but they in themselves won't guarantee a 5 or 6. However, many undeveloped examples make for weak—and low-scoring—essays.

What If I'm Not a "Writer"?

Writing essays may not be your favorite pastime, but you can still succeed on the SAT essay. If the essay is essentially well written, just staying on topic can earn you a good score. If your writing is weak, focus on building a well-supported argument; if you have that, other weaknesses and writing errors will be less important.

What's the Best Subject to Write About?

Examples based on literary or historical topics won't necessarily receive a higher score than an essay based on personal experience. Choose examples that you can write about with confidence; don't try to impress the readers. If you do choose personal experience, try to choose examples that focus on self-improvement, positive acts, or creative work. Remember that colleges may use these essays as additional personal statements.

What's the Best Way to Practice?

There is simply no substitute for writing essays under test-like conditions. Practice writing as many essays as possible between now and test day. And it's also a good idea to practice at the same time of day that you will be writing on test day.

Be hard on yourself. Don't allow yourself any extra minutes to complete an essay, and don't look at essay topics in advance. And practice writing on *no more* than a total of 46 lines on two pages.

After each practice essay, score yourself based on the guidelines provided in this book. As part of your self-evaluation, determine which types of examples are most useful to you and what types of errors you make most often.

Then analyze how well you followed Kaplan's methods in constructing your essay and what you might focus on for improvement. Do you have a tendency to rush your plan, or do you find that you haven't left two minutes to proofread? Practice to make your pacing reliable.

Finally, get a second opinion. Ask someone else to read and critique your practice essays. If you know someone else who's taking the SAT, you might agree to assist each other in this way. Knowing whether another person can follow your reasoning is the single most important learning aid you can have for the essay.

What If English Isn't My Native Language?

The SAT essay section can be a special challenge for the international student or English-Language Learner here in the United States. The SAT essay is different from the Test of English as a Foreign Language (TOEFL) essay because the prompt can be more complex and may use language that is harder to understand. But you don't need complex sentences. Keep your usage as simple as you need to ensure control; this isn't the time for experimental writing.

On the SAT, you will be taking a position on the prompt, *something that sometimes but not always happens on the TOEFL*. However, you will still be planning your essay using all same the tools covered in this book. Practice deciphering the prompts and writing essays. Make a special point of leaving time to proofread your essays after you've finished them, and revise anything that makes your writing unclear. There's a strong connection between your English reading skills and your writing skills, so keep reading as well.

HOW TO WRITE A HIGH SCORING SAT ESSAY: THE TOWF METHOD

A few things to keep in mind before we begin: you're not expected to produce a perfect piece of writing. The graders know that you have only 25 minutes to think about, write, and proofread your work, and they are trained to view and evaluate your essay on the basis of a timed first draft. But while they expect to see a few minor mistakes, they also expect an organized and read-able piece of writing that makes an argument supported by relevant examples. In this chapter, we'll show you how to accomplish this task.

Many scores are lower than they could be simply because these standard directions are ignored: present a point of view, and provide support for it. Understanding the prompt doesn't mean there is a right or wrong answer—you have to decide what you will choose as your position, and then back up your ideas with examples.

Kaplan's THINK-ORGANIZE-WRITE-FIX (TOWF) method will help you to develop an effective essay. After you have read the quote(s) and the assignment, do the following:

Step 1: THINK about the topic and brainstorm (pre-writing). (2 minutes)

Step 2: ORGANIZE your paragraphs. (5 minutes)

Step 3: WRITE your essay. (15 minutes)

Step 4: FIX any mistakes. (3 minutes)

Here's our minute-by-minute rundown of the TOWF method:

Step 1: Think about the Topic and Brainstorm (Pre-Writing)

This step takes 2 minutes. That leaves you 23 minutes to organize, write, and fix your essay. You do not have to write anything during these 2 minutes. There's plenty of time for that later. Use these precious seconds for thinking and nothing else.

The assignment question you're given is going to be very broad. To narrow it down, you need to come up with an argument that specifically addresses the topic. Let's say you get a quote or two with the following assignment question:

"Do you agree with the idea that the strong do what they wish?"

The assignment will ask you to use concrete examples from personal experience, current events, history, the arts, or science and technology to support your position. There is no need to directly refer to the quote(s) in your essay. You may if you wish, but it is there primarily as "food for thought," to help give the assignment some context and elaboration. The most important thing you need to do is to provide examples to support your position.

Pick a Side

First, you must decide whether to agree or disagree with the topic statement. You might *disagree* because you've seen that the United States doesn't boss around Canada or Mexico, even though it could. You might *agree* because a hawk can wipe out a whole duck family without fear of retribution because it has no natural enemies—you saw it happen yourself last week. Or you might *agree* because your boss delegates all the menial jobs to you and your friends while she does nothing except sit on her…chair.

> **Tip:** If you think better with a pen in your hand, you can brainstorm under the prompt in the test booklet. Use quick pros and cons charts, webs, lists, or other tools you've used in school to help develop your thoughts.

Choose Your Examples

Once you have picked your side, you must choose examples that back up your argument. Think up two or three examples that you can write about intelligently and passionately. You could use an example from history, like the relationship between the United States and Canada. You could use the relationship between a predator and its prey, like a hawk hunting ducklings. You could use an example from your life, like how your boss makes you clean out the grease traps at the restaurant while she talks loudly on her cell phone about nothing of any importance whatsoever.

Use Specific Evidence

You've got to cite evidence to support your example. You might want to discuss a fair trade agreement between the United States and Canada. You might want to discuss how hawks can and do eat up to ten ducklings a day in the spring. Or you might want to discuss how your boss made you stay late to mop the roof (mop the roof!) while she heated and then ate three chicken pot pies (three!). Remember, picking a side without having a good reason is *not* convincing and won't get you your highest essay score.

Step 2: Organize Your Paragraphs

This step takes up to five minutes. That may seem like a lot of time to spend before you write a single sentence. But taking a few minutes to organize and outline what you want to say is definitely worth it and will make the process of writing the essay a lot easier and faster once you start it.

So you have your argument, your examples, and your evidence in your head. It's time to plan your essay. As you practice outlining, use a small piece of scratch paper or write in the margins of this book. Remember: You won't receive any additional scratch paper on test day, but there should be some blank space under the essay question in your test booklet. Your outline does not need to be excessively long or detailed, and it will not be seen or evaluated by the graders. You're preparing an outline for your *own* organizational purposes and so that you won't forget any of your important points or examples once you actually start writing.

Tip: Now is not the time to completely overhaul your writing style. If you have been trained to write an introductory paragraph that begins with an attention getter and ends with a thesis statement, continue doing what you've been doing.

Here is how your essay paragraphs should be organized:

First Paragraph:

• Clearly state your argument in your thesis statement. (Choosing to write an essay with an implied thesis may be a risk if you are not an advanced writer. Make sure your point is stated clearly.)

• Briefly mention the evidence that you're going to cite in support of that argument.

Middle Paragraphs (2–3):

• Explore and explain your evidence in detail. These paragraphs demonstrate how the evidence supports the argument.

• Develop a few strong examples rather than briefly listing many undeveloped examples. The SAT graders value depth over breadth—meaning a few well-developed supporting points are better than many undeveloped supporting details.

Last Paragraph:

• Briefly summarize your argument.

• If you are short on time, you should at least write a brief conclusion.

So sticking with the mean boss example, an outline might look like this:

"Do you agree with the idea that the strong do what they wish?"

P1: I agree. Personal experience. My boss at Pizza Paradise is good example. Does no work herself and makes the rest of us do all the work.

P2: Me mopping the roof/her eating pot pies.

P3: Me cleaning grease traps/her talking on phone.

P4: My friend washing her car/her polishing her fingernails.

P5: These three examples show how the strong do what they wish.

Step 3: Write Your Essay

The writing step of your essay should take about 15 minutes. That's plenty of time to write three to five solid paragraphs if you work from a prepared outline.

To write your strongest essay, follow your outline. You spent five minutes thinking about and organizing your essay, so stick to it! Don't freak out and write from the opposing point of view or distract yourself with what *isn't* in your outline. That said, if you come up with the perfect example halfway through your essay, replace it in your outline, see how it works, then continue. But *try, try, try* not to erase and rewrite any big chunks of text. Trust yourself.

You also need to write clearly and concisely, using complete sentences and proper grammar. In the next two chapters, we will provide you with 22 principles of good writing. If you use them on test day, your essay *will* be well written. But you only have 15 minutes, so write fast! Here is a quickly written essay about that boss:

> **"Do you agree with the idea that the strong do what they wish?"**

> I think the statement the strong *do what they wish* is true. I have seen it happen in the world, where a strong country doesn't pay attention to weaker countries. I have seen it in nature, where animals eat weaker ones. I have also experienced it in real life at my job at Pizza Paradise.

> My boss at Pizza Paradise's name is Jillian. She is manager of the pizza restaurant. She always makes me and my friends who work there do all the work. I'm not sure if she does anything at all! For example, last week, she made me mop the roof. The roof is made of asphalt. Mopping doesn't do much good. While I was mopping, she sat inside eating three Pizza Paradise pot pies. She got to do exactly what she wanted, because she's the boss.

> The week before that, Jillian made me clean the grease traps. That's not even technically my job at all—I'm supposed to make the pizzas, not clean grease traps. But I did it anyway, because she's my boss. The whole time, she just talked on her cell phone to someone about knitting. I'm sure whoever she was talking to couldn't wait to get off the phone.

> Another even worse example is when she made my friend Pat wash her Trans Am while she painted her fingers. That's just not right. Cleaning grease traps and the roof is at least something to do with work. Washing her car has nothing to do with work. But my friend was afraid to get fired, so he did it to her Trans Am anyway. I don't think she even thanked him.

> All three of these exampels show how strong people get to do what they want. My boss has all the power at work, and she used it to make me mop the roof and clean the grease traps. She also used it to make my friend wash her car. We couldn't do anything about it, and she did what she wished.

Step 4: Fix Any Mistakes

This step takes three minutes. It involves proofreading and fixing your essay. Hopefully, all you'll need to do is fix minor grammatical and/or spelling errors, change a few words here and there, and maybe add a sentence or two for clarity's sake. If you need to delete a phrase, line, or an entire sentence, simply draw a line through it—called *strikethrough*—and insert your correction directly above or to the side.

If you spend the bulk of the 25 minutes thinking about, outlining, and writing the essay, the repair step should entail nothing more than putting the finishing touches on an already strong essay.

Here is our fixed essay:

> I think the statement "the strong *do what they wish*" is true. <u>I have seen it happen in world affairs,</u> where a strong country doesn't pay attention to weaker countries. I have seen it in nature, where <u>predators eat other, weaker animals</u>. I have also experienced it in real life at my job at Pizza Paradise.

<u>My boss's name is Jillian; she is the manager of the Pizza Paradise restaurant</u>. She always makes me and my friends who work there do all the work. I'm not sure if she does anything at all! For example, last week, she made me mop the roof. The roof is made of asphalt. Mopping doesn't do much good. While I was mopping, she sat inside eating three Pizza Paradise pot pies. She got to do exactly what she wanted.

The week before that, Jillian made me clean the grease traps. That's not even technically my job at all—I'm supposed to make the pizzas, not clean grease traps! But I did it anyway, because she's my boss. The whole time, she just talked on her cell phone to someone about knitting. I'm sure whoever she was talking to couldn't wait to get off the phone.

Another even worse example is when she made my friend Pat wash her Trans Am while she painted her <u>fingernails</u>. That's just not right. Cleaning grease traps and the roof is at least something to do with work. Washing her car has nothing to do with work whatsoever. But my friend was afraid to get fired, <u>so he washed her Trans Am anyway</u>. I don't think she even thanked him.

All three of these <u>examples</u> show how strong people get to do what they want. My boss has all the power at work, and she used it to make me mop the roof and clean the grease traps. She also used it to make my friend wash her car. We couldn't do anything about it <u>because we need our jobs, and therefore have to accept the fact that the strong do what they wish</u>.

PRACTICING THE STEPS

Okay, now it's your turn to practice. Let's go through each of the steps.

Practice: Thinking about the Topic and Brainstorming (Pre-Writing)

Here are three sample assignment essay questions with accompanying quotes. Look at your watch. Spend exactly two minutes thinking about and brainstorming how you would write an essay answering these three questions. While you're thinking and brainstorming, remember to pick a side, choose examples, and use specific evidence!

Directions: Consider carefully the following statements and the assignment below it:

> "I never saw an ugly thing in my life: for let the form of an object be what it may—light, shade, and perspective will always make it beautiful."
>
> —John Constable

> "If there is one thing worse than being an ugly duckling in a house of swans, it's having the swans pretend there's no difference."
>
> —Teena Booth

Assignment: Is it true that there are no ugly things?

Directions: Consider carefully the following statements and the assignment below it:

"College isn't the place to go for ideas."

—Helen Keller

"Next in importance to freedom and justice is popular education, without which neither freedom nor justice can be permanently maintained."

—James A. Garfield

Assignment: Does higher education stifle ideas and freedom, or is it essential to them?

Directions: Consider carefully the following statements and the assignment below it:

"All paid jobs absorb and degrade the mind."

—Aristotle

"To find out what one is fitted to do, and to secure an opportunity to do it, is the key to happiness."

—John Dewey

Assignment: What do you think of the view that paid jobs might be bad for you?

Practice: Organizing

Read the following essay directions and outline an essay on the assignment. (We'll stick with the same question we used last time to illustrate how the given quotes and examples outside of personal experience may be used.) Your outline should include the argument you're making, the evidence that supports your argument, and how this information will be arranged in three to five paragraphs.

You will have 25 minutes to write your essay in your test booklet (two pages).

Directions: Consider carefully the following statement and the assignment below it.

"Justice is nothing more than the interest of the stronger."

—Thrasymachus

Assignment: Is it true that the strong do what they wish?

In an essay, support your position by discussing an example (or examples) from literature, science and technology, the arts, current events, or your own experience or observation.

Again, use a small piece of scratch paper for your outline, or make notes in this book's margins (like you'll do in your test booklet on test day). When you're done, compare your outline to the sample outline below. Again, these are the ideas the author thought of for this topic. But your actual outline notes in practice and and on test day may be briefer—outline only as much as is necessary to recall your ideas and keep them organized.

P1 (intro):

a. Rome: greatest military power in ancient world; invaded weaker neighbors

b. Examples: Punic Wars: destroyed Carthage; conquest of Gaul and Eastern Mediterranean lands

P2:

a. Punic Wars: lasted over 100 years, ended with destruction of Carthaginian Empire

b. Why Rome fought these wars: to strip Carthage (major rival) of territory and wealth

c. Within a century, Rome took all of Carthage's territory and seaborne commerce

P3:

a. The Romans initially moved into Gaul in retaliation

b. But Romans also had territorial and commercial ambitions in Gaul

P4:

a. Rome took advantage of civil strife in Eastern Mediterranean lands

b. Rome wanted these lands because: wealthier than Western Med. lands and they secured Rome's control over Med. Sea

P5 (concl):

a. Restate general argument in different words

b. Quickly refer to any additional evidence

Practice: Writing

From *Pizza Paradise* to the Punic Wars. This outline illustrates a different approach to the assignment from that of our first sample essay. This proves our point—there is not only "one way" to write these essays. You have to use *your* knowledge and *your* experiences.

Now that you're done with your outline, you're ready to start writing. Start your practice with the essay topic that you just outlined. Here's the topic again, with directions like the ones you'll see on test day. Write your essay on the next pages.

You will have 25 minutes to write your essay in your test booklet (two pages).

Directions: Consider carefully the following statement and the assignment below it.

> "Justice is nothing more than the interest of the stronger."
> —Thrasymachus

Assignment: Is it true that the strong do what they wish?

In an essay, support your position by discussing an example (or examples) from literature, science and technology, the arts, current events, or your own experience or observation.

Write your essay on the lines provided. You have 25 minutes.

_____

_____

_____

_____

_____

_____

_____

_____

_____

_____

_____

_____

_____

_____

Practice: Fixing

When you are done writing, take two minutes to fix any mistakes. Look for grammar and spelling errors, fix any sentences that could use a little freshening up, and, if necessary, add or revise a sentence or two for clarity. Try not to make any drastic changes at this late stage; use the time that remains for fine-tuning.

HOW YOUR ESSAY IS GRADED

To help you get a sense of how your essay might be graded, we have included a sample high-scoring essay. Compare your essay to the one below, which merits a grade of 6. By asking and answering these questions, you'll get a sense of how well you've done.

- Is your essay's argument as clear and straightforward?
- Does your essay use supporting evidence as effectively?
- Is your essay as well organized?
- Is your essay about the same length?
- Does your sentence structure vary throughout the essay?
- Does your essay use an appropriate range of vocabulary?

Grade 6 Essay

Rome, which was the greatest military power in the ancient world, routinely invaded and conquered its weaker neighbors. It did so in order to increase its territory and wealth. That Rome was ruthless in pursuit of its own self-interest is illustrated by its treatment of the Carthaginians, the Gauls, and the peoples of the Near East. The Romans were in power, so they did as they pleased.

The Punic Wars between Rome and Carthage lasted for over 100 years and ended with the complete destruction of the Carthaginian empire. In 146 BC, Roman legions finally captured and burned Carthage itself, selling the city's survivors into slavery. As a result of its victory, Rome acquired territory in the Mediterranean and North Africa that it had long wanted to dominate. It also took control of seaborne trade in the region—trade that Carthage had previously dominated. In other words, Rome fought the Punic Wars in order to eliminate its major territorial and commercial rival in the Mediterranean and North African region.

The Romans initially invaded Gaul (located in southern France and northern Italy) in order to retaliate against "barbarian" tribes that had earlier sacked Rome and aided the Carthaginians in the Punic Wars. But later Roman attacks and conquests, which resulted in much suffering among the people of Gaul, were motivated by territorial and commercial ambitions. Gaul's land was very fertile, and control of it provided Rome with a secure source of food. Furthermore, Rome's treasury grew by heavily taxing those who used the area's well-developed trade routes.

Rome also exploited civil unrest in the Near East in order to expand its empire. Those who came under its control received harsh treatment, with many being killed or sold into slavery. Why was Rome interested in Near Eastern lands? It had two reasons. First, these lands contained great wealth, which Rome needed to run its empire. Second, control of the Near East served a vital strategic purpose; it prevented other powers from threatening Roman dominance of the Mediterranean Sea.

In sum, then, Rome did not hesistate to use force to accomplish its territorial and economic goals. In the short run, militaristic behavior enabled the empire to become stronger and more prosperous. In the long run, however, Rome's ruthless behavior was its undoing. The hatred that Roman conquests generated among non-Romans led to constant revolts, which eventually undermined the very foundations of the empire.

THREE PRACTICE ESSAY TOPICS

The following pages contain three practice essay topics. Give yourself 25 minutes. This is your chance to put TOWF to work:

THINK about the topic and brainstorm (pre-writing). (2 minutes)

ORGANIZE the paragraphs. (5 minutes)

WRITE your essay. (15 minutes)

FIX any mistakes. (3 minutes)

After you finish each topic, you'll find three sample essays—a strong essay, a mediocre essay, and a weak essay. You'll also find sample grader comments explaining why these essays are strong, mediocre, or weak. Use these essays and comments to judge the quality of your own essays. Determine your strengths and weaknesses, and then work on the weak spots.

Topic 1

You will have 25 minutes to write your essay in your test booklet (two pages).

Directions: Consider carefully the following statements and the assignment below it.

> "The fearless are merely fearless. People who act in spite of their fear are truly brave."
>
> —James A. LaFond-Lewis

> "I must not fear. Fear is the mind-killer. Fear is the little-death that brings total obliteration. I will face my fear. I will permit it to pass over me and through me. And when it has gone past I will turn the inner eye to see its path. Where the fear has gone there will be nothing. Only I will remain."
>
> —Frank Herbert

Assignment: Do you agree with the idea that people can exercise control over their fear, or does fear control people? In an essay, support your position by discussing an example (or examples) from literature, science and technology, the arts, current events, or your own experience or observation.

Prepare your outline; then write your essay on the lines provided.

Topic 1 Sample Essays

Grade 5 Essay

Some people learn about courage on the battlefeild. Some learn courage in natural disasters such as earthquakes and floods. I really learned the meaning of courage from my grandmother, her life and death, and the way she never let her fears consume or control her life.

My grandmother's name was Francine, but everyone called her Pip. She once told me that when she was growing up, if something was cool, people would say, "it's a pip." And she deserved the nickname. In the few faded snapshots of her childhood, you can see she was pretty, always smiling, and had a lively personality. It looks like she was always having fun.

Unfortunately, the man Pip married was killed in a car accident. She was alone with her two small children, my mother and my Aunt Jenny. Pip's husband had left behind a sizeable debt and no insurance. But with the help of kind relatives, Pip managed to raise the two girls, working two, and sometimes three, jobs to pay off the debts. In those days, a single mother and working, that took real courage. When her children were grown up, Pip took classes at a local college and got her diploma. She always said graduating was the proudest day of her life, and to me that diploma represents how no challenge was too scary for her to conquer.

When I was 13, Pip got sick with cancer. We'd go and visit her in the hospital, and she'd while away the time telling us stories about her life, from girlhood to being the oldest "kid" in her college class. It was like she was making us feel better, instead of the other way around. Pip was actually cheerful in the face of death, which is the scariest situation of all.

Pip's life proves that no matter how frightening a circumstance may be, a person can conquer their fears with the right attitude and the determination to do it. Pip relied on only herself, and always acted in spite of her fears. None of the scary situations Pip encountered in her life were ever able to hold her down. She is definitely the best example of courage I know.

Grader's comments: This is a solid essay. It's well organized and flows logically. Moreover, the evidence cited in the passage supports the author's convincing position. There are some minor errors in spelling and diction, but the overall grammar is effective.

Grade 3 Essay

I think people can control fear. My life has been, not easy, but not threatened by a war or poverty, so I don't know if I really know what courage is yet. Suffering is the thing that really teaches courage.

There are many examples all around us. Firemen risk their lives every single day. Policemen get shot at, even paramedics and doctors who treat AIDS. Astronauts could blow up or be lost in space. The writer who wrote satanic verse had courage. They put a price on his head. Hiding everyday, not knowing if the next stranger on the street is going to kill you because of that which you wrote. Getting out of bed in the morning takes courage if you're in his shoes.

And school teaches you that scientists also are brave when people don't believe their ideas but they stick to their guns and history proves them right. Like Galileo, he thought the earth went around the sun. The authorites said you can't say that, but of course now we know he was right. Other examples of courage are a fighter pilot behind enemy lines and the person who fights off a mugging. I think that all these examples prove that fear doesn't

Grader's comments: This essay is limited. It takes a position and is filled with evidence, but the author neglects to develop his ideas. The author simply provides a string of unconnected facts. Moreover, this essay contains numerous and significant grammatical problems.

Grade 1 Essay

I controlled my fear when I did my first back dive. I didn't let how scared I was stop me.

From the time since childhood, I could do a front dive but not a back one. No way! It just was just to scary. But thanks to my brother one day he showed me. We were at this pool but before the diving board. He put his hands on my back and said lean back and I did. Now I felt how to do it right, and got up on the board. I was scared, but my brother said breath and I did and did the dive!

Other examples of courage are Gandhi and Martin Luther King.

Grader's comments: This essay doesn't fulfill the writing assignment. The author's story of overcoming his fear of a back dive is potentially a good example, but it is poorly developed, thinly supported, and contains many major errors in grammar, style, and spelling. Furthermore, in an abrupt transition from personal experience to history, the final sentence simply names two men of courage without explaining why they were courageous.

Topic 2

You will have 25 minutes to write your essay in your test booklet (two pages).

Directions: Consider carefully the following statement(s) and the assignment below it.

> "The ultimate measure of a man is not where he stands in moments of comfort and convenience, but where he stands at times of challenge and controversy."
>
> —Martin Luther King, Jr.

> "Our greatest glory is not in never falling, but in rising every time we fall."
>
> —Confucius

Assignment: Do you agree with the idea that being resilient in response to challenge or failure is essential for success? In an essay, support your position by discussing an example (or examples) from literature, science and technology, the arts, current events, or your own experience or observation.

Prepare your outline; then write your essay on the lines provided.

Topic 2 Sample Essays

Grade 5 Essay

It's important to learn how to be resilient and to bounce back from failure or obstacles, and this can be done if one has the right perspective. People with this attitude are bouyant, not easily discouraged, and welcome challenges and adversity. I can think of no better example than in sixth grade, when I broke my hand. I fell off my bicycle one day and broke it, and the doctor put it in a cast.

Now the cast was a real obstacle and made life very difficult for me. But rather than giving up and buckling under all the pressure, I learned to rise to the challenge before me. It was on my right hand, the one I write with. It looked like homework would be impossible, but I learned to type with one hand and did my English and social studies work on the typewriter, and my Mom wrote out my math homework based on answers I gave her. The experience sure helped my typing! It also made me learn the value of work, and gave me a chance to really learn to appreciate my mother.

In addition, having the cast was an excuse to improve my basketball game. Instead of not practicing at all because I had a cast on, I was determined to not let it stop me from trying to improve my game. I was a decent dribbler, but most comfortable with my right hand. But with the cast on I was forced to practice dribbling with my left hand, and now I can go either way.

Finally there was one other unexpected benefit. In Art Class, I was never very good. But one day, with my hand still in the cast, I tried drawing with my left hand. To my surprise, I was much better at it than ever before! The cast is long gone, but I still draw left-handed and am really quite good at it. Maybe I'd never have known about this ability if I hadn't ever had the cast. It proves the importance of being resilient in a bad situation, and getting up again after a challenge or hardship.

Grader's comments: This essay demonstrates a strong grasp of the writing assignment. The author states a thesis, provides a relevant example, and discusses that example in a clear and convincing way. There are a few minor grammatical errors, but these mistakes don't affect the generally high quality of the essay.

Tip: Although a five paragraph essay is not required to receive a high grade, a focused argument with highly supported and detailed examples is required.

Grade 3 Essay

To say that "our greatest glory is not in never falling, but in rising every time we fall" is to be resilient. Some people just always look on the bright side, and are able to overcome there challenges.

Dorothy in The Wizard of Oz is stranded by the tornado and can't go home. So she takes the opportunity to make friends with Scarecrow etc, and to rid the world of wicked witches. Her optimism wins her the right to go back to Kansas. Ophelia in Hamlet however, is not so resilient. She and Hamlet fall in love but then he pushes her away. She doesn't understand why and kills herself.

In the real world, Marie Curie was told women couldn't be scientists but perservered and discovered radium. Now there are more woman scientists than ever.

I like to think I'm resilient too. If somebody tells me I can't do something, I just try harder until I can. I rise to the challenge. Take field hockey. I went out as a freshman and barely made the team, but worked and worked and this year was a starter on the varsity. We came in second in the league. Life is like that if you can bounce back. Don't get discouraged. Every cloud has a silver lining. So if you are resilient, you will keep trying no matter what and something good may come out of it.

Grader's comments: Even though the author attempted with some success to fulfill the assignment, her essay contains many grammatical problems. Moreover, the examples from literature and history are underdeveloped, especially in paragraph 3, and confused. The author doesn't really explain how the obstacles she mentions became opportunities for the individuals in question. Finally, the author's personal experience of overcoming an obstacle doesn't tell us much about how she overcame it.

Grade 1 Essay

I don't agree with the idea that being resilent is essential for success. Some challenges are just that and nothing is going to change it. Like if I wanted to be a NBA basketball player. In the NBA you have to be tall as a tree, and I'm the shortest person in the whole school. Back in elementery school too. So I'm never going to opportunity to play the NBA.

And if you die young like from leukemia. That doesn't give you the chance to do anything with your life no matter what you do. So it depends on the challenge. I mean let's be realistic. Trying your best isn't always going to help you out no matter what. Not in every situation. It just depends.

Grader's comments: This essay is deficient in both development and presentation. It's perfectly acceptable for the author to disagree with the stimulus question, but she provides hardly any argument in support of that position. The ideas that are presented are extremely thin, and there's little logical organization to them. Finally, this essay's prose seriously violates the rules of standard written English. For example, it's filled with sentence fragments.

Topic 3

You will have 25 minutes to write your essay in your test booklet (two pages).

Directions: Consider carefully the following statements and the assignment below it.

> "War does not determine who is right—only who is left."
> —Bertrand Russell

> "We shall defend our island, whatever the cost may be, we shall fight on the beaches, we shall fight on the landing grounds, we shall fight in the fields and in the streets, we shall fight in the hills; we shall never surrender."
> —Sir Winston Churchill

Assignment: Do you agree with the idea that war is never justified? In an essay, support your position by discussing an example (or examples) from literature, science and technology, the arts, current events, or your own experience or observation.

Prepare your outline; then write your essay on the lines provided.

Topic 3 Sample Essays

Grade 4 Essay

We are a violent species. We have been fighting wars since before recorded history. The first wars were fought over territory, or perhaps for possession of precious natural resources, such as the use of a stream. In the past several thousand years, inumerable wars have been fought for the acquisition of political or relgious supremacy.

I am totally against war, and would like to see it banished from human affairs. It is my belief, however, that fighting a war is justified in a few special circumstances, such as when freedom or survival is at stake. The American Revolution, for instance, was justifiable. The colonists rebelled in order to gain the right to worship as they pleased and to gain freedom from taxation without representation. World War II was a just war, with the Allies fighting to stop Hitler from achieving world domination. But wars fought in the name of religious freedom can become unjustified, and lead to persecution and massacres. Starting the war in what was formerly Yugoslavia wasn't justified. Ethnic prejudice is not the same as fighting for self-rule or survival. "Ethnic cleansing" led to the kind of massacres mentioned above.

There should be a world court to peacefully mediate disputes between countries or groups of people. The United Nations has tried to fill this role for 50 years, but doesn't have enough power to enforce its decisions. If we had a global organization powerful enough to do so, we might have a world with only justified wars or, better still, no wars at all.

Grader's comments: This is an adequate essay. The author has responded to the stimulus with an argument, but not one that precisely fulfills the writing assignment. A firm position was never really taken. The writing itself shows a reasonable familiarity with the conventions of standard written English.

Grade 3 Essay

War is justified in certain circumstances, such as self-defense. If one country attacks another country, the second country has the right to defend itself in order to survive. When the Japanese attacked Pearl Harbor, this gave us the right to fight World War II.

Aggression not in self-defense is not justified. All Quiet on the Western Front by Remarque is a prime example of the horrors of unjustified war. The German soldiers in World War 1 are portrayed in the novel like lambs to the slaughter, pawns in their leader's unjust war for domination of Europe.

What holds true for countries also holds true for people. A person only has the right to defend him or her self with deadly force if their life is threatened. It's called justifiable homicide. Personal freedom is also worth fighting for. That's why Black South Africans were justified to fight against apartheid.

Life in the United States, however does not require most of us to fight for survival. This is probably why people like violent movies. They watch stars (Stallone, Shwarzenegger, Van Damme) act out their own private fantasies of destruction, and no one gets hurt. Buildings get blown up with no loss of innocent life, its just a set, The bullets aren't real. Maybe we could put end to wars if leaders of countries would watch more violent movies!

Grader's comments: Here's another example of an essay in which the author doesn't precisely fulfill the writing assignment. Moreover, this essay wanders from idea to idea without much linkage. Also, it's filled with grammatical flaws—to the point of damaging its presentation of ideas.

Grade 2 Essay

It is hard to choose between these statements! I am against loss of life in any form. So war is never justified. But what about in the case of attack. Somebody attacks you, its right to fight back even if they die in the process. So the second statement is true too.

The Viet Nam war was not justified. We sent young Americans over there and alot of them didn't come back. There was alot of unrest at home with the antiwar Movement. Veterans had night mares for years and trouble getting jobs. And the VietNamese had to rebuild there country because it was all bombed out. So the circumstances were not right for us in this case. But if during the cold war the Russians had bombed us, we would be justified in bombing back. It's a matter of self-defense.

So if I have to choose, I'd take the second statement. That way you keep your options open.

Grader's comments: This essay doesn't really address the writing assignment. Moreover, it's seriously flawed because of its vague ideas, unsatisfactory organization, and poor grammar. The author would have been better served by choosing one side or the other, instead of waffling on the issue. Nevertheless, the essay contains the kernel of a coherent argument and does provide a bit of evidence in support of that argument; hence, it merits a 2 instead of a 1.

CHAPTER 3 SUMMARY

The SAT essay is graded on a number of different factors. The three most important ones are:

1. Length (3–5 paragraphs, each paragraph 2–5 sentences)

2. Content (address the topic, write to persuade)

3. Neatness (if they can't read it, you'll get a low score)

Kaplan has a great method called TOWF for writing a high-scoring essay:

THINK about the topic and brainstorm. (2 minutes)

ORGANIZE your paragraphs. (5 minutes)

WRITE your essay. (15 minutes)

FIX any mistakes. (3 minutes)

Four additional tips to keep in mind:

1. Decipher the Prompt

Even though you will be writing under time constraints (25 minutes to write an intro, sentences that express your logical and persuasive ideas in the paragraphs that follow, and a strong conclusion), the first thing, of course, is to read the essay prompt. Make sure you understand and address the assignment question.

Deciphering the steps of the prompt is your most important task. Even the very best written essay will not score well if it does not fulfill the expectations of the prompt.

2. Plan Ahead

Give yourself a hand by outlining and planning ahead. Quickly jot down your ideas in order to organize your thoughts and remember your main points.

3. Watch Your Language

Be sure your sentences are constructed so that your ideas are clear and understandable. Vary your sentence structure, sometimes using simple sentences and other times using compound and complex structures. Good grammar is essential: your writing must follow the general rules of standard written English. We'll delve further into SAT essay style in the next chapter.

4. Don't Sweat the Small Stuff

Do not obsess over every little thing. If you cannot remember how to spell a word, just keep going. Even the top-scoring essays will have flaws. The essay readers understand that you are writing first-draft essays. They will not be looking to take points off for minor errors.

However, if your essay is too insubstantial or littered with misspellings and grammar mistakes, the reader may conclude that you have a serious communication problem and score your essay accordingly. Your score can also suffer if your writing is unclear due to errors or sloppy presentation and the reader cannot understand what you are trying to say.

Chapter Four: **Writing Direct Statements**

In the previous chapter we had you write a few sample essays and compare them to good essays and not-so-good essays. How did yours compare? If they're on the not-so-good side, don't worry just yet. This chapter explains how to write phrases and sentences the SAT graders will like. Learning to directly state your point will improve your writing for the SAT as well as for college.

KEEP IT SIMPLE

Let's start with the single most important thing to bear in mind when writing an essay: keep it simple. It's so important that we're going to repeat it.

Keep It Simple, Smarty

Just remember to **KISS**! And no, we're not asking you to pucker up. We're encouraging you to *keep it simple, smarty*.

KISS applies to:

- Word choice
- Sentence structure
- Argument

This means you should, whenever possible, use simple words, simple sentences, and a simple argument.

Simple Words

Obsessing over how to use or even spell a big word correctly can throw off your train of thought. It's just not worth the effort. Bigger is NOT always better when it comes to vocabulary. When in doubt or pressed for time, stick to the simple words you know.

Simple Sentences

Complicated and wordy sentences are more likely to be filled with grammar errors. Again, considering the time constraints involved with timed essay writing, you will do yourself a favor by keeping your sentences simple and easy to follow.

Simple Arguments

The more convoluted your argument is, the more likely you are to write convoluted paragraphs. A clear, straightforward approach will lead to the clear, straightforward paragraphs that graders prefer.

With That Said

Graders don't expect eloquence in a 25-minute essay assignment, but they do want to see effective, logical writing.

Ten Style Commandments

Each of these strategies is followed by some weak sentences for you to improve through revising. Answers to all of the practice questions are at the end of the chapter starting on page 78.

Commandment One: Avoid Wordiness

Do not use several words when one word will do. Avoid *at the present time* or *at this point in time* when the simpler *now* will do.

Wordy: I am of the opinion that the aforementioned managers should be advised that they will be evaluated with regard to the utilization of responsive organizational software for the purpose of devising a responsive network of customers.

Concise: We should tell the managers that we will evaluate their use of flexible computerized databases to develop a customer's network.

Writing Drill 1

Improve the following sentences by omitting or replacing wordy phrases. Write your revised sentences on the lines that follow. Answers begin on page 77.

1. The agency is not prepared to undertake expansion at this point in time.

   Rewrite: _____

   _____

2. In view of the fact that John has prepared with much care for this presentation, it would be a good idea to award him with the project.

   Rewrite: _____

   _____

3. The airline has a problem with always having arrivals that come at least an hour late, despite the fact that the leaders of the airline promise that promptness is a goal which has a high priority for all the employees involved.

Rewrite: _____

_____

4. In spite of the fact that she only has a little bit of experience in photography right now, she will probably do well in the future because she has a great deal of motivation to succeed in her chosen profession.

Rewrite: _____

_____

5. The United States is not in a position to spend more money to alleviate the suffering of the people of other countries, considering the problems of its own citizens.

Rewrite: _____

_____

6. Although not untactful, George is a man who says exactly what he believes.

Rewrite: _____

_____

7. Accuracy is a subject that has great importance to English teachers and company presidents alike.

Rewrite: _____

_____

8. The reason why babies often cry when a stranger picks them up is that they experience fear of those with whom they are not familiar.

Rewrite: _____

_____

9. Ms. Miller speaks with a high degree of intelligence with regard to many aspects of modern philosophy.

Rewrite: _____

_____

10. The best of all possible leaders is one who listens and inspires simultaneously.

    Rewrite: _____

    _____

Commandment Two: Don't Be Redundant Over and Over Again

Redundancy means "needlessly repeating an idea." It's redundant to write "a beginner lacking experience." The word "beginner" by itself implies lack of experience. It's redundant to write "don't be redundant over and over again." The word "redundant" implies repetition.

So watch out for words that add nothing to the sentence. This chart lists some common redundant phrases and how to fix them.

Redundant	Concise
refer back	refer
few in number	few
small-sized	small
grouped together	grouped
in my own personal opinion	in my opinion
end result	result
serious crisis	crisis
new initiatives	initiatives

Writing Drill 2

Repair the following sentences by eliminating redundancies. Answers begin on page 77.

1. All these problems have combined together to create a serious crisis.

2. A staff that large in size needs an effective supervisor who can get the job done.

3. He knows how to follow directions and he knows how to do what he is told.

4. The writer's technical skill and ability do not mask his poor plot line.

5. That monument continues to remain a significant tourist attraction.

6. The recently observed trend of spending on credit has created a middle class that is poorer and more impoverished than ever before.

7. Those who can follow directions are few in number.

8. She has deliberately chosen to change careers.

9. Dialogue opens up many doors to compromise.

10. The ultimate conclusion is that environmental and economic concerns are intertwined.

Commandment Three: Avoid Needless Qualification

Always remember: You are trying to persuade the reader with your essay. What's the best way to persuade someone? Should you force them to see things your way with a bunch of exclamation points and extreme language, or should you be reasonable?

We're confident that you are a reasonable writer, so use reason when writing your SAT essay. There won't be any single, clear-cut "answer" to the essay topic, so don't overstate your case. Use qualifiers like *fairly*, *rather*, *somewhat*, and *relatively* once in a while. This lets the reader know that you are being reasonable, not absolute or irrational.

However, using qualifiers too often weakens your essay. It makes you sound like you are not sure of what you're writing. And, like wordy phrases, qualifiers can add bulk to your writing without adding substance. The key to a successful essay is to balance your opinions with the occasional qualifier and to state your facts neutrally. A fact will speak for itself.

Wordy (too many qualifiers): This *rather* serious breach of etiquette *may possibly* shake the very foundations of the diplomatic community.

Concise: This serious breach of etiquette *may* shake the foundations of the diplomatic community.

Avoid overusing the word *very*. Some writers use this intensifying adverb before almost every adjective in an attempt to be more forceful. They should try a more varied approach. If you need to add emphasis, look for a stronger adjective (or verb). For example:

Weak: Novak is a very good pianist.

Strong: Novak is a virtuoso pianist. OR: Novak plays beautifully.

Redundant	Concise
more unique	unique
the very worst	the worst
completely full	full
absolutely ultimate	ultimate

Excessive qualification detracts from the quality of your argument and can lead to redundancy, wordiness, and a weak position.

Writing Drill 3

Eliminate needless qualification in the following sentences. Write your answers on the lines that follow. Answers begin on page 77.

1. Ms. Wangiru is a fairly excellent teacher.

   Rewrite: _____

   _____

2. Ferrara seems to be sort of a slow worker.

   Rewrite: _____

   _____

3. There are very many reasons technology has not permeated all countries equally.

   Rewrite: _____

   _____

4. It is rather important to pay attention to all the details of a murder trial as well as to the "larger picture."

   Rewrite: _____

   _____

5. You yourself are the very best person to decide what you should do for a living.

   Rewrite: _____

   _____

6. It is possible that the author overstates his case somewhat.

   Rewrite: _____

   _____

7. The president perhaps should use a certain amount of diplomacy before he resorts to force.

   Rewrite: _____

   _____

8. In Italy I found about the best food I have ever eaten.

   Rewrite: _____

   _____

9. Needless to say, children should be taught to cooperate at home and in school.

   Rewrite: _____

   _____

10. The travel agent does not recommend the trip to Seattle, since it is possible that the weather may be inclement.

Rewrite: _____

_____

Commandment Four: Don't Write Just to Fill Up Space

If you have something to say, just say it. If you need to smooth over a change of subject, do so with a transitional word or phrase, rather than with a meaningless sentence. This strategy has a bunch of "don'ts":

- Don't write a sentence that gets you nowhere. Make every sentence count.
- Don't ask a question only to answer it. Get to the point.
- Don't write a whole sentence only to announce that you're changing the subject. Instead, make use of transitional words and phrases to keep the transition smooth.

Wordy: Which idea of the author's is more in line with what I believe? This is a very interesting question…
Concise: The author's beliefs are similar to mine.

Get to the point quickly and stay there. Simplicity and clarity win points on the SAT exam.

Writing Drill 4

Rewrite each of these two-sentence statements as one concise sentence on the lines that follow. Answers begin on page 77.

1. In the late 20th century, the earth can be characterized as a small planet. Advanced technology has made it easy for people who live vast distances from each other to communicate.

   Rewrite: _____

   _____

2. What's the purpose of getting rid of the chemical pollutants in water? People cannot safely consume water that contains chemical pollutants.

   Rewrite: _____

   _____

3. Napoleon suffered defeat in Russia because most of his troops perished in the cold. Most of his men died because they had no winter clothing to protect them from the cold.

   Rewrite: _____

   _____

4. Third, I do not believe those who argue that some of Shakespeare's plays were written by others. There is no evidence that other people had a hand in writing Shakespeare's plays.

Rewrite: _____

_____

5. Which point of view is closest to my own? This is a good question. I agree with those who say that the United States should send humanitarian aid to areas of need.

Rewrite: _____

_____

6. Frank Lloyd Wright was a famous architect. He was renowned for his ability to design buildings that blend into their surroundings.

Rewrite: _____

_____

7. Who was Julius Caesar? He was a leader of the Roman Empire.

Rewrite: _____

_____

8. He was not in class today. The teacher refused to let him into class because he showed up ten minutes late.

Rewrite: _____

_____

9. The fire burned thousands of acres of forest land. Many trees were destroyed by the fire.

Rewrite: _____

_____

10. A lot of people find math a difficult subject to master. They have trouble with math because it requires very precise thinking skills.

Rewrite: _____

_____

Commandment Five: Avoid Needless Self-Reference

Another waste of time and space in your writing is to overly clarify your opinion. You can assume that the reader knows that you, as the writer of the essay, are the one who believes, thinks, and feels the things that you are writing. In that way, phrases like *I feel*, *I believe*, and *it's my opinion that…* are obvious and unnecessary.

Weak: I am of the opinion that air pollution is a more serious problem than the government has led us to believe.

Forceful: Air pollution is a more serious problem than the government has led us to believe.

Self-reference is another form of qualifying what you say—a very obvious form. One or two self-references in an essay might be appropriate, just as the use of qualifiers like *probably* and *perhaps* can be effective if you practice using them sparingly. Practice is the only sure way to improve your writing.

Weak: I happen to think that teenagers should spend more time reading books than watching TV.

Forceful: Teenagers should spend more time reading books than watching TV.

Writing Drill 5

Rewrite these sentences to eliminate needless self-references on the lines that follow. Answers begin on page 77.

1. I feel we ought to pay teachers more than we pay senators.

   Rewrite: _____

   _____

2. The author, in my personal opinion, is stuck in the past.

   Rewrite: _____

   _____

3. I do not think this argument can be generalized to most business owners.

   Rewrite: _____

   _____

4. My own experience shows me that food is the best social lubricant.

   Rewrite: _____

   _____

5. I doubt more people would vote even if they had more information about candidates.

   Rewrite: _____

   _____

6. Although I am no expert, I do not think privacy should be valued more than social concerns.

   Rewrite:_____

   _____

7. My guess is that most people want to do good work, but many are bored or frustrated with their jobs.

   Rewrite:_____

   _____

8. I must emphasize that I am not saying the author does not have a point.

   Rewrite:_____

   _____

9. If I were a college president, I would implement several specific reforms to combat apathy.

   Rewrite:_____

   _____

10. It is my belief that either alternative would prove disastrous.

   Rewrite:_____

   _____

Commandment Six: Use the Active Voice

Put verbs in the active voice whenever possible. In the active voice, the subject performs the action: *We decide now.* In the passive voice, the subject is the receiver of the action and is often only implied: *It will be decided now.*

Avoid the passive voice EXCEPT in the following cases:

- When you do not know who performed the action: *The letter was opened before I received it.*
- When you prefer not to refer directly to the person who performs the action: *An error has been made in computing this data.*

   Passive: The estimate of this year's tax revenues was prepared by the General Accounting Office.
   Active: The General Accounting Office prepared the estimate of this year's tax revenues.

Passive sentences are weak. They are usually the product of writing before you think. To change from the passive to the active voice, ask yourself who or what is performing the action. In the previous example, the General Accounting Office (GAO) is performing the action. Therefore, the GAO should be the subject of the sentence.

Writing Drill 6

Replace the passive voice with the active voice wherever possible. Rewrite the sentences on the lines that follow. Answers begin on page 77.

1. That movement was led by brave but misguided men.

   Rewrite: _____

   _____

2. The bill was passed by congress in time, but it was not signed by the president until the time for action had passed.

   Rewrite: _____

   _____

3. Advice is usually requested by those who need it least; it is not sought out by the truly lost and ignorant.

   Rewrite: _____

   _____

4. That building should be relocated where it can be appreciated by the citizens.

   Rewrite: _____

   _____

5. Garbage collectors should be generously rewarded for their dirty, smelly labors.

   Rewrite: _____

   _____

6. The conditions of the contract agreement were ironed out minutes before the strike deadline.

   Rewrite: _____

   _____

7. The minutes of the City Council meeting should be taken by the city clerk.

   Rewrite: _____

   _____

8. With sugar, water, or salt, many ailments contracted in less-developed countries could be treated.

   Rewrite: _____

   _____

9. Test results were distributed with no concern for confidentiality.

   Rewrite: _____

   _____

10. The report was compiled by a number of field anthropologists and marriage experts.

    Rewrite: _____

    _____

Commandment Seven: Avoid Weak Openings

Try not to begin a sentence with *there is, there are, it would be, it could be, it can be,* or *it is.* These roundabout expressions usually indicate that you are trying to distance yourself from the position you are taking.

Weak openings usually result from writing before you think. They happen when you are hedging until you figure out what you want to say.

Weak: There are several reasons why Andre and his brother will not share an apartment.

Strong: Andre and his brother will not share an apartment for several reasons.

Writing Drill 7

Rewrite these sentences to eliminate weak openings on the lines that follow. Answers begin on page 77.

1. It would be unwise for businesses to ignore the illiteracy problem.

   Rewrite: _____

   _____

2. It can be seen that in many fields experience is more important than training.

   Rewrite: _____

   _____

3. There are several reasons why this plane is obsolete.

   Rewrite: _____

   _____

4. It would be of no use to reprimand the class for its poor reading scores without addressing the inexperience of the teacher.

   Rewrite: _____

   _____

5. There are many strong points in the candidate's favor; intelligence, unfortunately, is not among them.

   Rewrite: _____

   _____

6. It is difficult to justify building a more handsome prison.

   Rewrite: _____

   _____

7. It has been decided that we, as a society, can tolerate homelessness.

   Rewrite: _____

   _____

8. There seems to be little doubt that Americans like watching television better than conversing.

   Rewrite: _____

   _____

9. It is clear that cats make better pets than mice.

   Rewrite: _____

   _____

10. It is obvious that intelligence is a product of environment and heredity.

    Rewrite: _____

    _____

Commandment Eight: Don't Be Vague

Avoid vague references, indirect language, and general wordiness. Choose specific, descriptive words. Vague language weakens your writing because it forces the reader to guess what you mean instead of allowing the reader to concentrate fully on your ideas and style. The essay topics you'll see on the exam will be open-ended, but not so obscure that you won't be able to come up with any specific examples or concrete information. Your argument will be more forceful if you stick to the specifics.

> **Weak:** Chantal is highly educated.
> **Strong:** Chantal has a master's degree in business administration.
>
> **Weak:** Chantal is a great communicator.
> **Strong:** Chantal speaks persuasively.

Notice that, sometimes, to be more specific and concrete, you use more words than you might with vague language. But this strategy does NOT conflict with the goal of being concise. Being concise means eliminating *unnecessary* words. Getting specific sometimes means adding necessary words.

Writing Drill 8

Rewrite these sentences to replace vague language with specific, concrete language on the lines that follow. Answers begin on page 77.

1. Water is transformed into steam when the former is heated up to 100 degrees Celcius.

    Rewrite: _____

    _____

2. Many people imitate others before achieving creativity. Artists, for example, often imitate other artists as they learn their craft.

    Rewrite: _____

    _____

3. Arthur is a careless person.

    Rewrite: _____

    _____

4. Experts think that banks are contributing to the current economic downturn by constantly raising their interest rates.

    Rewrite: _____

    _____

5. She told us that she was going to go to the store as soon as her mother came home.

    Rewrite: _____

    _____

6. A radar unit is a highly specialized piece of equipment.

   Rewrite: _____

   _____

7. The principal told Jayden that he shouldn't even think about coming back to school until he changed his ways.

   Rewrite: _____

   _____

8. The detective had to seek the permission of the lawyer to question the suspect.

   Rewrite: _____

   _____

9. The executive assistant was unable to complete the task that had been assigned.

   Rewrite: _____

   _____

Commandment Nine: Avoid Clichés

Time pressure and anxiety may make you lose focus. That's when clichés can slip into your writing. Clichés are overused expressions, which can make you sound lazy. Keep them out of your essay.

Weak: Performance in a crisis is the acid test for a leader.

Strong: Performance in a crisis is the best indicator of a leader's abilities.

Putting a cliché in quotation marks in order to distance yourself from the cliché does not strengthen the sentence: *Aunt Violet never "ran from a fight," but she didn't stand up for her convictions, either.* If anything, the presence of quotation marks around a cliché just makes the weak writing more noticeable. Always substitute more specific language for a cliché.

Writing Drill 9

Make the following sentences more direct and original by replacing clichés and rewrite them on the lines that follow. Answers begin on page 77.

1. Beyond the shadow of a doubt, Jefferson was a great leader.

   Rewrite: _____

   _____

2. I have a sneaking suspicion that families spend less time together than they did 15 years ago.

   Rewrite: _____

   _____

3. The pizza delivery man arrived in the sequestered jury's hour of need.

   Rewrite: _____

   _____

4. Trying to find the employee responsible for this embarrassing information leak is like trying to find a needle in a haystack.

   Rewrite: _____

   _____

5. Both strategies would be expensive and completely ineffective, so it's six of one and half a dozen of the other.

   Rewrite: _____

   _____

6. The military is putting all its eggs in one basket by relying so heavily on nuclear missiles for the nation's defense.

   Rewrite: _____

   _____

7. Older doctors should be required to update their techniques, but you can't teach an old dog new tricks.

   Rewrite: _____

   _____

8. You have to take this new fad with a grain of salt.

   Rewrite: _____

   _____

9. The politician reminds me of Abraham Lincoln: he's like a diamond in the rough.

   Rewrite: _____

   _____

10. A ballpark estimate of the number of fans in the stadium would be 120,000.

    Rewrite: _____

    _____

Commandment Ten: Avoid Jargon

Jargon comes in two categories of words. The first jargon category is the specialized vocabulary of a group. This is language that only one group of people—such as doctors, computer programmers, or baseball managers—uses.

The second category of jargon is complex language that makes many students' essays hard to read.

> **Using jargon:** The international banks are cognizant of the new law's significance.
>
> **Jargon-free:** The international banks are aware of the new law's significance.

You will not impress anyone with big words that do not fit the tone or context of your essay, especially if you misuse them.

If you are not certain of a word's meaning, leave it out. An appropriate word, even a simple one, will add impact to your argument. As you come across words you are unsure of, ask yourself, "Would a reader in a different field be able to understand exactly what I mean from the words I've chosen?" and "Is there any way I can say the same thing more simply?"

> **Using jargon:** The new law would negatively impact each of the nations involved.
>
> **Jargon-free:** The new law would hurt each of the nations involved.

(*Impact* is also used to mean *affect* or *benefit*.)

Below are some words that have been overused by certain groups and can sound like jargon.

Jargon Hit List

prioritize	parameter (boundary, limit)
optimize	user-friendly
time frame	utilize (use)
input/output	finalize (end, complete)
mutually beneficial	bottom line
conceptualize (imagine, think)	right-size
maximize	bandwidth
designate	blindside
originate (start, begin)	downside
facilitate (help, speed up)	ongoing (continuing)

Writing Drill 10

Replace the jargon in the following sentences with more appropriate language and rewrite them on the lines that follow. Answers begin on page 77.

1. We anticipate utilizing hundreds of paper clips in the foreseeable future.

   Rewrite: _____

   _____

2. The research-oriented person should not be hired for a people-oriented position.

   Rewrite: _____

   _____

3. Educationwise, our schoolchildren have been neglected.

   Rewrite: _____

   _____

4. Foreign diplomats should always interface with local leaders.

   Rewrite: _____

   _____

5. Pursuant to your being claimed as a dependent on the returns of another taxpayer or resident wage earner, you may not consider yourself exempt if your current income exceeds 500 dollars.

   Rewrite: _____

   _____

6. There is considerable evidentiary support for the assertion that Vienna sausages are good for you.

   Rewrite: _____

   _____

7. With reference to the poem, I submit that the second and third stanzas connote a certain despair.

   Rewrite: _____

   _____

8. Allow me to elucidate my position: This horse is the epitome, the very quintessence of equine excellence.

   Rewrite: _____

   _____

9. In the case of the recent railway disaster, it is clear that governmental regulatory agencies obfuscated in the preparation of materials for release to the public through both the electronic and print media.

   Rewrite: _____

   _____

10. Having been blindsided by innumerable unforeseen crises, this office has not been able to prepare for the aforementioned exigencies.

    Rewrite: _____

    _____

CHAPTER 4 SUMMARY

The most important thing to keep in mind while writing your essay is to KISS or keep it simple, smarty.

KISS applies to:

- Word choice
- Sentence structure
- Argument

Graders understand you are under time pressure, so small mistakes aren't a huge deal as long as you don't repeat them.

Ten Style Commandments:

1. Avoid wordiness.
2. Don't be redundant.
3. Avoid needless qualification.
4. Don't write just to fill up space.
5. Avoid needless self-reference.
6. Use the active voice.
7. Avoid weak openings.
8. Don't be vague.
9. Avoid clichés.
10. Avoid jargon.

ANSWERS AND EXPLANATIONS

Many items in the writing drills could have more than one possible correct answer. In those cases, we've suggested sample correct answers. Keep that in mind as you compare your answers to ours.

Drill 1: Avoid Wordiness

1. The agency is not prepared to expand now.

2. Since John has prepared for this presentation so carefully, we should award him the project.

3. Flights are always at least an hour late on this airline, though its leaders promise that promptness is a high priority for all its employees.

4. Although she is inexperienced in photography, she will probably succeed because she is motivated.

5. The United States cannot spend more money to alleviate other countries' suffering when its own citizens suffer.

6. Although tactful, George says exactly what he believes.

7. Accuracy is important to English teachers and company presidents alike.

8. Babies often cry when strangers pick them up because they fear unfamiliarity.

9. Ms. Miller speaks intelligently about many aspects of modern philosophy.

10. The best leader is one who listens and inspires simultaneously.

Drill 2: Don't Be Redundant

1. All these problems have combined to create a crisis.

2. A staff that large needs an effective supervisor.

3. He knows how to follow directions.

4. The writer's technical skill does not mask his poor plot line.

5. That monument remains a significant tourist attraction.

6. The recent trend of spending on credit has created a more impoverished middle class.

7. Few people can follow directions.

8. She has chosen to change careers.

9. Dialogue opens many doors to compromise.

10. The conclusion is that environmental and economic concerns are intertwined.

Drill 3: Avoid Needless Qualification

1. Ms. Wangiru is a good teacher.

2. Ferrara is a slow worker.

3. For many reasons, technology has not permeated all countries equally.

4. In a murder trial, it is important to pay attention to the details as well as to the "larger picture."

5. You are the best person to decide what you should do for a living.

6. The author overstates his case somewhat.

7. The president should use diplomacy before he resorts to force.

8. In Italy, I found the best food I have ever eaten.

9. Children should be taught to cooperate at home and in school.

10. The travel agent said not to go to Seattle, since the weather may be inclement. (Saying "it is possible that the weather may be inclement" is an example of redundant qualification, since both *possible* and *may* indicate uncertainty.)

Drill 4: Don't Write Just to Fill Up Space

1. Advanced technology has made it easy for people who live vast distances from each other to communicate.

2. People cannot safely consume water that contains chemical pollutants.

3. Napoleon suffered defeat in Russia because most of his troops perished in the cold.

4. No present evidence suggests that Shakespeare's plays were written by others.

5. I agree with those who say that the United States should send humanitarian aid to areas of need.

6. The architect Frank Lloyd Wright was famous for his ability to design buildings that blend into their surroundings.

7. Julius Caesar was a leader of the Roman Empire.

8. The teacher refused to let him into class because he showed up ten minutes late.

9. Many trees were destroyed by the fire that burned thousands of acres of forest land.

10. A lot of people find math a difficult subject because it requires very precise thinking skills.

Drill 5: Avoid Needless Self-Reference

1. We ought to pay teachers more than we pay senators.

2. The author is stuck in the past.

3. This argument cannot be generalized to most business owners.

4. Food is perhaps the best social lubricant.

5. More people would not vote even if they had more information about candidates.

6. Privacy should not be valued more than social concerns.

7. Most people want to do good work, but many are bored or frustrated with their jobs.

8. The author has a point.

9. College presidents should implement several specific reforms to combat apathy.

10. Either alternative would prove disastrous.

Drill 6: Use the Active Voice

1. Brave but misguided men led that movement.

2. Congress passed the bill in time, but the president did not sign it until the time for action had passed.

3. Those who need advice least usually request it; the truly lost and ignorant do not seek it.

4. We should relocate that building where citizens can appreciate it.

5. City government should generously reward garbage collectors for their dirty, smelly labors.

6. Negotiators ironed out the conditions of the contract agreement minutes before the strike deadline.

7. The city clerk should take the minutes of the City Council meeting.

8. With sugar, water, or salt, doctors can treat many of the ailments that citizens of less-developed countries contract.

9. The teacher distributed test results with no concern for confidentiality.

10. A number of field anthropologists and marriage experts compiled the report.

Drill 7: Avoid Weak Openings

1. Businesses ignore the illiteracy problem at their own peril.

2. Experience is more important than training in many fields.

3. This plane is obsolete for several reasons.

4. The class cannot be reprimanded for poor reading scores without also addressing the inexperience of the teacher.

5. The candidate has many strong points; intelligence, unfortunately, is not among them.

6. The city cannot justify building a more handsome prison.

7. We, as a society, have decided to tolerate homelessness.

8. Americans must like watching television better than conversing.

9. Cats make better pets than mice.

10. Intelligence is a product of environment and heredity.

Drill 8: Don't Be Vague

1. When water is heated to 100 degrees Celsius, it turns into steam.

2. The Hudson River school painters imitated European painting techniques before developing their own distinctly American style.

3. Arthur often forgets to do his chores.

4. Many economists think that rising bank interest rates have contributed to the current economic downturn.

5. Pop culture has a strong influence on the identity and socialization of modern teens.

6. A radar unit registers the distance and characteristics of aircraft.

7. The principal told Jayden that he could not return to school until his behavior improved.

8. We muster courage to overcome fear of rejection when striking up conversation with a stranger, or fear of failure when performing onstage or on the field.

9. The executive assistant was unable to type the document.

Drill 9: Avoid Clichés

1. Jefferson was certainly a great leader.

2. Families probably spend less time together than they did 15 years ago.

3. The pizza delivery man arrived just when the sequestered jury most needed him.

4. Trying to find the employee responsible for this embarrassing information leak may be impossible.

5. Both strategies would be expensive and completely ineffective: they have an equal chance of failing.

6. The military should diversify its defense rather than rely so heavily on nuclear missiles.

7. Older doctors should be required to update their techniques, but many seem resistant to changes in technology.

8. You need not take this new fad very seriously; it will surely pass.

9. The politician reminds me of Abraham Lincoln with his rough appearance and warm heart.

10. I estimate that 120,000 fans were in the stadium. (Even when a cliché is used in its original context, it sounds old.)

Drill 10: Avoid Jargon

1. We expect to use hundreds of paper clips in the next two months.

2. A person who likes research should not be hired for a position that requires someone to interact with customers all day.

3. Our schoolchildren's education has been neglected.

4. Foreign diplomats should always talk to local leaders.

5. If someone claims you as a dependent on a tax return, you may still have to pay taxes on your income in excess of 500 dollars.

6. Recent studies suggest that Vienna sausages are good for you.

7. When the poet wrote the second and third stanzas, he must have felt despair.

8. This is a fine horse.

9. Government regulatory agencies were not honest in their press releases about the recent railway accident.

10. Having spent our time responding to many unexpected problems this month, we have not been able to prepare for these longer-term needs.

Chapter Five: **Getting the Mechanics of Writing Right**

Studying this chapter will help you prepare for both the essay and the multiple-choice sections of the SAT. It contains the 12 rules that apply to *all* writing. Remember, essay graders will not mark you down for the occasional errors common to first-draft writing. A lone sentence fragment or a slight problem with subject-verb agreement is to be expected. What is important is that you do not make these mistakes *repeatedly*, as this may indicate to the reader that you lack an under-standing of some of the basic rules of writing and grammar.

Think of this section as a reminder. It will help you grasp the finer points of good writing while refreshing the solid writing skills you've developed over the years. If you feel overwhelmed, stop and take a break. You need time to absorb the information. So go slow. But be sure to do the exercises, and then compare your answers to ours. Make sure you understand the error in each sentence so you can always avoid the mistake in your writing come test time.

As you work through this chapter, you will come across a few technical words that describe par-ticular functions that words have in a sentence. You will not be expected to know these terms on the Writing section. Just understand what the part of speech does in the sentence so that you can recognize an error when you see one.

Answers to all of the practice questions are at the end of the chapter starting on page 107.

Rule 1: Avoid Slang and Colloquialisms

Conversational speech is filled with slang and colloquial expressions. *Do not use slang in your essay!* Slang terms and colloquialisms can be confusing to the reader, since these expressions are not universally understood. They also can make you sound like a lazy writer.

> **Incorrect:** He is really into skateboards.
> **Correct:** He enjoys skateboarding.

> **Incorrect:** She plays a wicked game of tennis.
> **Correct:** She excels in tennis.

> **Incorrect:** Myra has got to go to Memphis for a week.
> **Correct:** Myra must go to Memphis for a week.

Incorrect: Joan has been doing science for eight years now.

Correct: Joan has been a scientist for eight years now.

Incorrect: The blackened salmon's been one of the restaurant's most popular entrées.

Correct: The blackened salmon has been one of the restaurant's most popular entrées.

With a little thought, you will find the right word. Using informal language and unclear contractions is risky. Play it safe by sticking to standard usage.

Writing Drill 1

Replace the informal elements of the following sentences with more appropriate terms on the lines that follow. Answers begin on page 107.

1. Cynthia Larson sure knows her stuff.

   Rewrite: _____

   _____

2. The crowd was really into watching the fire-eating juggler, but then the dancing horse grabbed their attention.

   Rewrite: _____

   _____

3. As soon as the Human Resources department checks out his résumé, I am sure we will hear gales of laughter issuing from the office.

   Rewrite: _____

   _____

4. Having something funny to say seems awfully important in our culture.

   Rewrite: _____

   _____

5. The chef has a nice way with striped bass: his sauce was simple, but the effect was sublime.

   Rewrite: _____

   _____

6. Normal human beings can't cope with repeated humiliation.

   Rewrite: _____

   _____

7. The world hasn't got much time to stop polluting; soon, we all will have to wear face masks.

   Rewrite: _____

   _____

8. If you want a good cheesecake, you must make a top-notch crust.

   Rewrite: _____

   _____

9. International organizations should try and cooperate on global issues like hunger.

   Rewrite: _____

   _____

10. The environmentalists aren't in it for the prestige; they really care about protecting the spotted owl.

    Rewrite: _____

    _____

Rule 2: Avoid Sentence Fragments and Run-On Sentences

Technically, a sentence fragment has no independent clause (see box below). A run-on sentence has two or more independent clauses that are improperly connected. While writing under pressure, it's easy to lose track and end up with a sentence fragment or a run-on. Here are some tips on how to avoid these common problems.

Independent Clauses 101: Avoiding Sentence Fragments and Run-On Sentences

Several rules depend on your ability to identify an *independent clause*—a group of words that can stand alone as its own grammatically correct sentence. Understanding how independent clauses function in sentences is essential to avoiding grammatical mistakes.

An independent clause includes a subject, verb, and a complete thought; whereas a *dependent clause* is missing one or more of the key parts of a sentence. Let's examine the sentence below:

She likes to eat meatloaf sandwiches when she's hiking.

The independent clause in this sentence is *she likes to eat meatloaf sandwiches.* The clause has a subject, a verb, and a complete thought. No additional information is required. The dependent clause—*when she's hiking*—isn't a complete thought and depends on the independent clause that precedes it.

A complete sentence must include at least one independent clause. A line without an independent clause is a *sentence fragment*—and is missing the subject, verb, and/or a complete thought. For instance, the phrase *a slice of cheese pizza to go* is missing a verb and is not a complete thought.

Sentences may have more than one independent clause, but the clauses must be connected properly; otherwise, you create a run-on sentence. *Run-ons* are sentences that do not properly connect two or more independent clauses. Let's look at the following run-on sentence:

She would like a meatloaf sandwich, I'd like a cheese pizza.

This sentence contains two independent clauses which could each stand alone as a complete sentence. As this sentence is written, the only thing connecting the two independent clauses is a comma, which is not strong enough by itself to connect two independent clauses. This creates a run-on sentence.

Now that you know how to identify an independent clause, keep reading to find out how to fix specific problems with sentence fragments, run-ons, and comma splices.

Sentence Fragments

Every sentence in formal expository writing must have an independent clause. An independent clause contains a subject and a predicate and does not begin with a subordinate conjunction such as one of these:

after	if	than	whenever
although	in order that	though	where
as	provided that	unless	whether
because	since	until	while
before	so that		

Incorrect: Global warming. That is what the scientists and journalists are worried about this year.
Correct: Global warming is the cause of concern for scientists and journalists this year.

Incorrect: Seattle is a wonderful place to live. Having mountains, ocean, and forests all within easy driving distance. If you can ignore the rain.
Correct: Seattle is a wonderful place to live, with mountains, ocean, and forests all within easy driving distance. However, it certainly does rain often.

Incorrect: Why do I think the author's position is preposterous? Because he makes generalizations that I know are untrue.
Correct: I think the author's position is preposterous because he makes generalizations that I know are untrue.

Beginning single-clause sentences with coordinate conjunctions—*and, but, or, nor, yet, so,* and *for*—is acceptable in moderation (although some graders may object to beginning a sentence with *and*). For example:

Correct: Most people would agree that indigent patients should receive wonderful health care. But every treatment has its price.

Run-On Sentences

Time pressure may also cause you to mistakenly write two or more sentences as one. Watch out for independent clauses that are not joined with any punctuation at all or are joined only with a comma.

Sample run-on sentence: Current insurance practices are unfair, they discriminate against the people who need insurance most.

You can repair run-on sentences including the one above in any of three ways:

1. Use a period.
2. Use a semicolon.
3. Use a conjunction.

Run-on sentence revision using a period: Using a period enables you to make separate sentences of the independent clauses. *Current insurance practices are unfair. They discriminate against the people who need insurance most.*

Run-on sentence revision using a semicolon: A semicolon functions as a "weak period." In other words, it is a shorter pause than what you would do for a period, but longer than an ordinary comma. It separates independent clauses, but signals to the reader that the ideas in the clauses are related. *Current insurance practices are unfair; they discriminate against the people who need insurance most.*

Run-on sentence revision using a conjunction: The third method of repairing a run-on sentence is usually the most effective. Use a conjunction to turn an independent clause into a dependent one and to make explicit how the clauses are related. You may also use a coordinating conjunction with a comma to connect the two clauses. *Current insurance practices are unfair in that they discriminate against the people who need insurance most.*

Another common cause of run-on sentences is the misuse of adverbs like *however, nevertheless, furthermore, likewise,* and *therefore.*

Run-on sentence: Current insurance practices are discriminatory, furthermore they make insurance too expensive for the poor.

Revised: Current insurance practices are discriminatory. Furthermore, they make insurance too expensive for the poor. (A semicolon may also be used in place of the period between *discriminatory* and *furthermore.*)

Writing Drill 2

Repair the following by eliminating sentence fragments and run-on sentences on the lines that follow. Answers begin on page 107.

1. The academy has all the programs Angie will need. Except the sports program, which has been phased out.

   Rewrite: _____

   _____

2. Leadership ability. That is the elusive quality which our current government employees have yet to capture.

   Rewrite: _____

   _____

3. Antonio just joined the athletic club staff this year but Barry has been with us since 1993, therefore we would expect Barry to be more skilled with the weight-lifting equipment.

   Rewrite: _____

   _____

4. There is time to invest in property. After one has established oneself in the business world, however.

   Rewrite: _____

   _____

5. Sentence fragments are often used in casual conversation, however they should not be used in written English under normal circumstances.

   Rewrite: _____

   _____

Rule 3: Use Commas Correctly

When using the comma, follow these six guidelines:

1. Use commas to separate items in a series. If more than two items are listed in a series, they should be separated by commas. The final comma—the one that precedes the word *and*—is not strictly required.

   Correct: My recipe for buttermilk biscuits contains flour, baking soda, salt, shortening, and buttermilk.

   Correct: My recipe for chocolate cake contains flour, baking soda, sugar, eggs, milk, and chocolate.

2. Do not place commas before the first element of a series or after the last element.

Incorrect: My investment advisor recommended that I construct a portfolio of, stocks, bonds, commodities futures, and precious metals.

Correct: My investment advisor recommended that I construct a portfolio of stocks, bonds, commodities futures, and precious metals.

Incorrect: The elephants, tigers, and dancing bears, were the highlights of the circus.

Correct: The elephants, tigers, and dancing bears were the highlights of the circus.

3. Use commas to separate two or more adjectives before a noun; do not use a comma after the last adjective in the series.

Incorrect: I can't believe you sat through that long, dull, uninspired, movie three times.

Correct: I can't believe you sat through that long, dull, uninspired movie three times.

Incorrect: The manatee is a round, blubbery, bewhiskered, creature whose continued presence in American waters is endangered by careless boaters.

Correct: The manatee is a round, blubbery, bewhiskered creature whose continued presence in American waters is endangered by careless boaters.

4. Use commas to set off parenthetical clauses and phrases. A parenthetical expression is one that is not necessary to the main idea of the sentence.

Correct: Gordon, who is a writer by profession, bakes an excellent cheesecake.

The main idea here is that Gordon bakes an excellent cheesecake. The intervening clause merely serves to identify Gordon; thus, it should be set off with commas.

Incorrect: The newspaper, that has the most insipid editorials, is the *Daily Times*.

Correct: The newspaper that has the most insipid editorials is the *Daily Times*.

Incorrect: The newspaper which has the most insipid editorials of any I have read won numerous awards last week.

Correct: The newspaper, which has the most insipid editorials of any I have read, won numerous awards last week.

In the first example, the clause beginning with *that* defines which paper the author is discussing. In the second example, the main point is that the newspaper won numerous awards, and the intervening clause beginning with *which* identifies the paper.

5. Use commas after most introductory phrases.

Incorrect: Having watered his petunias every day during the drought Harold was very disappointed when his garden was destroyed by insects.

Correct: Having watered his petunias every day during the drought, Harold was very disappointed when his garden was destroyed by insects.

Incorrect: After the banquet Harold and Martha went dancing.

Correct: After the banquet, Harold and Martha went dancing.

6. Use commas to separate independent clauses (clauses that could stand alone as complete sentences) connected by coordinate conjunctions such as *and, but, not, yet*, etc.

Incorrect: Susan's old car has been belching blue smoke from the tailpipe for two weeks but it has not broken down yet.

Correct: Susan's old car has been belching blue smoke from the tailpipe for two weeks, but it has not broken down yet.

Incorrect: Zachariah's pet frog eats 50 flies a day yet it has never gotten indigestion.

Correct: Zachariah's pet frog eats 50 flies a day, yet it has never gotten indigestion.

Here's a final word on commas: it is incorrect to use a comma to separate the two parts of a compound verb.

Incorrect: Barbara went to the grocery store, and bought two quarts of milk.

Correct: Barbara went to the grocery store and bought two quarts of milk.

Incorrect: Zachariah's pet frog eats 50 flies a day, and never gets indigestion.

Correct: Zachariah's pet frog eats 50 flies a day and never gets indigestion.

Writing Drill 3

Correct the punctuation errors in the following sentences by inserting the proper punctuation marks or crossing out unnecessary ones. Answers begin on page 107.

1. Peter wants me to bring records games candy and soda to his party.

2. I need, lumber, nails, a hammer and a saw to build the shelf.

3. It takes a friendly energetic person to be a successful salesman.

4. I was shocked to discover that a large, modern, glass-sheathed, office building had replaced my old school.

5. The country club, a cluster of ivy-covered whitewashed buildings was the site of the president's first speech.

6. Pushing through the panicked crowd the security guards frantically searched for the suspect.

7. Despite careful analysis of the advantages and disadvantages of each proposal Harry found it hard to reach a decision.

Rule 4: Use Semicolons Correctly

Follow these two guidelines for correct semicolon usage:

1. A semicolon may be used instead of a coordinate conjunction such as *and, or,* or *but* to link two closely related independent clauses.

> **Incorrect:** Whooping cranes are an endangered species; and they are unlikely to survive if we continue to pollute.

> **Correct:** Whooping cranes are an endangered species; they are unlikely to survive if we continue to pollute.

> **Correct:** Whooping cranes are an endangered species, and they are unlikely to survive if we continue to pollute.

> **Correct:** Whooping cranes are an endangered species; there are only 50 whooping cranes in New Jersey today.

2. A semicolon also may be used between independent clauses connected by words like *therefore, nevertheless,* and *moreover*.

> **Correct:** The staff meeting has been postponed until next Thursday; therefore, I will be unable to get approval for my project until then.

> **Correct:** Farm prices have been falling rapidly for two years; nevertheless, the traditional American farm is not in danger of disappearing.

Writing Drill 4

Fix the following sentences, if necessary, on the lines that follow. Answers begin on page 107.

1. Morgan has five years' experience in karate; but Thompson has even more.

   Rewrite: _____

   _____

2. Very few students wanted to take the class in physics, only the professor's kindness kept it from being canceled.

   Rewrite: _____

   _____

3. You should always be prepared when you go on a camping trip, however you must avoid carrying unnecessary weight.

   Rewrite: _____

   _____

Rule 5: Use Colons Correctly

When you see a colon, it means "something's coming!" Follow these three rules for correct colon usage:

1. In formal writing, the colon is used only as a means of signaling that what follows is a list, definition, explanation, or concise summary of what has gone before. The colon usually follows an independent clause, and it will frequently be accompanied by a reinforcing expression like *the following*, *as follows*, or *namely*, or by an explicit demonstrative like *this*.

   Correct: Your instructions are as follows: read the passage carefully, answer the questions on the last page, and turn over your answer sheet.

   Correct: This is what I found in the refrigerator: a moldy lime, half a bottle of stale soda, and a jar of peanut butter.

   Correct: The biggest problem with the country today is apathy: the corrosive element that will destroy our democracy.

2. Be careful not to put a colon between a verb and its direct object.

   Incorrect: I want: a slice of pizza and a small green salad.

   Correct: This is what I want: a slice of pizza and a small green salad.

Here, the colon serves to announce that a list is forthcoming.

   Correct: I don't want much for lunch: just a slice of pizza and a small green salad.

Here, what follows the colon defines what *I don't want much* means.

3. Context will occasionally make clear that a second independent clause is closely linked to its predecessor, even without an explicit expression like those used above. In addition, a colon is appropriate, although a period will always be correct, too.

   Correct: We were aghast: the "charming country inn" that had been advertised in such glowing terms proved to be a leaking cabin full of mosquitoes.

   Correct: We were aghast. The "charming country inn" that had been advertised in such glowing terms proved to be a leaking cabin full of mosquitoes.

Writing Drill 5

Rewrite these sentences so they use colons correctly on the lines that follow. Answers begin on page 107.

1. I am sick and tired of: your whining, your complaining, your nagging, your teasing, and, most of all, your barbed comments.

   Rewrite: _____

   _____

2. The chef has created a masterpiece, the pasta is delicate yet firm, the mustard greens are fresh, and the medallions of beef are melting in my mouth.

Rewrite: _____

_____

3. In order to write a good essay, you must: practice, get plenty of sleep, and eat a good breakfast.

Rewrite: _____

_____

Rule 6: Use Hyphens and Dashes Correctly

Follow these seven guidelines to correct usage of hyphens and dashes:

1. Use the hyphen to separate a word at the end of a line.

   Correct: In this incredible canvas, the artist used only monochromatic elements.

2. Use the hyphen with the compound numbers twenty-one through ninety-nine, and with fractions used as adjectives.

   Incorrect: Sixty five students constituted a majority.
   Correct: Sixty-five students constituted a majority.

   Incorrect: A two thirds vote was necessary to carry the measure.
   Correct: A two-thirds vote was necessary to carry the measure.

3. Use the hyphen with the prefixes *ex, all, self*, and *semi*, and with the suffix *elect*.

   Incorrect: Semiretired executives are often called upon to assist others in starting new businesses.
   Correct: Semi-retired executives are often called upon to assist others in starting new businesses.

   Incorrect: The constitution protects against self incrimination.
   Correct: The constitution protects against self-incrimination.

   Incorrect: The president elect was invited to chair the meeting.
   Correct: The president-elect was invited to chair the meeting.

4. Use the hyphen with a compound adjective when it comes before the word it modifies, but not when it comes after the word it modifies.

   Correct: The no-holds-barred argument continued into the night.
   Correct: The argument continued with no holds barred.

5. Use the hyphen with any prefix used before a proper noun or adjective.

> **Incorrect:** His pro African sentiments were heartily applauded.
> **Correct:** His pro-African sentiments were heartily applauded.

> **Incorrect:** They believed that his activities were unAmerican.
> **Correct:** They believed that his activities were un-American.

6. Use a hyphen to separate component parts of a word in order to avoid confusion with other words or to avoid the use of a double vowel.

> **Incorrect:** Most of the buildings in the ghost town are recreations of the original structures.
> **Correct:** Most of the buildings in the ghost town are re-creations of the original structures.

> **Incorrect:** She took an antiinflammatory drug for her sports injury.
> **Correct:** She took an anti-inflammatory drug for her sports injury.

7. Use the dash to indicate an abrupt change of thought. In general, however, in formal writing, it's better to plan what you want to say in advance and avoid abrupt changes of thought.

> **Correct:** The inheritance must cover the entire cost of the proposal—Gail has no other money to invest.

> **Correct:** To get a high score—and who doesn't want to get a high score—you need to devote yourself to prolonged and concentrated study.

Writing Drill 6

Insert hyphens and dashes in the correct places in these sentences. Answers begin on page 107.

1. The child was able to count from one to ninety nine.

2. The adults only movie was banned from commercial TV.

3. John and his ex wife remained on friendly terms.

4. A two thirds majority would be needed to pass the budget reforms.

5. The house, and it was the most dilapidated house that I had ever seen was a bargain because the land was so valuable.

Rule 7: Use Apostrophes Correctly

Follow these three guidelines to correct apostrophe usage:

1. Use the apostrophe with contracted forms of verbs to indicate that one or more letters have been eliminated in writing. Generally, though, you should try to avoid contractions on the Writing section of the test.

One of the most common errors involving the apostrophe is using it in the contractions *you're* or *it's* to indicate the possessive form of *you* or *it*. Whenever you write *you're*, ask yourself whether you mean *you are*. If not, the correct word is *your*. Similarly, are you sure you mean *it is*? If not, use the possessive form *its*. Remember: You spell *his* and *hers* without an apostrophe, so you should spell *its* without an apostrophe as well.

> **Incorrect:** You're chest of drawers is ugly.
> **Correct:** Your chest of drawers is ugly.

> **Incorrect:** The dog hurt it's paw.
> **Correct:** The dog hurt its paw.

2. Use the apostrophe to indicate the possessive form of a noun.

> **Not possessive:** the boy, Harry, the children, the boys
> **Possessive:** the boy's, Harry's, the children's, the boys'

> **Correct:** I caught a glimpse of the fox's red tail as the hunters sped by.

The *'s* ending indicates that one fox is the owner of the tail.

> **Correct:** Ms. Fox's office is on the first floor.

One person possesses the office.

> **Correct:** The Foxes' apartment has a wonderful view.

There are several people named Fox living in the same apartment. First, you must form the plural, and then add the apostrophe to indicate possession.

3. The apostrophe is used to indicate possession only with nouns; in the case of pronouns, there are separate possessives for each person and number.

Pronoun	Possessive
her	hers
his	his
its	its
my	mine
our	ours
their	theirs
your	yours

The exception is the neutral *one*, which forms its possessive by adding an apostrophe and an *s*.

> **Correct:** One's attention should not waver during the test.

Writing Drill 7

Add apostrophes where needed and cross out unnecessary ones in the following sentences. Answers begin on page 107.

1. The presidents limousine had a flat tire.

2. You're tickets for the show will be at the box office.

3. The opportunity to change ones lifestyle does not come often.

4. The desks' surface was immaculate, but it's drawers were messy.

5. The cat on the bed is hers'.

Rule 8: Pay Attention to Subject-Verb Agreement

Singular subjects and plural subjects take different forms of the verb in the present tense. Usually the difference lies in the presence or absence of a final *s* (for example, *he becomes* and *they become*), but sometimes the difference is more radical (for example, *he is* and *they are*). You can usually trust your ear to give you the correct verb form. However, certain situations may cause difficulty, such as the following:

- When the subject and verb are separated by a number of words.
- When the subject is an indefinite pronoun like *anyone*.
- When the subject consists of more than one noun.

Don't let the words that come between the subject and the verb confuse you as to the number (singular or plural) of the subject. Usually one word can be pinpointed as the grammatical subject of the sentence. The verb, no matter how far removed, must agree with that subject in number.

Incorrect: The joys of climbing mountains, especially if one is a novice climber without the proper equipment, escapes me.

Correct: The joys of climbing mountains, especially if one is a novice climber without the proper equipment, escape me.

Incorrect: A group of jockeys who have already finished the first race and who wish to have their pictures taken are blocking my view of the horses.

Correct: A group of jockeys who have already finished the first race and who wish to have their pictures taken is blocking my view of the horses.

Here, the long prepositional phrase beginning with the preposition *of* qualifies the noun group. The subject of the sentence is the singular noun *group*, which takes the singular verb *is*.

Keep this rule in mind: a subject that consists of two or more nouns connected by *and* takes the plural form of the verb.

Incorrect: Karl and George has combined their expertise.

Correct: Karl and George have combined their expertise.

Incorrect: Karl, who is expert in cooking Hunan spicy duck, and George, who is expert in eating Hunan spicy duck, has combined their expertise to start a new restaurant.

Correct: Karl, who is expert in cooking Hunan spicy duck, and George, who is expert in eating Hunan spicy duck, have combined their expertise to start a new restaurant.

When the subject consists of two or more nouns connected by *or* or *nor*, the verb agrees with the closest noun.

Incorrect: Either the senators or the president are misinformed.

Correct: Either the senators or the president is misinformed.

Incorrect: Either the president or the senators is misinformed.

Correct: Either the president or the senators are misinformed.

There are some connecting phrases that look as though they should make a group of words into a plural but actually do not. The only connecting word that can make a series of singular nouns into a plural subject is *and*. In particular, these connecting words and phrases do not result in a plural subject:

along with   in addition to

as well as   together with

besides

Incorrect: The chairman, along with the treasurer and the secretary, are misinformed.

Correct: The chairman, along with the treasurer and the secretary, is misinformed.

If a sentence that is grammatically correct still sounds awkward, you should probably rephrase your thought.

Better: Along with the treasurer and the secretary, the chairman is misinformed.

Writing Drill 8

Fix or replace incorrect verbs in the following sentences on the lines that follow. Answers begin on page 107.

1. The logical structure of his complicated and rather tortuous arguments are always the same.

   Rewrite: _____

   _____

2. Both the young child and her grandfather was saddened for months after discovering that the oldest ice cream parlor in the city had closed its doors forever.

   Rewrite: _____

   _____

3. Hartz brought the blueprints and model that was still on the table instead of the ones that Mackenzie had returned to the cabinet.

Rewrite: _____

_____

4. A case of bananas have been sent to the local distributor in compensation for the fruit that was damaged in transit.

Rewrite: _____

_____

5. A total of 50 editors read each article, a process that takes at least a week, sometimes six months.

Rewrite: _____

_____

6. Neither the shipping clerk who packed the equipment nor the truckers who transported it admits responsibility for the dented circuit box.

Rewrite: _____

_____

7. Either Georgette or Robespierre are going to be asked to dinner by the madcap Calvin. I dread the result in either case.

Rewrite: _____

_____

8. I can never decide whether to eat an orange or a Belgian chocolate; each of them have their wondrous qualities.

Rewrite: _____

_____

9. Everyone in the United States, as well as the Canadians, expect the timber agreement to fall through.

Rewrite: _____

_____

Rule 9: Use Modifiers Correctly

In English, the position of a word within a sentence often establishes the word's relationship to other words in the sentence. This is especially true with modifying phrases. Modifiers, like pronouns, are generally connected to the nearest word that agrees with the modifier in person and number. If a modifier is placed too far from the word it modifies (the referent), the meaning may be lost or obscured. Notice in the following sentences that ambiguity results when the modifying phrases are misplaced in the sentence.

Avoid ambiguity by placing modifiers as close as possible to the words they are intended to modify.

Incorrect: Cheung and Martha sat talking about the movie in the office.

Correct: Cheung and Martha sat in the office talking about the movie.

Incorrect: They wondered how much the house was really worth when they bought it.

Correct: When they bought the house, they wondered how much it was really worth.

The phrases *in the office* and *when they bought it* act as modifiers. Modifiers can refer to words that either precede or follow them. Ambiguity can also result when a modifier is squeezed between two possible referents and the reader has no way to know which is the intended referent.

Incorrect: The dentist instructed him regularly to brush his teeth.

Correct: The dentist instructed him to brush his teeth regularly.

Incorrect: Tom said in the car he had a map of New Jersey.

Correct: Tom said he had a map of New Jersey in the car.

Be sure that the modifier is closest to the intended referent and that there is no other possible referent on the other side of the modifier.

All the previous sentences are examples of misplaced modifiers (modifiers whose placement makes the intended reference unclear). In addition to misplaced modifiers, watch for dangling modifiers (modifiers whose intended referents are not even present).

Incorrect: Coming out of context, Peter was startled by Julio's perceptiveness.

Correct: Julio's remark, coming out of context, startled Peter with its perceptiveness.

The modifying phrase *coming out of context* is probably not intended to refer to Peter, but if not, then to whom or what? Julio? Perceptiveness? None of these makes sense as the referent of *coming out of context*. What came out of context was more likely a statement or remark. This sentence is incorrect because there is no word or phrase that can be pinpointed as the referent of the opening modifying phrase. Rearrangement and rewording solve the problem.

Writing Drill 9

Rewrite these sentences to put modifiers closer to the words they modify on the lines that follow. Answers begin on page 107.

1. Renato advised him quickly to make up his mind.

   Rewrite: _____

   _____

2. I agree with the author's statements in principle.

   Rewrite: _____

   _____

3. Coming out of the woodwork, he was surprised to see termites.

   Rewrite: _____

   _____

4. The governor's conference met to discuss racial unrest in the auditorium.

   Rewrite: _____

   _____

5. Ms. Hernandez said in her office she had all the necessary documents.

   Rewrite: _____

   _____

6. All of his friends were not able to come, but he decided that he preferred small parties anyway.

   Rewrite: _____

   _____

7. Shoshana remembered she had to place a telephone call when she got home.

   Rewrite: _____

   _____

8. Jorge told Linda he did not like to discuss politics as they walked through the museum.

   Rewrite: _____

   _____

9. Having worked in publishing for ten years, Stokely's résumé shows that he is well qualified.

   Rewrite: _____

   _____

10. A politician would fail to serve her constituents without experience in community service.

    Rewrite: _____

    _____

Rule 10: Use Pronouns Correctly

A pronoun is a word that replaces a noun in a sentence. Every time you write a pronoun—*he, him, his, she, her, it, its, they, their, that*, or *which*—be sure there can be absolutely no doubt what its antecedent is. The antecedent is the particular noun a pronoun refers to or stands for. Careless use of pronouns can obscure your intended meaning.

You can usually *rearrange a sentence to avoid an ambiguous pronoun reference*.

   Incorrect: The teacher told the student he was lazy.

   (Does *he* refer to teacher or student?)

   Correct: The student was lazy, and the teacher told him so.

   Correct: The teacher considered himself lazy and told the student so.

   Incorrect: Sara knows more about history than Irina because she learned it from her father.

   (Does *she* refer to Sara or Irina?)

   Correct: Since Sara learned history from her father, she knows more than Irina does.

   Correct: Because Irina learned history from her father, she knows less about it than Sara does.

If you are worried that a pronoun reference will be ambiguous, rewrite the sentence so that there is no doubt. Do not be afraid to repeat the antecedent (the noun that the pronoun refers to) if necessary.

   Incorrect: I would rather settle in Phoenix than in Albuquerque, although it lacks wonderful restaurants.

   Correct: I would rather settle in Phoenix than in Albuquerque, although Phoenix lacks wonderful restaurants.

A reader must be able to pinpoint the pronoun's antecedent. Even if you think the reader will know what you mean, do not use a pronoun without a clear and appropriate antecedent.

   Incorrect: When you are painting, be sure not to get it on the floor.

   Correct: When you are painting, be sure not to get any paint on the floor.

It could refer to only the noun *paint*. But pronouns cannot refer to implied nouns.

Avoid using *this, that, it,* or *which* to refer to a whole phrase, sentence, or idea. Even when these pronouns are placed very close to their intended antecedents, the references may still be unclear. A good rule of thumb is to try not to begin a sentence with *this* or *that* unless the word accompanies a noun. For example, it's fine to say *This problem*… or *That situation*…

> **Incorrect:** Consumers use larger amounts of non-recyclable plastic every year. This will someday turn the earth into a giant trashcan.
>
> **Correct:** Consumers use larger amounts of non-recyclable plastic every year. This ever-growing mass of waste products will someday turn the earth into a giant trashcan.

> **Incorrect:** The salesman spoke loudly, swayed back and forth, and tapped the table nervously, which made his customers extremely nervous.
>
> **Correct:** The salesman spoke loudly, swayed back and forth, and tapped the table nervously, mannerisms which made his customers extremely nervous.

Also, unless you are talking about the weather, avoid beginning a sentence with *it*.

> **Incorrect:** It is difficult to distinguish between the scent of roses and that of tulips.
>
> **Correct:** To distinguish between the scent of roses and that of tulips is difficult.

Some indefinite pronouns will always go with singular verb forms, and some will always go with plural verb forms. See the lists below for common examples. Remember that *-body, -one,* and *-thing* pronouns are singular.

Singular Indefinite Pronouns

anybody	everybody	somebody	either	one
anyone	everyone	someone	neither	each
anything	everything	something	no one	

Plural Indefinite Pronouns

both	few	many	several

Relative Pronouns

who	whom	that	which

It may be difficult to decide which relative pronoun—*who,whom,that,* or *which*—to use.

> **Incorrect:** Those salespeople, whom have been calling all day, are harassing me.
>
> **Correct:** Those people, whom I have been calling all day, never returned my call.

One way to decide is to turn the clause into a question. Ask yourself, "I have been calling who or whom?" Answer your question, substituting a pronoun: "I have been calling *them*." In the second sentence, you would ask, "Who or whom has been calling all day?" Answer your question, substituting a pronoun: "*They* have been calling all day." If you use *her, him, them,* or *us* to answer the question, the appropriate relative pronoun is *whom*. If you use *she, he, they,* or *we* to answer the question, the appropriate relative pronoun is *who*.

More on Who vs. Whom

If you often confuse *who* and *whom*, you're not alone! Here's a quick tip to help you remember the difference between the two.

Who is always a subject. *Who* does the action.

> *Who is teaching him?*

If you substitute *he* or *she* in place of *who* (*she* is teaching him), you can confirm that *who* is indeed the subject. *Who* is doing the action.

Whom is always an object. *Whom* receives the action.

> *She is teaching whom?*

If you substitute *him* or *her* in place of *whom* (she is teaching *him*), you can confirm that *whom* is the object and is receiving the action (rather than doing the action).

That and *which* are often used interchangeably, but they shouldn't be. As a rule, use *which* if the relative clause is set off by commas (in other words, when the clause isn't crucial to the meaning of the sentence). Use *that* if the clause isn't set off by commas (when the clause is crucial to the meaning of the sentence).

> **Incorrect:** The movie, that was released two years behind schedule, was one of the few that were real box office hits this spring.
>
> **Correct:** The movie, which was released two years behind schedule, was one of the few that were real box office hits this spring.

> **Incorrect:** Maria wants the same toy which Lucy has.
>
> **Correct:** Maria wants the same toy that Lucy has.

Writing Drill 10

Correct the following sentences on the lines that follow. Answers begin on page 107.

1. Clausen's dog won first place at the show because he was well bred.

   Rewrite: _____

   _____

2. The critic's review made the novel a commercial success. He is now a rich man.

   Rewrite: _____

   _____

3. The military advisor was more conventional than his commander, but he was a superior strategist.

   Rewrite: _____

   _____

4. Sofia telephoned her friends in California before going home for the night, which she had not done for weeks.

   Rewrite: _____

   _____

5. Although Jaime hoped and dreamed he'd be selected for the job, it did no good. When he called them the next morning, they had hired someone else.

   Rewrite: _____

   _____

6. You must pay attention when fishing—otherwise, you might lose it.

   Rewrite: _____

   _____

7. Zolsta Karmagi is the better musician, but he had more formal training.

   Rewrite: _____

   _____

Rule 11: Pay Attention to Parallelism

Matching constructions must be expressed in parallel form. It is often rhetorically effective to use a particular construction several times in succession in order to provide emphasis. The technique is called parallel construction, and it is effective only when used sparingly. If your sentences are varied, a parallel construction will stand out. If your sentences are already repetitive, a parallel structure will further obscure your meaning. Here's how parallel construction should be used:

> *As a* leader, Lincoln inspired a nation to throw off the chains of slavery; *as a* philosopher, he proclaimed the greatness of the little man; *as a* human being, he served as a timeless example of humility.

The repetition of the italicized construction provides a strong sense of rhythm and organization to the sentence and alerts the reader to yet another aspect of Lincoln's character.

The most common mistake that students make in their essays with regard to parallelism is to fail to use parallel structure where it's needed. But sometimes students make the mistake of using parallel structure where it's not needed. Here's an example of how someone might make the mistake of using a parallel structure for dissimilar items.

Incorrect: They are sturdy, attractive, and cost only a dollar each.

The phrase *they are* makes sense preceding the adjectives *sturdy* and *attractive*, but cannot be understood before *cost only a dollar each*.

Correct: They are sturdy, attractive, and inexpensive.

Parallel constructions must be expressed in parallel grammatical form: all nouns, all infinitives, all gerunds, all prepositional phrases, or all clauses.

Incorrect: All students should learn word processing, accounting, and how to program computers.

Correct: All students should learn word processing, accounting, and computer programming.

This strategy applies to any words that might begin each item in a series: prepositions (*in, on, by, with*, etc.), articles (*the, a, an*), helping verbs (*had, has, would*, etc.), and possessives (*his, her, our*, etc.). Either repeat the word before every element in a series or include it only before the first item. Anything else violates the rules of parallelism.

In effect, your treatment of the series determines the form of all subsequent elements.

Incorrect: He invested his money in stocks, in real estate, and a home for retired performers.

Correct: He invested his money in stocks, in real estate, and in a home for retired performers.

Correct: He invested his money in stocks, real estate, and a home for retired performers.

When proofreading, check that each item in the series agrees with the word or phrase that begins the series. In the above example, *invested his money* is the common phrase that each item shares. You would read, *He invested his money in real estate, (invested his money) in stocks, and (invested his money) in a home for retired performers.*

Writing Drill 11

Correct the faulty parallelism in the following sentences on the lines that follow. Answers begin on page 107.

1. This organization will not tolerate the consumption, trafficking, or promoting the use of drugs.

   Rewrite: _____

   _____

2. The dancer taught her understudy how to move, how to dress, and how to work with choreographers and deal with professional competition.

   Rewrite: _____

   _____

3. Merrill based his confidence on the futures market, the bond market, and on the strength of the president's popularity.

   Rewrite: _____

   _____

4. The grocery baggers were ready, able, and were quite determined to do a great job.

   Rewrite: _____

   _____

Rule 12: Don't Shift Narrative Voice

Strategy 5 in the last chapter advised you to avoid needless self-reference. Since you are asked to write an explanatory essay, however, an occasional self-reference may be appropriate. You may even call yourself *I* if you want, as long as you keep the number of first-person pronouns to a minimum. Less egocentric ways of referring to the narrator include *we* and *one*. If these more formal ways of writing seem stilted, stay with *I*. Look at these three examples:

1. In my lifetime, I have seen many challenges to the principle of free speech.

2. We can see many challenges to the principle of free speech.

3. One must admit that there have been many challenges to the principle of free speech.

The method of self-reference you select is called the narrative voice of your essay. Any of the above narrative voices are acceptable. Nevertheless, whichever you choose, you must be careful not to shift narrative voice in your essay. If you use *I* in the first sentence, for example, do not use *we* in a later sentence.

Incorrect: In my lifetime, *I* have seen many challenges to the principle of free speech. *We* can see how a free society can get too complacent when free speech is taken for granted.

Correct: In *my* lifetime, *I* have seen many challenges to the principle of free speech. *I* can see how a free society can get too complacent when free speech is taken for granted.

Correct: In *our* lifetime, *we* have seen many challenges to the principle of free speech. *We* can see how a free society can get too complacent when free speech is taken for granted.

Likewise, it is wrong to shift from *you* to *one*.

Incorrect: Just by following the news, *you* can readily see how politicians have a vested interest in pleasing powerful interest groups. But *one* should not generalize about this tendency.

To correct the above sentence, you need to change one pronoun to agree with the other.

Correct: *We can readily see* (to agree with *but we should not generalize*)

Correct: *I can readily see* (to agree with *but I would not generalize*)

Correct: *One can readily see* (to agree with *but one should not generalize*)

Writing Drill 12

Rewrite these sentences to give them consistent points of view on the lines that follow. Answers begin on page 107.

1. I am disgusted with the waste we tolerate in this country. One cannot simply stand by without adding to such waste: living here makes you wasteful.

   Rewrite: _____

   _____

2. You must take care not to take these grammar rules too seriously, since one can often become bogged down in details and forget why he is writing at all.

   Rewrite: _____

   _____

3. We all must take a stand against waste in this country; otherwise, how will one be able to look at oneself in the mirror?

   Rewrite: _____

   _____

CHAPTER 5 SUMMARY

Essay graders will not take off a lot of points for small mistakes. But that doesn't mean that you shouldn't know the rules of good writing and that you shouldn't try to write the best essay you possibly can.

12 rules to good writing:

1. Avoid slang and colloquialisms.

2. Avoid sentence fragments and run-on sentences.

3. Use commas correctly.

4. Use semicolons correctly.

5. Use colons correctly.

6. Use hyphens and dashes correctly.

7. Use apostrophes correctly.

8. Pay attention to subject-verb agreement.

9. Use modifiers correctly.

10. Use pronouns correctly.

11. Pay attention to parallelism.

12. Don't shift narrative voice.

ANSWERS AND EXPLANATIONS

Many of the items in the writing drills could have more than one possible correct answer. In those cases, we've suggested sample correct answers. Keep that in mind as you compare your answers to ours.

Drill 1: Avoid Slang and Colloquialisms

1. Cynthia Larson is an expert.

2. The crowd was absorbed in watching the fire-eating juggler, but then the dancing horse caught their attention.

3. As soon as the Human Resources department tries to verify his résumé, I am sure we will hear gales of laughter issuing from the office.

4. Having something funny to say seems to be very important in our culture.

5. The chef prepares striped bass skillfully: his sauce was simple, but the effect was sublime.

6. Normal human beings cannot tolerate repeated humiliation.

7. The world does not have much time to stop polluting; soon, we all will have to wear face masks.

   (*Hasn't got* is both a contraction and an example of the colloquial substitution of *have got* for *have*.)

8. If you want a good cheesecake, you must make a superb crust.

9. International organizations should try to cooperate on global issues like hunger.

10. The environmentalists are not involved in the project for prestige; they truly care about protecting the spotted owl.

Drill 2: Avoid Sentence Fragments and Run-On Sentences

1. The second sentence is a fragment. Combine it with the first to create one complete sentence.

   Sample Rewrite:

   The private academy has all the programs Angie will need, except that the sports program has been phased out.

2. *Leadership ability* is a sentence fragment, since it has no predicate.

   Sample Rewrite:

   Leadership ability: that is the elusive quality that our current government employees have yet to capture.

3. Here we have a run-on sentence (two independent clauses linked by a comma and *therefore*).

   Sample Rewrite:

   Antonio just joined the athletic club staff this year, but Barry has been with us since 1993; therefore, we would expect Barry to be more skilled with the weight-lifting equipment.

4. The conjunction *after* makes the second group of words a sentence fragment.

   Sample Rewrite:

   There is time to invest in property, but only after one has established oneself in the business world.

5. Since transitional words like *however* do not subordinate a clause, this is a run-on sentence. You could either change the first comma to a semicolon or separate the clauses with a period.

   Sample Rewrite:

   Sentence fragments are often used in casual conversation. In written English, however, they should not be used under normal circumstances.

Drill 3: Use Commas Correctly

1. Peter wants me to bring records, games, candy, and soda to his party.

2. I need lumber, nails, a hammer and a saw to build the shelf.

3. It takes a friendly, energetic person to be a successful salesman.

4. I was shocked to discover that a large, modern, glass-sheathed office building had replaced my old school.

5. The country club, a cluster of ivy-covered whitewashed buildings, was the site of the president's first speech.

6. Pushing through the panicked crowd, the security guards frantically searched for the suspect.

7. Despite careful analysis of the advantages and disadvantages of each proposal, Harry found it hard to reach a decision.

Drill 4: Use Semicolons Correctly

1. Morgan has five years' experience in karate, but Thompson has even more.

2. Very few students wanted to take the class in physics; only the professor's kindness kept it from being canceled.

3. You should always be prepared when you go on a camping trip; however, you must avoid carrying unnecessary weight.

Drill 5: Use Colons Correctly

1. I am sick and tired of your whining, your complaining, your nagging, your teasing, and, most of all, your barbed comments.

2. The chef has created a masterpiece: the pasta is delicate yet firm, the mustard greens are fresh, and the medallions of beef are melting in my mouth.

3. In order to write a good essay, you must do the following: practice, get plenty of sleep, and eat a good breakfast.

Drill 6: Use Hyphens and Dashes Correctly

1. The child was able to count from one to ninety-nine.

2. The adults-only movie was banned from commercial TV.

3. John and his ex-wife remained on friendly terms.

4. A two-thirds majority would be needed to pass the budget reforms.

5. The house—and it was the most dilapidated house that I had ever seen—was a bargain because the land was so valuable.

Drill 7: Use Apostrophes Correctly

1. The president's limousine had a flat tire.

2. Your tickets for the show will be at the box office.

3. The opportunity to change one's lifestyle does not come often.

4. The desk's surface was immaculate, but its drawers were messy.

5. The cat on the bed is hers.

Drill 8: Pay Attention to Subject-Verb Agreement

1. The logical structure of his complicated and rather tortuous arguments is always the same.

2. Both the young child and her grandfather were saddened for months after discovering that the oldest ice cream parlor in the city had closed its doors forever.

3. Hartz brought the blueprints and model that were still on the table instead of the ones that Mackenzie had returned to the cabinet. (The restrictive phrase beginning with *that* defines the noun phrase *blueprints and model*.)

4. A case of bananas has been sent to the local distributor in compensation for the fruit that was damaged in transit.

5. A total of 50 editors reads each article, a process that takes at least a week, sometimes six months.

6. Neither the shipping clerk who packed the equipment nor the truckers who transported it admit responsibility for the dented circuit box.

7. Either Georgette or Robespierre is going to be asked to dinner by the madcap Calvin. I dread the result in either case.

8. I can never decide whether to eat an orange or a Belgian chocolate; each of them has its wondrous qualities.

   (Note that you must also change the possessive pronoun from *their* to *its*.)

9. Everyone in the United States, as well as the Canadians, expects the timber agreement to fall through.

Drill 9: Use Modifiers Correctly

1. *Quickly* is sandwiched between two verbs, and it could refer to either one.

   Sample Rewrite:

   Renato advised him to make up his mind quickly.

2. *In principle* probably modifies *agreed*, but its placement makes it appear to modify *statement*.

   Sample Rewrite:

   I agree in principle with the author's statements.

3. Termites are probably coming out of the woodwork, not the man.

   Sample Rewrite:

   He was surprised to see termites coming out of the woodwork.

4. Was the racial unrest in the auditorium, or was the conference merely held there?

   Sample Rewrite:

   The governor's conference met in the auditorium to discuss racial unrest.

5. Did she say it in her office? Were the documents in her office? Or both?

   Sample Rewrite:

   Ms. Hernandez said that she had all the necessary documents in her office.

6. If none of his friends came, it must have been a small party indeed.

   Sample Rewrite:

   Not all of his friends were able to come, but he decided that he preferred small parties anyway.

7. Did she remember when she got home? Or did she have to call when she got home?

   Sample Rewrite:

   When she got home, Shoshana remembered she had to place a telephone call.

8. Either he didn't like discussing politics in the museum, or he didn't like discussing it at all.

   Sample Rewrite:

   As they walked through the museum, Jorge told Linda he did not like to discuss politics.

9. Was it Stokely's résumé that worked in publishing for ten years?

   Sample Rewrite:

   Stokely, who has worked in publishing for ten years, appears from his résumé to be well qualified.

10. It is the person holding the job, not her constituents, that requires experience in community service.

    Sample Rewrite:

    A politician without experience in community service would fail to serve her constituents.

Drill 10: Use Pronouns Correctly

1. The structure of the sentence might leave us wondering whether Clausen or his dog was well bred. Instead, use the impersonal *it*.

   Sample Rewrite:

   Clausen's dog won first place at the show because it was well bred.

2. It's not clear who *he* is. No antecedent exists in the sentence for it. *Critic's* can't be the antecedent of *he* because it's the possessive form.

   Sample Rewrite:

   The critic's review made the novel a commercial success, and the novelist is now a rich man.

3. We cannot tell from the context whether the military advisor or his superior was the superior strategist.

   Sample Rewrite:

   The military advisor was more conventional than his commander, but the advisor was a superior strategist.

4. *Which* is the problem here: we do not know whether Sofia had not spent the night at home in weeks or whether she had not telephoned her friends in weeks.

Sample Rewrite:

Because she had not telephoned her California friends in weeks, Sofia called them before she went home for the night.

5. Referring to some ambiguous *they* without identifying who they are beforehand is incorrect.

Sample Rewrite:

Jaime wanted the job badly, but when he called the employer the next morning, he found that the company had hired someone else.

6. We don't know exactly what *it* is, but we can assume that it is a fish.

Sample Rewrite:

You must pay attention when fishing—otherwise, you might lose your catch.

7. We do not know whether *he* refers to Zolsta or to the unnamed lesser musician.

Sample Rewrite:

Zolsta Karmagi is the better musician, but Sven Wonderup had more formal training.

Drill 11: Pay Attention to Parallelism

1. This organization will not tolerate the consumption, trafficking, or promotion of drugs.

2. The dancer taught her understudy how to move, dress, work with choreographers, and deal with professional competition.

3. Merrill based his confidence on the futures market, the bond market, and the strength of the president's popularity.

4. The grocery baggers were ready, able, and determined to do a great job.

Drill 12: Don't Shift Narrative Voice

1. I am disgusted with the waste we tolerate in this country. We cannot simply stand by without adding to such waste: living here makes all of us wasteful.

2. You must take care not to take these grammar rules too seriously, since you can often become bogged down in details and forget why you are writing at all.

3. We must all take a stand against waste in this country; otherwise, how will we be able to look at ourselves in the mirror?

When using *we*, you must make sure to use the plural form of verbs and pronouns.

Multiple Choice

Chapter Six: **Identifying Sentence Errors**

This chapter builds on what you've already reviewed in chapters 4 and 5 on direct writing and mechanics skills. It will help you improve and prepare for the grammar questions in the SAT Multiple-Choice Writing section.

Luckily, the majority of Identifying Sentence Errors questions test a limited amount of grammar. If you know the kind of grammar the SAT usually tests, and if you familiarize yourself with the SAT's "spot-the-mistake" questions, you will do better on the Writing sections.

WHAT ARE IDENTIFYING SENTENCE ERRORS QUESTIONS?

All Identifying Sentence Errors questions are of the "spot-the-mistake" variety. You're given a sentence with four words or phrases underlined. The underlined parts are labeled (A) through (E). One of the underlined fragments may contain a grammar mistake. You're supposed to spot it and fill in the corresponding oval on your grid. If the sentence is mistake-free, the correct answer is (E) (no error). Here's an example:

> <u>Although</u> the number of firms declaring
>   A
> bankruptcy <u>keep</u> growing, the mayor <u>claims that</u> the
>   B   C
> city <u>is thriving.</u> <u>No error</u>
>   D   E

You need to decide which underlined word or phrase—if any—needs to be changed to make the sentence grammatically correct. You should assume that the parts of the sentence that are not underlined are correct, since they can't be changed.

KAPLAN

The Kaplan Four-Step Method for Identifying Sentence Errors

Here's our four-step method for answering Identifying Sentence Errors questions:

1. Read the whole sentence, "listening" for the mistake.

2. If you "heard" the mistake, choose it and you're done.

3. If not, read each underlined choice and eliminate choices that contain no errors.

4. If you're sure the sentence contains no errors, choose (E).

Try out our method on the example given earlier. Start by reading it to yourself.

> <u>Although</u> the number of firms declaring
>   A
> bankruptcy <u>keep</u> growing, the mayor <u>claims that</u> the
>   B   C
> city <u>is thriving</u>. <u>No error</u>
>   D   E

Did you hear the mistake? If so, your work is done for this question; fill in the appropriate oval and move on. If you didn't hear the mistake on the first reading, go back, read each underlined part, and start eliminating underlined parts that are right.

The word *although* seems fine in this context. The word *keep* is a plural verb, but its subject is *number*, which is singular. That seems to be a mistake. The phrase *claims that* sounds all right—it has a singular verb for a singular subject, *mayor*. Similarly, *is thriving* sounds all right, and it too provides a singular verb for the singular subject *city*. Choice (B) contains the mistake, so (B) is the correct answer.

This is a classic example because errors of subject-verb agreement are common on the Writing section. You'll learn more about the most common errors in the rest of this chapter. *This information is extremely valuable!* It's so much easier to spot errors when you know what to look for.

Keep in mind that not all the Identifying Sentence Errors questions on the Writing section contain errors. When you're reading each sentence just to spot mistakes, you may fall into the trap of spotting mistakes where there are none.

Remember, choice (E) (no error) is the correct answer about one in five times. If you find that for the 19 Identifying Sentence Errors questions you have chosen (E) only once or twice, chances are that you're spotting mistakes that aren't there.

COMMON WRITING SECTION MISTAKES

Don't, at this late point, start trying to learn all the rules of grammar. You won't have to recite them on the Writing section anyway. Instead, we'll show you the top 16 errors you need to watch out for. Once you are used to seeing these mistakes, you'll have an easier time spotting them on test day.

Each Common Mistake is followed by a quiz. Answers to all of the practice questions and the Practice Quiz are at the end of the chapter starting on page 141.

Common Mistake 1: Subject-Verb Agreement When Subject Follows Verb

Singular subjects call for singular verbs. Plural subjects call for plural verbs. Simple, right? Subject-verb agreement under normal circumstances is not difficult for native speakers of English. You know better than to say *Americans is...* or *The building are...* But in certain situations, subject-verb agreement can be tricky because it is not so obvious what the subject of the sentence is.

For example, it's tricky when the subject comes after the verb, as it does in clauses beginning with *there is* or *there are*. Take a look:

> Despite an intensive campaign to encourage conservation, there *is* many Americans who have not accepted recycling as a way of life.

This sentence demonstrates *the most common* of all subject-verb agreement errors found on the Writing section. It generally occurs once or twice on each test. The subject of the sentence is not *there*. The subject is *Americans*, which is plural. Therefore, the singular verb is incorrect; *is* should be replaced by the plural verb *are*. Watch out whenever you see *there is* or *there are* on the Writing section!

Here's another example in which the subject follows the verb:

> High above the Hudson River *rises* the gleaming skyscrapers of Manhattan.

This sentence is tricky because there is a singular noun, *the Hudson River*, before the verb *rises*. But the later noun *skyscrapers* is actually the subject. Think about it. What's doing the rising? It's not the river, but the skyscrapers. The subject is plural, and so the verb should be *rise*.

Common Mistake 1: Drill

Change the italicized verbs in the sentences that contain errors in subject-verb agreement. Write "correct" if the verb is correct. Answers are on page 136.

1. According to a noted meteorologist, there *is* various explanations for the accelerating rate of global warming.

2. In this critically acclaimed film, there *is* a well-developed plot and an excellent cast of characters.

3. Through the locks of the Panama Canal *passes* more than 50 ships each day.

4. There *are* a number of state legislatures currently debating strict environmental laws.

5. If there *is* competing proposals, your idea may not be acted upon until next week.

6. There *is* at least five types of climbing rose and a unique variety of small fir in the Botanical Gardens.

7. Despite numerous professed sightings, there *is* still no conclusive evidence of extraterrestrial beings.

Common Mistake 2: Subject-Verb Agreement When Subject and Verb Are Separated

The SAT has another way to complicate a simple thing like subject-verb agreement. Some additional information about the subject is inserted before the verb appears.

Expect to see at least one question like this on the Writing section:

> The local congressman, a reliable representative of both community and statewide interests, *are* among the most respected persons in the public sector.

The way to determine whether the verb agrees with the subject is to identify the subject of the sentence. You see the plural *community and statewide interests* right in front of the verb *are*, but that's not the subject. It's part of the modifying phrase that's inserted after the subject *congressman*, which is singular, and the correct verb should be singular, *is*.

Don't let intervening phrases fool you! In this example, the commas are a tip-off that the verb is separated from the subject. Another tip-off is a preposition like *of*:

> The collection of paintings entitled "Clammy Clam Clams" *are* one of the most widely traveled exhibits in recent years.

Again, you should first find the subject of the sentence. The subject is *collection*. The phrases that follow the subject—*of paintings* and *entitled "Clammy Clam Clams"*—merely modify the subject. The true subject is singular, and so the verb should be *is*.

The SAT writers like this type of question because the intervening modifying phrases or clauses can cause you to lose track of the subject. These phrases simply modify the subject they follow *without changing its number*. Don't be fooled by the placement of these intervening phrases.

Common Mistake 2: Drill

Circle the verb in parentheses that agrees with the subject. Answers are on page 136.

1. Multipurpose vehicles, which can be very useful on rough terrain, (is/are) now banned in many states.

2. The level of chemicals and other air pollutants (is/are) now monitored in many offices.

3. The fundamental hitting skills of Rick Reuschel (goes/go) largely unnoticed by the average fan.

4. A community as diverse as Los Angeles (attracts/attract) immigrants from many countries.

5. One-way tickets for domestic travel (is/are) often more expensive than round-trip fares.

6. So-called "bullet trains" from Tokyo to Osaka (completes/complete) the 300-mile trip in about two hours.

7. Donations to the church-sponsored orphanage (is/are) up by 50 percent over last year.

8. Einstein's theory of relativity (ranks/rank) with the most developed hypotheses involving space and time.

Common Mistake 3: Subject-Verb Agreement When the Subject Seems Plural

Sometimes the sentence includes what appears to be, but in fact is not, a plural subject. Here's an example:

> Neither ambient techno nor trance *were* a part of mainstream listening habits in the United States ten years ago.

This sentence is tough because it has two subjects, but these two singular subjects do not add up to a plural subject. When the subject of a sentence is in the form *neither _____ nor _____* or in the form *either _____ or _____*, and the nouns in the blanks are singular, the verb should be singular. In the sentence above, it's as if *ambient techno* and *trance* act as subjects one at a time. So the verb should be the singular *was*. If the nouns in a neither-nor or either-or construction are plural, then a plural verb is correct.

Here are some other constructions that seem to make plural subjects, but actually don't:

- _____ along with _____
- _____ as well as _____
- _____ in addition to _____

In these constructions, the noun in the first blank is the true subject and what follows is, grammatically speaking, just an intervening modifying phrase. If the first noun is singular, the verb should be singular. Look at this sentence:

> Poor pitching, along with injuries and defensive lapses, *are* among the problems that plague last year's championship team.

The phrase *along with injuries and defensive lapses* is a modifying phrase that separates the subject *poor pitching* from the verb *are*. This sentence is tricky because there seem to be three problems that plague the baseball team. But, in fact, phrases like *along with* or *in addition to* do not work in the same way as the conjunction *and* does. If the above sentence had begun *Poor pitching, injuries, and defensive lapses,* the plural verb *are* would have been correct. As written, however, the sentence has only one subject, *poor pitching*, and its verb should be *is*.

Beware those fake compound subjects!

Common Mistake 3: Drill

Circle the verb in parentheses that agrees with the true subject. Answers are on page 136.

1. The fishing industry, along with railroad safety issues, (is/are) of great concern to the state assembly.

2. Either the manager or one of his coaches usually (removes/remove) a pitcher from the mound.

3. Both the word *scuba* and the word *radar* (is/are) acronyms.

4. Auto exhaust, in addition to industrial pollution, (is/are) a cause of smog in Southern California.

5. It is said that neither poor weather nor poor health (keeps/keep) a postman from making his rounds.

Common Mistake 4: Confusion of Simple Past and Past Participle

A typical error tested on the Writing section is confusion between the simple past and the past participle forms of a verb. A past participle form may be sneakily substituted for the simple past form, as in this sentence:

> Several passersby *seen* the bank robber leaving the scene of his crime.

The verb form *seen* is the past participle and should be used only with a helping verb *have* or *be*. This sentence requires the simple past form *saw*.

It's safe to say that the Writing section will almost *always* have a question in which the simple past is used with a helping verb, or in which the past participle is used without a helping verb. So these are good mistakes to be able to spot.

For regular verbs, the simple past and past participle are identical, ending in -*ed*. But irregular verbs like *see* usually have two different forms for simple past and past participle. The following is a list of irregular verbs that have appeared on the SAT. These are the simple past and past participle forms that are most often confused. Instead of listing them alphabetically, we have grouped them by pattern.

IRREGULAR VERBS

Infinitive	Simple Past	Past Participle (has/have + _____)
break	broke	broken
speak	spoke	spoken
freeze	froze	frozen
forget	forgot	forgotten
get	got	gotten
ride	rode	ridden
rise	rose	risen
arise	arose	arisen
drive	drove	driven
write	wrote	written
eat	ate	eaten
fall	fell	fallen
give	gave	given
take	took	taken
shake	shook	shaken
see	saw	seen
ring	rang	rung
sing	sang	sung
sink	sank	sunk
shrink	shrank	shrunk
drink	drank	drunk
begin	began	begun
swim	swam	swum
run	ran	run
come	came	come
become	became	become
do	did	done
go	went	gone
blow	blew	blown
grow	grew	grown
know	knew	known
throw	threw	thrown
fly	flew	flown
draw	drew	drawn

Note the patterns. Verb forms that end in -oke, -oze, -ot, -ode, -ose, -ove, -ote, -ang, -ank, -an, -am, -ame, -ew, or -ook are simple past. Verb forms that end in -en, -wn, -ung, -unk, -un, -um, -ome, and -one are past participles. Train your ear for irregular verb forms that aren't already second nature to you.

Common Mistake 5: Confusion of Infinitive and Gerund

Some questions test your sense of idiomatic use of English. What they're testing is whether you know what combinations of words *sound* right or which words sound right in particular contexts.

For example, there is generally at least one question in which the infinitive is used where a gerund would be appropriate, or vice versa:

> Team officials heralded Cap Day as an attempt *at attracting* a larger
> turnout of fans.

This sentence is unidiomatic. There's no grammar rule that explains why it's wrong to say *an attempt at attracting*. If you have a good sense of idiom, your ear tells you it should be an *attempt to attract*. This sentence confuses the *-ing* gerund form with the *to* + verb infinitive form. Here's another sentence that should sound wrong:

> Surveillance cameras are frequently placed in convenience stores to
> prevent customers *to shoplift*.

After *prevent*, you don't use the infinitive but rather the word *from* plus the gerund. The sentence should end: *to prevent customers from shoplifting*.

Why? There's no real grammatical reason. That's just the way we say and write it in English. You have to trust yourself on these. Studying lists of all the infinitive/(preposition +) gerund combinations that could possibly appear on the Writing section would not be a good use of your time. But don't worry; you don't need to see every possible combination in advance. Just remember to pay attention whenever an infinitive or gerund is underlined on the test.

The infinitive form of a verb is the *to* form.

> *To run*

The gerund form of a verb is the *-ing* form.

> *Running*

Common Mistake 5: Drill

Identify and correct the sentences that confuse gerund and infinitive. Write the correct forms of the italicized verbs on the lines that follow. If the sentence is already correct, write "correct." Answers are on page 136.

1. The International Olympic Committee does not allow professional tennis players over 21 years of age *to competing* in the Games.

   _____

2. Our directors plan *increasing* the number of workers in the plant by 500.

   _____

3. Any parent would see the value *to set* a curfew for his or her child.

_____

4. Questioning a store owner's right *of installing* a surveillance camera is not the purpose of this City Council meeting.

_____

5. The trade agreement is designed to prevent Japan *from limiting* the amount of its imports.

_____

6. Through this new ad campaign, we hope *for tripling* our gross income by the end of the year.

_____

7. We did not succeed *to discourage* him from going alone.

_____

8. The teachers' union is eager *to resolve* the contractual disagreement with the school board.

_____

Common Mistake 6: Non-Idiomatic Preposition after Verb

The Writing section also tests your recognition of prepositions that combine idiomatically with certain verbs. Here's a sentence that uses the wrong preposition:

> City Council members frequently meet until the early morning hours in order to *work in* their stalemates.

It's not always wrong to write *work in*. You might use *work in* to speak about the field one works in or the place one works in. But this combination does not correspond to the meaning of this sentence. The writer means to say *work through* or *work out*—that is, overcome the stalemates.

Here's another sentence with the wrong preposition:

> The singer's new CD was *frowned at* by many parents because of its violent lyrics.

That's just not the way we say it in English. The preferred verb-preposition combination is *frowned upon*. That's the idiomatic expression. Once again, this is an area where you'll have to trust your ear. Just remember to pay attention and think for a moment when you see an underlined preposition after a verb.

More verb-preposition idioms are listed on the next page.

Commonly Tested Verbs and Prepositions

abide by	consist of	object to
abide in	contribute to	participate in
accuse of	count (up)on	pray for
agree to	cover with	prevent from
agree with	decide (up)on	prohibit from
agree on	depend (up)on	protect from
apologize for	differ about	provide with
apply for	differ from	recover from
apply to	differ over	rely (up)on
approve of	differ with	rescue from
argue about	discriminate against	respond to
argue with	distinguish from	stare at
arrive at	dream about	stop from
believe in	dream of	subscribe to
blame for	escape from	substitute for
care about	excel in	succeed in
care for	excuse for	thank for
charge for	forget about	vote for
charge with	forgive for	wait for
compare to	hide from	wait on
compare with	hope for	work with
complain about	insist (up)on	worry about

Common Mistake 7: Wrong Word

The English language contains many pairs of words that sound alike but are spelled differently and have different meanings. Expect to encounter one or two questions that test your ability to distinguish between these problematic word pairs. Here are some examples:

ACCEPT/EXCEPT: To *accept* is to take or receive something that is offered: *Dad said he would accept my apology for putting a dent in his new car, but then he grounded me for two weeks.*

To *except* is to leave out or exclude: *The soldier was excepted from combat duty because he had poor field vision. Except* is usually used as a preposition meaning "with the exception of, excluding": *When the receptionist found out that everyone except him had received a raise, he demanded a salary increase as well.*

ADAPT/ADOPT: To *adapt* is to change oneself or change something to become suitable for a particular condition or use: *Fred tried to adapt his Volkswagen for use as a submarine by gluing the windows shut and attaching a periscope to the roof.*

To *adopt* is to make something one's own: *My neighbors decided to adopt a child.*

AFFECT/EFFECT: To *affect* is to have an influence on something: *Al refused to let the rain affect his plans for a picnic, so he sat under an umbrella and ate potato salad.*

To *effect* is to bring something about or cause something to happen: *The young activist received an award for effecting a change in her community.* An *effect* is an influence or a result: *The newspaper article about homeless animals had such an effect on Richard that he brought home three kittens from the shelter.*

Most often, *affect* is used in its verb form, and *effect* is used in its noun form.

AFFLICT/INFLICT: To *afflict* is to torment or distress someone or something. It usually appears as a passive verb: *Jeff is afflicted with severe migraine headaches.*

To *inflict* is to impose punishment or suffering on someone or something: *No one dared displease the king, for he was known to inflict severe punishments on those who upset him.*

ALLUSION/ILLUSION: An *allusion* is an indirect reference to something, a hint: *I remarked that Sally's boyfriend was unusual looking; this allusion to his prominent tattoos did not please Sally.*

An *illusion* is a false, misleading, or deceptive appearance: *A magician creates the illusion that something has disappeared by hiding it faster than the eye can follow it.*

EMIGRATE/IMMIGRATE: To *emigrate* is to leave one country for another country, and it is usually used with the preposition *from*: *Many people emigrated from Europe in search of better living conditions.*

To *immigrate* is to enter a country to take up permanent residence there, and it is usually used with the preposition *to*: *They immigrated to North America because land was plentiful.*

EMINENT/IMMINENT: Someone who is *eminent* is prominent or outstanding: *The eminent archeologist Dr. Wong has identified the artifact as prehistoric in origin.*

Something that is *imminent* is likely to happen soon, or is impending: *After being warned that the hurricane's arrival was imminent, beachfront residents left their homes immediately.*

LAY/LIE: To *lay* is to place or put something down, and this verb usually does have a "something"—a direct object—following it. The form *laid* serves as the simple past and the past participle of *lay*. *Before she begins her pictures, Emily lays all of her pencils, brushes, and paints on her worktable to avoid interruptions while she draws and paints.*

To *lie* is to recline, or to be in a lying position or at rest. This verb never takes a direct object: You do not lie anything down. The simple past form of *lie* is *lay*; the past participle is *lain*. Notice that the past form of *lie* is identical with the present form of *lay*. This coincidence complicates the task of distinguishing the related meanings of *lay* and *lie*: *Having laid the picnic cloth under the sycamore, they lay in the shady grass all last Sunday afternoon.*

Okay fine. Let's let this one lie for now.

LEAVE/LET: To *leave* is to depart, or to allow something to remain behind after departing, or to allow something to remain as it is. One irregular verb form, *left*, serves as the simple past and the past participle: *I boarded my plane and it left, leaving my baggage behind in Chicago.* When *leave* is used in the third sense—to allow something to remain as it is—and followed by *alone*, this verb does overlap with *let*: *If parents leave* (or *let*) *a baby with a new toy alone, she will understand it as quickly as if they demonstrated how the toy works.*

To *let* is to allow, or to rent out. These are the verb's core meanings, but it also combines with several different prepositions to produce various specific senses. *Let* is irregular. One form serves as present, past, and past participle. *The French border police would not let the Dutch tourist pass without a passport.*

RAISE/RISE: To *raise* is to lift up, or to cause to rise or grow, and it usually has a direct object: You *raise* dumbbells, roof beams, tomato plants, children. *Raise* is a completely regular verb: *The trade tariff on imported leather goods raised the prices of Italian shoes.*

To *rise* is to get up, to go up, to be built up. This verb never takes a direct object: you do not *rise* something. The past and past participle forms are irregular; *rose* is the simple past, and *risen* is the past participle. *Long-distance commuters must rise early and return home late.*

SET/SIT: The difference between *set* and *sit* is very similar to the difference between *lay* and *lie* and between *raise* and *rise*. To *set* is to put or place something, to settle or arrange it. But *set* takes on other specific meanings when it combines with several different prepositions. *Set* is an irregular verb in that one form serves as present, past, and past participle. *Set* usually takes a direct object: you *set* a ladder against the fence, a value on family heirlooms, a date for the family reunion. *The professor set the students' chairs in a semicircle in order to promote open discussion.*

To *sit* is to take a seat or to be in a seated position, to rest somewhere, or to occupy a place. This verb does not usually take a direct object, although you can say: *The usher sat us in the center seats of the third row from the stage.* The irregular form *sat* serves as past and past participle. Usually, no direct object follows this verb: *The beach house sits on a hill at some distance from the shoreline.*

Common Mistake 8: Wrong Tense

Here's a sentence with a verb in the wrong tense:

> Over the last half-century, the building of passenger airliners *had grown* into a multibillion-dollar industry.

In a one-verb sentence like this one, time-descriptive phrases help you determine what the time frame of a sentence is. The action being described is a process that began during the last half-century and that is continuing to the present day. Any action starting in the past and continuing today is expressed by a verb in the present perfect tense. The present perfect form of this verb is *has grown*. Using the verb *had* makes it seem that passenger airliners aren't being made anymore. That can't be! With practice, you'll be able to spot mistakes like this with confidence.

Another type of sentence testing verb tense might have two verbs in it. Here's an example:

> Many superb tennis players turn professional at an alarmingly early age, but because of their lack of physical stamina, *suffered* early in their careers.

When there are two verbs in a sentence, first study the time relation between the verbs, and determine whether it is logical as presented. In this sentence, the verb in the first clause of this sentence is *turn*, a present-tense verb. The action is not occurring at any specified occasion, but in the general present. The verb *suffered* is in the simple past, but it should remain in the general present, even though the phrase *early in their careers* may suggest a past time. Be sure that there is a logical relation between the verbs when two are presented in the same sentence.

Common Mistake 8: Drill

Are the italicized words in the following sentences grammatically correct? If not, replace the incorrect phrase with the correct phrase in the blank provided. Answers are on page 136.

1. Scientists have noted how coastlines change subtly and land masses *will shrink* _____ infinitesimally as the polar ice caps begin to melt.

2. Accounts of their voyages reveal that some of the first Europeans to travel to the North American continent *think* _____ they had landed in Asia.

3. At art auctions during the last few years, paintings by some acknowledged masters *will have brought* _____ prices in the millions.

4. The country's land reform law *is* _____ first proposed by a coalition government in 1945 and included farmers who lost their farms during collectivization.

5. As a result of the recent economic recession, many graduating law students *have had* _____ difficulty finding jobs even in large, well-established firms.

6. The Port Huron Statement, an outline of the values and goals of the Students for a Democratic Society, *was having* _____ a major impact on social protest in the decade following its 1962 publication.

7. To get to the theater, which is on the East Side, wait at the corner until the express bus _____ *came*.

8. As the ninth inning began, his manager reminded "Doc" Gooden that he *has hit* _____ the lead-off batter in the first inning.

Common Mistake 9: Number Agreement Problems

The Writing section also tests a particular error of modification involving number. For instance, a noun may be plural while a phrase describing the noun belongs with a singular noun. That sounds complicated, but fortunately, you don't need to be able to explain the grammar involved. You just need to be able to spot this type of mistake. Here's an example:

> The advertisement in the newspaper requested that only persons
> *with a high school diploma* apply for the position.

Nouns in a sentence must have logical number relations. The noun in question, the subject of the second clause of this sentence, is *persons*, a plural noun. However, the noun *diploma* is singular. Because the phrase is singular, it seems to say that this group of people shares one diploma, when in fact each person should have his or her own diploma. The underlined phrase should read *with high school diplomas*.

Here's an example of number disagreement in which a singular noun is coupled with a plural subject:

> The economies of Romania and Albania are considered by many to
> be *a symbol* of the failure of the command market structure.

Again, identify the subject of the sentence, *economies*. The noun that corresponds to the subject is *symbol*, a singular noun. There is no agreement in number between *economies* and *symbol*. Each individual economy is a symbol; both economies wouldn't be a single symbol. The plural form, *symbols*, makes this sentence grammatically correct. Make sure that the nouns in a sentence that should logically agree in number do agree.

Common Mistake 9: Drill

Place a check next to the following sentences that contain an error in number agreement. Answers are on page 136.

❑ 1. Rising stock value and capital liquidity are considered by financiers to be *a requirement* for healthy investment.

❑ 2. The two-piece bathing suit is considered by many to be *a throwback* to the 1960s.

❑ 3. The rubble of Berlin and the division of Germany were *a reminder* of the defeat of the Axis powers in World War II.

❑ 4. Many question the validity of laws that do not allow people *with a child* to rent certain apartments.

❑ 5. Students *in a college T-shirt* will be admitted to the concert for free.

❑ 6. Few could foresee the Model T and Model A, produced by Ford in the early twentieth century, as *the prototype* of today's automobile.

❑ 7. Armed with their bank *account*, corporate raiders schemed to overtake many of America's leading industries.

❑ 8. One of the eels of the Muraenidae family, the moray is feared *as a lethal aquatic vertebrate*.

Common Mistake 10: Pronoun in the Wrong Number

You'll be tested on your ability to tell whether a noun and the pronoun that refers to that noun agree in number. A singular pronoun should be used to refer to a singular noun; a plural pronoun should be used with a plural noun. In the following example, the pronoun does not match its antecedent in number:

> The typical college student has difficulty adjusting to academic
> standards much higher than those of *their* school.

The subject of the sentence is *student*, a singular noun. The pronoun *their* should refer to a plural noun, but in this sentence it refers back to *student*. Therefore, the pronoun should be the singular form *his* or *her*, not the plural form *their*. Look for the same kind of mistake in the next sentence:

> Most infants, even unusually quiet ones, will cry with greater inten-
> sity when *it* begins teething.

The error in this sentence is just the opposite from that in the first example. The subject is *infants*, a plural noun. But the pronoun that refers back to this plural noun is *it*, a singular form. The correct form of the pronoun is *they*, which refers back to the plural subject. Be sure that a pronoun agrees with its antecedent in number.

Common Mistake 10: Drill

Are the following sentences grammatically correct? Note the incorrect sentences and replace the italicized words with the correct forms in the blank lines provided. Answers are on page 136.

1. The appreciation shown to the dance troupe was a symbol of the school's gratitude for *their* _____ hard work.

2. The mayor welcomed the foreign delegation by presenting *them* _____ with a key to the city.

3. Crowds of tennis fans love his style of play, because the tennis star frequently appeals to *them* _____ for support.

4. The Internal Revenue Service is annually derided by critics who claim that *their* _____ instruction manuals for filing taxes are too cryptic.

5. A typical bank will reject an application for a loan if *their* _____ credit department discovers that the applicant is unemployed.

6. Investors who lost money in the stock market crash generally recouped *his*_____ losses over the next 18 months.

7. The committee asserts that the venture capitalist has not proven quite as philanthropic as *their* _____ public relations campaign suggests.

8. The waitresses in this elegant restaurant can receive up to 80 percent of *her* _____ salary in tips.

Common Mistake 11: Pronoun in the Wrong Case in Compound Noun Phrases

When two subjects act on the same verb, we call this a *compound subject*. Can you identify the compound in the sentence below and the error in the choice of pronoun?

> Him and the rest of the team stopped by the ice cream shop for
> milkshakes after the game.

In this sentence, the compound subject is *Him and the rest of the team*. To identify the error, you should isolate the pronoun from the compound. Take away the second part of the compound, and you are left with *him*. You wouldn't say "Him stopped by the ice cream shop," would you? The correct subject pronoun form for this sentence is *he*.

Can you identify and isolate the incorrect pronoun in the following sentence?

> Uncle John and Aunt Rosie join my parents and I for dinner every Thursday.

In this sentence, the compound noun phrase in question is *my parents and I*, the object of the verb. Ignoring the phrase *my parents*, you can now read the sentence: *Uncle John and Aunt Rosie join I for dinner every Thursday*. The pronoun *I* is the incorrect form of the personal pronoun; the correct form is *me*, the object form. *My parents and* I would be correct only as the subject of the sentence.

Common Mistake 11: Drill

For the following exercise questions, single out the pronoun from the rest of the compound. Then determine what role the pronoun plays in the sentence, and put the pronoun into the correct form.

Circle the pronoun in parentheses that makes the sentence grammatically correct. Answers are on page 136.

1. The other drivers and (I/me) pulled over until the heavy rains passed.

2. I did not receive the final draft of the report until it was approved by my supervisor and (he/him).

3. (We/Us) and the high school band accompanied the team to the stadium on the chartered bus.

4. Our professor forgot to distribute the new Bunsen burner kit to my lab partner and (I/me).

5. (She/Her) and her parents set off yesterday on a three-week cruise of the North Atlantic.

6. It was surprising to hear the minister address my new wife and (I/me) as "Mr. and Mrs. Murphy."

7. The legal authorities questioned (she/her) and the other students involved in the incident for two hours before dropping the charges.

8. (We/Us) and the other team combined for 16 runs and 23 hits in the seven-inning game.

Common Mistake 12: Pronoun Shift

"Pronoun shift" is a switch in pronoun person or number within a given sentence. Here's an example:

> One cannot sleep soundly if *you* exercise vigorously before retiring to bed.

The subject in the first clause is *one*, and the subject in the second clause is *you*. These two pronouns refer to the same performer of two actions, so they should be consistent in person and number. If you see the pronoun *one* in one part of a sentence, then *one* should also be used elsewhere in the sentence. The sentence should not shift to the second-person *you* form.

Look for another kind of pronoun shift in this sentence:

> If someone loses his way in the airport, *they* can ask any employee for directions.

The subject is *someone* in the first clause, but *they* in the second clause. Clearly, both pronouns refer to the same agent; the performer of both actions, losing and asking, is the same. This switch in number from singular to plural is not grammatically correct. In creating such a sentence, sneaky SAT writers play on a common logical confusion. In English, singular words like *one*, *someone*, and *a person* can represent people in general. So can plural words like *people* or *they*. Be on the lookout when general statements use pronouns, and consider whether these pronouns are consistent.

Common Mistake 12: Drill

Identify the sentences that include a pronoun shift, and replace the incorrect italicized words with the correct forms in the blanks provided. Answers are on page 136.

1. When we gather during the Thanksgiving holidays, *you* _____ cannot help appreciating family and friends.

2. One cannot gauge the immensity of the Empire State Building until *you* _____ stands atop the building.

3. As you arrive in New York City's Grand Central Terminal, *one* _____ can easily imagine that station as the most elaborate in all of the United States.

4. You may not be fond of Shakespeare, but the theater company guarantees *you* _____ will be impressed with the quality of acting in this production.

5. You should not even attempt to pass your driving test unless *one* _____ have learned to parallel park.

6. When they grew up in my grandfather's neighborhood during the Great Depression, *you* _____ could feel the despair that gripped the nation.

7. Whenever we read about a plane crash, even as infrequent flyers, *you* _____ become concerned about air safety.

8. When one considers the vastness of the universe, one cannot help being struck by *your* _____ own insignificance.

Common Mistake 13: Pronoun with Ambiguous Reference

There are two ways the Writing section might test your ability to recognize ambiguous pronoun reference. First, a sentence may be given in which it is impossible to determine to what noun the pronoun refers. Take a look at this example:

> The United States entered into warmer relations with China after *its* compliance with recent weapons agreements.

To which country does the pronoun *its* refer? Grammatically and logically, either country could be the antecedent of the pronoun. With the limited information provided by this sentence alone, you simply can't determine which country the pronoun stands in for. Its reference is ambiguous.

Pronoun reference can also be ambiguous if the pronoun's antecedent is not explicitly stated in the sentence:

> After the derailment last month, *they* are inspecting trains for safety more often than ever before.

The question to ask about this sentence is: who is *they*? There is no group of people identified in this sentence to whom the pronoun could refer. You can logically infer that *they* refers to agents of a railroad safety commission, but because these inspectors are not explicitly mentioned in the sentence, the personal pronoun cannot be clear. Be sure to locate the antecedent of any under-lined pronoun in a sentence.

Fixing problem sentences such as these requires rewriting the sentence. For the SAT, you'll have to be able to identify the problem.

Common Mistake 13: Drill

Read the following sentences and circle the pronouns with ambiguous reference. Answers are on page 136.

1. The company chairman contacted the marketing director after he failed to attend the sales meeting.

2. Temporary loss of hearing is a common occurrence at rock concerts where they sit too close to the mammoth speakers.

3. The small claims court lawyer won the case for the defendant once she proved her innocence with legal documents.

4. Jurors are told to disregard the race of the participants in a trial when they come into the courtroom.

5. When an old friend came to town last week, he asked what plays they were presenting on Broadway.

6. The manager benched the star player after he criticized the pitcher's lack of intensity.

7. Dozens of students rallied against administration officials to protest the music they were playing on the college radio station.

8. When the painters work on your neighbors' laundry room, make sure that they do not get paint on their clothes.

Common Mistake 14: Faulty Comparison

Most faulty comparisons happen when two things that logically cannot be compared are compared. A comparison can be faulty either logically or grammatically. Look for the faulty comparison in this sentence:

> A Nobel Peace Prize winner and the author of several respected novels, Elie Wiesel is a name still less well known than last year's Heisman Trophy winner.

In every sentence, you should first identify what things or actions are being compared. In this sentence, *name* is compared to *last year's Heisman Trophy winner*. This comparison is faulty because a person's name is compared to another person. If the first item were simply *Elie Wiesel*, then the comparison would be valid.

Try to identify the faulty comparison in the next sentence:

> To lash back at one's adversaries is a less courageous course than attempting to bring about reconciliation with them.

The comparison in this sentence is logically correct in that two actions are compared. But the problem lies in the grammatical form of the words compared. An infinitive verb, *to lash*, expresses the first action, but a gerund, *attempting*, expresses the second action. These forms should match in order to make the comparison parallel. If *lashing* replaced *to lash*, the comparison would be grammatically parallel and logically valid. Check all comparisons for logic and grammatical consistency.

Common Mistake 14: Drill

Which of the following sentences contain faulty comparisons? Correct the phrases that contain errors of comparison on the lines that follow. Answers are on page 136.

1. Like many politicians, the senator's promises sounded good but ultimately led to nothing.

   Rewrite: _____

   _____

2. As a manager and a problem solver, the governor was considered as creative as, or more creative than, writing and painting.

   Rewrite: _____

   _____

3. Marine zoologists who have trained porpoises maintain that porpoises have powers of attention more sustained than chimpanzees.

   Rewrite: _____

   _____

4. The United States scientist's assumption, unlike Germany's Professor Heisenberg, was that the release of atomic energy would be sudden and violent.

   Rewrite: _____

   _____

5. Although some traditionalists still prefer typewriters to computers, most people agree that word processors are a great boon.

   Rewrite: _____

   _____

6. The nonviolent resistance philosophy of Thoreau, Ghandi, and King holds that it is better to go to jail than submitting to an unjust law.

   Rewrite: _____

   _____

7. The cost of a year at college these days is greater than a house was when my father was a boy.

   Rewrite: _____

   _____

8. According to some medievalists, women were treated with far greater respect during the Middle Ages than many countries in the twentieth century.

   Rewrite: _____

   _____

Common Mistake 15: Misuse of Adjective or Adverb

These questions test your ability to recognize misuses of one-word modifiers. Keep in mind that adjectives modify nouns, and adverbs modify verbs, adjectives, and other adverbs. Now ask yourself what the italicized word is intended to modify as you look at the sentence below:

> The applicants for low-interest loans hoped to buy *decent* built
> houses for their families.

The word *decent* is an adjective. However, a word in this position should describe how the houses were built. A word that modifies an adjective like *built* is an adverb. So the word needed in this sentence is an adverb, *decently*. Notice also that this adverb ends in *-ly*, which is the most common adverbial ending.

Now take a look at this sentence:

> The critics who reviewed both of David Eggers's novels like the second one *best*.

The word *best* is a superlative modifier. (It's an adverb in this sentence, but *best* can also be an adjective.) Superlative adverbs and adjectives (adverbs and adjectives ending in *-est*, such as *biggest*, *loudest*, *fastest*) should express comparisons between three or more things or actions.

This sentence compares critics' responses to two novels by David Eggers. Comparative adverbs and adjectives (ending in *-er*, such as *bigger*, *louder*, *faster*) should express comparisons between two things or actions. Instead of *best*, this sentence needed the comparative modifier *better*. Remember that some adjectives and adverbs, usually those of two or more syllables, form the comparative with *more* instead of the *-er* ending. And *most* instead of the *-est* ending converts some modifiers to superlatives. For example: *big*, *bigger*, and *biggest*; *frustrated*, *more frustrated*, and *most frustrated*.

Trust your ear to distinguish adjectives from adverbs on the Writing section questions, but do "listen" carefully. Pay close attention when you decide whether a sentence needs a comparative or superlative modifier.

Common Mistake 15: Drill

Circle the option in parentheses that makes the sentence grammatically correct. Answers are on page 136.

1. Global warming would increase more (gradual/gradually) if solar energy sources were more fully exploited.

2. Eliminating (commercial/commercially) prepared sauces and seasonings is a good way to reduce the amount of sodium in your diet.

3. Although many people feel that parapsychology, the study of psychic phenomena, is completely frivolous, others take it very (serious/seriously).

4. Among the many problems facing the nation's schools today, the high dropout rate may be the (more/most) distressing.

5. The reading list for the course included short stories by five American authors, but most students found those by Poe (more/most) effective.

6. Archeologists excavating the ancient Inca site removed soil very (slow/slowly) to protect any buried artifacts.

7. Although Delacroix is best known for the drama of his large canvases, many of his smaller works capture heroic themes just as (forceful/forcefully).

8. When movies were cheaper to produce than they are now, young directors were able to make films (easier/more easily).

Common Mistake 16: Double Negative

Don't use no double negatives on the Writing section! Get it? In standard written English, it is incorrect to use two negatives together unless one is intended to cancel out the other. Notice the two negative words in this sentence:

> James easily passed the biology exam *without hardly* studying his lab notes.

Without is a negative, as is any word that indicates absence or lack. *Hardly* is a less familiar negative; it also denotes a scarcity of something, but perhaps not a total absence.

Now look at this sentence:

> In the history of the major leagues, *barely no one* has maintained higher than a .400 batting average for an entire season.

Clearly, *no one* is a negative, but so is *barely*. Just as *hardly* does, this word indicates a scarcity of something, or almost a total absence. Be on the lookout for negatives that are not obviously negative, such as *hardly*, *barely*, and *scarcely*.

Common Mistake 16: Drill

Which of the following sentences contain inappropriate double negatives? Reach each sentence and circle the double negatives, if any. Answers are on page 136.

1. Until Copernicus proposed his theory, scarcely no one believed that the sun was the center of the universe.

2. The decline of outmoded industries has resulted in an unstable economy, since no easy way of retraining workers has never been found.

3. Many submarine volcanoes lie at such great depth that eruptions occur without hardly any release of gas or steam.

4. Charles Dickens had not written fiction for scarcely three years when he became a best-selling novelist.

5. Practically no big-time college football team has enjoyed success on the gridiron without increasing overall athletic department revenues.

6. Because consumer electronics are so affordable today, hardly no college student needs to go without a personal stereo.

7. Last summer's extended drought means there may not be scarcely enough wheat to satisfy the growing demand.

8. The author's latest work is so powerfully written and emotionally charged that hardly any commentators have criticized it.

CHAPTER 6 SUMMARY

Identifying Sentence Errors questions test your knowledge of:

- Basic grammar
- Sentence structure
- Word choice

All Identifying Sentence Errors questions are "spot-the-mistake" questions, and Kaplan has a four-step method for spotting mistakes:

Step 1. Read the whole sentence, "listening" for the mistake.

Step 2. If you "heard" the mistake, choose it and you're done.

Step 3. If not, read each underlined choice, and eliminate choices that contain no errors.

Step 4. If you're sure the sentence contains no errors, choose E.

There are 16 mistakes the SAT likes to test. Most of these will appear on your administration of the SAT:

1. Subject-verb agreement: when subject follows verb

2. Subject-verb agreement: when subject and verb are separated

3. Subject-verb agreement: when the subject seems plural

4. Confusion of simple past and past participle

5. Confusion of infinitive and gerund

6. Non-idiomatic preposition after verb

7. Wrong word

8. Wrong tense

9. Number agreement problems

10. Pronoun in the wrong number

11. Pronoun in the wrong case in compound noun phrases

12. Pronoun shift

13. Pronoun with ambiguous reference

14. Faulty comparison

15. Misuse of adjective or adverb

16. Double negative

CHAPTER SIX DRILLS: ANSWERS AND EXPLANATIONS

Common Mistake 1: Drill

1. are 2. are 3. pass 4. correct 5. are 6. are 7. correct

Common Mistake 2: Drill

1. are 2. is 3. go 4. attracts 5. are 6. complete 7. are 8. ranks

Common Mistake 3: Drill

1. is 2. removes 3. are 4. is 5. keeps

Common Mistake 5: Drill

1. to compete 2. to increase/on increasing 3. of setting 4. to install 5. correct 6. to triple 7. in discouraging 8. correct

Common Mistake 8: Drill

1. shrink 2. thought 3. have brought/brought 4. was 5. correct 6. had 7. comes 8. had hit

Common Mistake 9: Drill

1. requirements 2. correct 3. reminders 4. with children 5. in college T-shirts 6. prototypes 7. accounts 8. correct

Common Mistake 10: Drill

1. its 2. it 3. correct 4. its 5. its 6. their 7. his or her 8. their

Common Mistake 11: Drill

1. I 2. him 3. We 4. me 5. She 6. me 7. her 8. We

Common Mistake 12: Drill

1. we 2. one/she/he (stands) 3. you 4. correct 5. you (have) 6. they 7. we 8. one's/her/his

Common Mistake 13: Drill

1. he 2. they 3. she/her 4. they 5. they 6. he 7. they 8. they/their

Common Mistake 14: Drill

1. faulty, Like those of many politicians 2. faulty, than he was as a writer and painter 3. faulty, than those of chimpanzees 4. faulty, unlike Germany's Professor Heisenberg's 5. correct 6. faulty, than to submit to an unjust law 7. faulty, than the cost of a house 8. faulty, than they are in many countries

Common Mistake 15: Drill

1. gradually 2. commercially 3. seriously 4. most 5. most 6. slowly 7. forcefully 8. more easily

Common Mistake 16: Drill

1. scarcely no one 2. no easy way has never been found 3. without hardly 4. had not written fiction for scarcely three years 5. Correct 6. hardly no 7. may not be scarcely enough. 8. correct

SHARPEN YOUR SKILLS

Now use what you have learned in this chapter on this Practice Quiz. These questions are just like the ones that will be on the SAT.

For the questions you get wrong or have trouble with on this Practice Quiz, reread the part of this chapter about the specific mistake that was being tested. Make sure you fully understand what the mistake was and why you missed it.

IDENTIFYING SENTENCE ERRORS PRACTICE QUIZ

Directions: The following sentences test your knowledge of grammar, usage, diction (choice of words), and idiom.

Some sentences are correct.

No sentence contains more than one error.

You will find that the error, if there is one, is underlined and lettered. Elements of the sentence that are not underlined will not be changed. In choosing answers, follow the requirements of standard written English.

If there is an error, select the <u>one underlined part</u> that must be changed to make the sentence correct and fill in the corresponding oval on your answer sheet.

If there is no error, fill in answer oval (E).

1. <u>Even when</u> shrouded by the morning fog,
      A
   Mt. Hood <u>looked</u> more <u>dramatically</u> beautiful
          B   C
   to us than <u>any mountain</u>. <u>No error</u>
             D   E

2. <u>Today's</u> athlete may feel such <u>great</u> pressure
      A   B
   <u>to succeed</u> at every level of competition that
      C
   <u>they begin</u> taking drugs at an early age. <u>No error</u>
       D   E

3. <u>Bicycling</u>, as well as walking and jogging,
      A
   <u>reduce</u> <u>one's</u> <u>dependence on</u> motorized
     B   C   D
   transportation. <u>No error</u>
               E

4. Children from two-parent homes, <u>according</u> to
                              A
   a <u>recent</u> clinical study, <u>are</u> as susceptible to
      B   C
   peer pressure <u>as</u> children with only one parent.
              D
   <u>No error</u>
     E

5. The volunteer librarian <u>is</u> <u>extremely</u> concerned
                    A   B
   <u>in</u> the appallingly low rate of adult literacy in
    C
   <u>his</u> community. <u>No error</u>
     D   E

6. The wrestlers knew that fasting <u>could be</u>
                         A
   dangerous, but <u>them</u> and their teammates
               B
   were desperate <u>to</u> lose weight <u>before</u> the
             C   D
   championship match. <u>No error</u>
               E

7. Artifacts from Sumerian Ur, <u>though less well</u>
                                              A
   <u>known</u> <u>than</u> other archaeological discoveries,
    B   C
   <u>is</u> sophisticated in both design and execution.
    D
   <u>No error</u>
    E

8. Whenever we <u>travel</u> abroad, a <u>sense of</u>
                      A   B
   excitement and an anticipation of being

   in a foreign land <u>overtake</u> <u>you</u>. <u>No error</u>
                            C   D   E

9. My older brother and <u>me</u> <u>shared</u> a ten-speed
                            A   B
   bicycle <u>until</u> he passed <u>his</u> driver's examination
            C   D
   and received his license. <u>No error</u>
                                    E

10. The chairwoman felt that she <u>could not</u> give in
                                      A
    <u>with</u> his demands, <u>which</u> she thought were
     B   C
    <u>completely</u> unreasonable. <u>No error</u>
     D   E

11. <u>One</u> can learn more <u>about</u> new computers by
     A   B
    actually working with <u>them</u> than one can by
                            C
    <u>merely</u> reading the instruction manual.
     D
    <u>No error</u>
     E

12. To expand the newspaper's <u>coverage of</u>
                                    A
    local politics, <u>they</u> transferred a <u>popular</u>
                      B   C
    columnist <u>to</u> the City Desk. <u>No error</u>
               D   E

13. As one <u>roams</u> the <u>halls of</u> the National Gallery
               A   B
    of Art, <u>you</u> should appreciate not only the
              C
    <u>displays</u> of art, but the grandeur of the
     D
    building's architecture. <u>No error</u>
                                E

14. Before he <u>drunk</u> the poison, Socrates <u>joked</u>
                  A   B
    <u>gently</u> with his distraught and <u>grieving</u>
     C   D
    followers. <u>No error</u>
                 E

15. In <u>recently</u> constructed concert halls, there <u>is</u>
          A   B
    usually at least two <u>sets</u> of stairs at the rear <u>of</u>
                          C   D
    the balcony. <u>No error</u>
                   E

16. Many foreign electronics <u>companies</u> have
                                  A
    learned <u>to build</u> machines at lower cost by
              B
    using <u>inexpensive</u> produced <u>components</u>.
            C   D
    <u>No error</u>
     E

17. Although ecological awareness is

    <u>international</u>, there are <u>few if any</u> countries
          A   B

    <u>on the rise</u> <u>in which</u> no native species are
        C   D

    endangered. <u>No error</u>
                E

18. The <u>clean</u> cars and spacious <u>stations</u> of the
         A   B

    new subway system <u>is</u> a tribute to the
                   C

    project's <u>thousands of</u> laborers. <u>No error</u>
            D   E

19. <u>Some</u> settlers move to new countries simply
      A

    <u>because of</u> the compelling <u>natural</u> beauty
        B   C

    found in <u>them</u>. <u>No error</u>
           D   E

20. The Soviet Union had <u>not hardly</u> developed a
                   A

    spaceship <u>suitable</u> for lunar <u>travel</u> when the
            B   C

    first United States astronaut <u>landed on</u> the
                           D

    moon in 1969. <u>No error</u>
                E

21. The police officer <u>noticed</u> the wanted suspect
                A

    only after <u>he</u> <u>removed</u> his sunglasses and
            B   C

    <u>sat down</u> at the counter. <u>No error</u>
      D   E

22. Babar <u>was created</u> over 60 years ago <u>in</u> a
          A   B

    suburb of Paris <u>but</u> is <u>the most popular</u>
                C   D

    elephant in children's literature. <u>No error</u>
                            E

23. Unemployment compensation <u>was developed</u> to
                      A

    aid <u>those</u> people <u>between</u> jobs or otherwise
        B   C

    temporarily <u>without a position</u> of employment.
                 D

    <u>No error</u>
     E

24. The triathlete <u>had swam</u> three miles <u>before</u> leg
               A   B

    cramps <u>caused</u> her to <u>withdraw from</u> the
          C   D

    competition. <u>No error</u>
               E

25. The speaker <u>whom</u> the graduating class <u>chose</u>
             A   B

    <u>to deliver</u> their commencement address was
      C

    an <u>imminent</u> authority on international
         D

    diplomacy. <u>No error</u>
            E

26. The jazz band <u>was forced</u> <u>to return</u> the gate
              A   B

    receipts after <u>they</u> had arrived at the arena one
              C

    hour <u>late</u>. <u>No error</u>
        D   E

27. By the time <u>today's</u> freshmen complete <u>their</u>
                A   B

    engineering degrees, the job market

    <u>in their field</u> <u>has become</u> quite robust.
        C   D

    <u>No error</u>
      E

28. <u>On</u> the executive board of the <u>publishing</u>
     A   B

    company <u>sits</u> five women <u>and</u> four men.
          C   D

    <u>No error</u>
      E

29. Today, <u>when</u> Indian leaders sue to regain
          A

    <u>ancestral</u> lands, the government often <u>offered</u>
       B   C

    <u>to settle</u> the disputes out of court. <u>No error</u>
      D   E

30. Borges, <u>probably</u> the most <u>innovative</u> writer of
              A   B

    the twentieth century, <u>brought</u> to literature a
                       C

    fresh <u>concept of</u> the nature of fiction. <u>No error</u>
          D   E

IDENTIFYING SENTENCE ERRORS PRACTICE QUIZ ANSWERS AND EXPLANATIONS

1.   D

The comparison between Mt. Hood and any mountain is illogical. Mt. Hood is itself a mountain, so it cannot be contrasted with every member of its own class of things, mountains. The underlined phrase should be *any other mountain*.

2.   D

Apparently, the plural pronoun *they* refers to the subject of this sentence. But the subject is *athlete*, a singular noun even though it represents a whole class of athletes. A singular form of the personal pronoun, *he* or *she*, corresponds to the subject in number. Of course, with a singular pronoun, the verb *begin* also changes to *begins*.

3.   B

Reduce is a plural form of the verb *to reduce*. But the subject of this verb is bicycling, a gerund, and a gerund is always singular. The phrase between commas, *as well as walking and jogging*, may seem to make the subject plural. But a phrase following a subject, set off by commas, and introduced by a compound preposition like *as well as* or *in addition to*, is not treated as part of a sentence's subject. *Bicycling* remains the singular subject requiring a singular verb, *reduces*.

4.   E

There is no error in this sentence. The comparison here is both logical and idiomatic.

5.   C

In this context, the adjective *concerned* requires a different preposition, *about* instead of *in*. By itself, the word *concerned* can take three different prepositions—*about*, *in*, or *with*—but each combination produces a different meaning.

6.   B

Them is the object form of the personal pronoun that could refer to the wrestlers. But the pronoun serves as a subject in this sentence—*them...were desperate*—so it should be in subject form, *they*.

7.   D

The only verb in the sentence is the singular *is*. However, the subject of the sentence is *artifacts*, a plural noun. A long phrase separating the subject and its verb makes it harder to "listen" for agreement, but the verb should be plural, *are*.

8.   D

We and *you* are not interchangeable in this sentence, though either one could be grammatically correct. But when two pronouns within one sentence refer to the same performer of actions, the pronouns should be consistent. Here, because it's underlined, *you* can change to match *we*.

9.   A

Me is part of the subject of this sentence; the position of the pronoun makes that obvious. But the form of the pronoun signals that it's an object. To be part of the subject, the pronoun should have the subject form, *I*. It's *Is hared*, not *me shared*.

10.   B

The idiomatic verb-preposition combination *give in to* means "submit to," and that is the meaning of the verb in this sentence. The preposition *with* is simply unidiomatic in this usage.

11.   E

There is no error in this sentence. The parallel construction in this sentence balances perfectly.

12.   B

They has no antecedent in this sentence. A personal pronoun cannot refer to an unstated noun.

13.   C

One and *you* are not interchangeable in this sentence. Either *one* and *he* or *you* could be used, but both *one* and *you* cannot refer to the same performer of actions within one sentence. Because *you* is underlined, it can change to be consistent with *one*.

14.   A

This sentence requires the simple past of the verb *to drink*, which is *drank*. The form given in this sentence is the past participle.

15. B

The only verb in the sentence is the singular *is*. The subject of the sentence is *sets*, a plural noun. The word *there* preceding *is* serves to delay the subject *sets*. The subject is no longer in the position where we expect to find it, before the verb. Nevertheless, the verb should be plural—*are*—to agree with the plural subject.

16. C

Inexpensive seems to modify the word *produced* and to describe how the components were produced. But adverbs describe how an action is done, so the adjective *inexpensive* needs an adverbial ending. The word needed is the adverb *inexpensively*.

17. E

There is no error in this sentence.

18. C

The only verb in the sentence is the singular *is*. But this sentence has two plural subjects, *cars* and *stations*. The verb should be plural, *are*, to correspond with the plural subjects.

19. D

The pronoun *them* is ambiguous; although you may assume it refers to the *countries*, grammatically it might as easily refer to the *settlers*.

20. A

Hardly is a modifier that negates the word it modifies. In this sentence, it negates *developed*. *Not* also negates *developed* and creates a double-negative construction where only one negation is intended. Such double negatives are substandard usage in modern English.

21. B

It is unclear to whom the pronoun *he* refers. Because the singular pronoun *he* could agree with either noun, *officer* or *suspect*, the pronoun's reference is unclear and the noun should be restated.

22. C

This sentence is grammatically correct, but logically faulty. The conjunction *but* expresses a contrast, but the two predicates express no contrast. Babar's great and lasting popularity is not at odds with his creation in France over 60 years ago. So the *but* is not a logical way to link the two predicates.

23. D

The singular noun *position* should be the plural noun *positions*. As the phrase stands in the given sentence, *people... without a position of employment* seems to say that many persons lack the same position of employment, while of course, many unemployed people lack many different positions.

24. A

Swam is the simple past tense of the verb *to swim*. But the required verb tense in this sentence is the past perfect because the triathlete *had swum* before *cramps caused her to withdraw*. The past perfect is formed with an auxiliary verb, *had*, and the past participle, *swum*, not *swam*.

25. D

The words *imminent* and *eminent* are easily confused. *Imminent* means "likely to occur at any moment"; it is familiar and appropriate in the phrase "imminent disaster." But *eminent*, the word this sentence needs, means "highly regarded."

26. C

They seems to refer to the first subject, *jazz band*. But *jazz band* is a singular noun, although a band is made up of several musicians. The band must be singular because it acts as a unit, arriving late and disappointing the audience. The pronoun referring to the band should be *it*.

27. D

The verb phrase in the second clause is *has become*, a verb in the present perfect tense. The present perfect should express recently completed or past but continuing action: *times have changed* (and they still do). But the future time established in the first clause requires a future perfect verb in the second clause: *the job market…will have become.*

28. C

The verb *sits* is singular, but the subject of the sentence, *five women and four men*, is plural. The subject appears in an unusual position following the verb. Nevertheless, the correct verb is the plural *sit*.

29. C

The verb *offered* is in the past tense. But the first word of the sentence, *today*, indicates that the action takes place in the present. Therefore, the verb should be in the present tense, *offers*.

30. E

There is no error in this sentence.

Chapter Seven: **Improving Sentences**

Just like Identifying Sentence Errors questions, the large majority of Improving Sentences questions relate to a surprisingly limited number of grammatical issues. The main difference between the two question types is that while the errors in the Identifying Sentence Errors questions consist of single words or short phrases, the errors in Improving Sentences questions generally involve the structure of the whole sentence. So Improving Sentences questions can be a little trickier and more involved.

WHAT ARE IMPROVING SENTENCES QUESTIONS?

Remember our "spot-the-mistake" strategy? We've got a similar strategy for Improving Sentences. In addition to finding the mistake in each sentence, you have to pick the answer choice that best corrects it. Like we said, a little trickier.

So in each of these questions, you're given a sentence, part or all of which is underlined. There are five answer choices: the first one (choice (A)) reproduces the underlined part of the sentence exactly, and the other four rephrase the underlined portion in various ways.

Here's an example:

> The Emancipation Edict freed the Russian serfs <u>in 1861;</u>
> <u>that being four years</u> before the Thirteenth Amendment
> abolished slavery in the United States.
>
> (A) in 1861; that being four years
> (B) in 1861 and is four years
> (C) in 1861 and this amounts to four years
> (D) in 1861, being four years
> (E) in 1861, four years

You have to pick the best choice to replace the underlined portion of the sentence. The correct answer must produce a sentence that's not only grammatically correct, but also effective: it must be clear, precise, and free of awkward verbiage.

The Kaplan Four-Step Method for Improving Sentences

Step 1. Read the sentence carefully, listening for a mistake.

Step 2. Identify the error(s).

Step 3. Predict a correction.

Step 4. Check the choices for a match that doesn't introduce a new error.

Let's use this method on the example given earlier.

1. Read the sentence *carefully*, listening for a mistake.

The stem sentence just doesn't sound right.

2. Identify the error(s).

The semicolon and phrase *that being* seem like the wrong way of joining the two parts of the sentence.

3. Predict a correction.

The semicolon and *that being* seem unnecessary. Joining the two sentence fragments with a simple comma would probably work. (Incidentally, answer choices that contain the word *being* are usually wrong.) Plug in your choice to be sure it sounds best. Choice (E) has just a comma. Is that enough?

4. Check the choices for a match that doesn't introduce a new error.

All the answer choices begin with *in 1861* and end with *four years*, so you have to look at what's between to see what forms the best link. Scan the choices, and you'll find that the *an dis* in (B), the *and this amounts to* in (C), and the *being* preceded by a comma in (D) are no better than choice (A)—the original sentence.

Choice (E) is the best way to rewrite the underlined portion of the sentence, so (E) is the correct answer.

Remember: Not every sentence contains an error. **Choice (A) is correct about one-fifth of the time.** In any event, since you should begin by reading the original sentence carefully, you should never waste time reading choice (A).

COMMON IMPROVING SENTENCES MISTAKES

Answering Improving Sentences questions correctly begins with simply reading the sentence carefully. So read carefully! We can't say that often enough. The error, if there is one, will often be obvious to you at the first reading.

If it isn't, remember that only a rather limited range of grammar rules is tested. For that reason, we're going to give you a comprehensive survey of the grammatical problems that actually occur with some frequency on Improving Sentences questions. Once your ear has become attuned to the Improving Sentences section's favorite grammar mistakes, you'll have an easier time identifying them on test day. So here are the top five mistakes.

Answers to all of the practice questions and the Practice Quiz are at the end of the chapter starting on page 166.

Common Mistake 1: Run-On Sentences

The Writing section usually includes one or two run-on sentences. In a typical run-on sentence, two independent clauses, each of which could stand alone as a complete sentence, are erroneously joined together. They either have no punctuation or, most often, just a comma. Here's an example:

> The decrease in crime can be attributed to a rise in the number of police officers, more than 500 joined the force in the last year alone.

Both clauses in this sentence are independent; each could stand alone as a sentence. It is therefore incorrect to join them with just a comma between them. There are several ways to correct run-on sentences. One way is simply to change the comma into a period, producing two separate sentences:

> The decrease in crime can be attributed to a rise in the number of police officers. More than 500 joined the force in the last year alone.

Note: This method is never used on the Writing section.

A second way is to change the comma into a semicolon. A semicolon can be described as a "weak period." It's used to indicate that two clauses are grammatically independent but that the ideas expressed are not so independent as to warrant separate sentences. Substituting a semicolon for the comma would make this sentence correct:

> The decrease in crime can be attributed to a rise in the number of police officers; more than 500 joined the force in the last year alone.

Note: Inserting a semicolon for the given comma is the method Writing section writers use most frequently.

Tip: Commas and Independent Clauses
Is the chapter 5 review still fresh in your mind? Yes? Then you should recall that an independent clause is a group of words capable of standing on its own to form a sentence. You cannot use a comma alone to connect two independent clauses. This creates a run-on sentence.

There are other ways to join two independent clauses. In the next example, the two clauses are independent, but one is logically subordinate to the other. To make the correction, you can convert the clause expressing the subordinate idea into a grammatically subordinate, or dependent, clause. Sound confusing? It's not. Let's try an example. Identify the two clauses in this sentence:

> Liquor companies are now introducing low-alcohol and alcohol-free beverages, litigation against distillers continues to increase year after year.

Although the clauses in this sentence are grammatically independent, they are not unrelated. Logically, the first clause depends on the second one; it seems to express a response to what is described in the second clause. You can logically infer that the liquor companies are introducing these products because the number of litigations against them is great. So a good way to correct the error in this sentence would be to make the first clause grammatically dependent on the second clause, as follows:

> Although liquor companies are now introducing low-alcohol and alcohol-free beverages, litigation against distillers continues to increase year after year.

A fourth way to correct a run-on sentence is simply to reduce the two independent clauses to one. This can be done in sentences in which the independent clauses have the same subject. You can compress the two clauses into one independent clause with a compound predicate. Let's look:

> The Humber Bridge in Britain was completed in 1981, it is the longest single-span suspension bridge in the world.

In this sentence, the pronoun *it*, the subject of the second clause, refers to Humber Bridge, the subject of the first clause. To correct this sentence, remove both the comma and the pronoun *it*, and insert the coordinating conjunction *and*. The sentence now reads:

> The Humber Bridge in Britain was completed in 1981 and is the longest single-span suspension bridge in the world.

Now the sentence consists of one independent clause with a compound predicate and only one subject.

A fifth and very common way to join two independent clauses is by using a comma and a coordinate conjunction.

> The decrease in crime can be attributed to a rise in the number of police officers, more than 500 joined the force in the last year alone.

The two independent clauses can be most logically connected here by using a coordinate conjunction along with a comma. (Remember, coordinating conjunctions include: *for, and, nor, but, or, yet,* and *so.*) By using one of these conjunctions, let's correct this sentence to be:

> The decrease in crime can be attributed to a rise in the number of police officers, for more than 500 joined the force in the last year alone.

Common Mistake 1: Drill

Choose the answer that produces the most effective, clear, and exact sentence. Answers are on page 161.

1. Hockney's most arresting work has been produced at his home in <u>Los Angeles, he moved there</u> from his native Britain.

   (A) Los Angeles, he moved there

   (B) Los Angeles; he moved there

   (C) Los Angeles, but he moved there

   (D) Los Angeles and he moved there

   (E) Los Angeles he moved there

2. Banquets are frequently thrown to honor guests in a Chinese <u>home, they often feature</u> shark fin as the main dish.

   (A) home, they often feature

   (B) home; often feature

   (C) home and often feature

   (D) home and they often feature

   (E) home, these often feature

3. <u>Many well-heeled taxpayers pay</u> less than 10 percent of their annual income to the Internal Revenue Service, some middle-income taxpayers pay a much larger percentage annually.

   (A) Many well-heeled taxpayers pay

   (B) However, many well-heeled taxpayers pay

   (C) With many well-heeled taxpayers which pay

   (D) Many a well-heeled taxpayer pays

   (E) Although many well-heeled taxpayers pay

4. Most western European countries have decreased their consumption of fossil <u>fuels, a number of eastern European countries, however, have</u> not done so.

(A) fuels, a number of eastern European countries, however, have

(B) fuels, however a number of eastern European countries have

(C) fuels, while on the other hand a number of eastern European countries have

(D) fuels; a number of eastern European countries, however, have

(E) fuels, a number however of eastern European countries have

Common Mistake 2: Faulty Coordination/Subordination

These two kinds of errors occur when sentence clauses are joined incorrectly. Faulty coordination and faulty subordination are closely related, but require separate explanations.

Faulty Coordination

Coordination between two clauses is faulty if it doesn't express the logical relation between the clauses. Often, this error involves a misused conjunction. A conjunction is a connective word joining two clauses or phrases in one sentence. The most common conjunctions are:

- And
- But
- Because
- However

Identify the conjunction in the following sentence. Why does it fail to connect the clauses logically?

> Ben Franklin was a respected and talented statesman, and he was most famous for his scientific discovery of electricity.

To identify and correct the faulty coordination, determine what the relationship between the sentence's two clauses really is. Does the simple additive connective word *and* best express the relationship?

The writer states two facts about Ben Franklin: he was a talented statesman and he made a scientific discovery. Although these two facts are quite distinct, the writer joins the two ideas with the conjunction *and*, which normally expresses a consistency between two equally emphasized facts.

This is an error in coordination.

A better way to coordinate these two contrasting ideas would be to use the conjunction *but*, which indicates some contrast between the two clauses. In this sentence, *but* points to a common expectation. An individual usually distinguishes herself or himself in one field of accomplishment: in politics *or* in science, *but* not in both. So Franklin's distinction in two diverse fields seems to contradict common expectations and calls for a *but*.

Faulty Subordination

Faulty subordination is most commonly found on the Writing section in a group of words that contains two or more subordinate, or dependent, clauses but no independent clause. There are several connective words that, when introducing a sentence or clause, always indicate that the phrase that follows is dependent or subordinate. They are:

- Since
- Because
- So that
- If

Whenever a dependent clause begins a sentence, an independent clause must follow some-where in the sentence. Look at the group of words below and identify the faulty subordination:

> Since the small electronics industry is one of the world's fastest growing sectors, because demand for the computer chip continues to be high.

Since indicates that the first clause in this group of words is subordinate and needs to be preced-ed or followed by an independent clause. But *because* in the second clause indicates that the second clause is also subordinate. The "sentence" is faulty because there is no independent clause to make the group of words grammatically complete. The second connective word, *because*, should be eliminated in order to make the group of words a complete and logical sen-tence. With this revision, the *since* clause expresses a cause, and the independent clause expresses an effect or result:

> Since the small electronics industry is one of the world's fastest growing sectors, demand for the computer chip continues to be high.

Common Mistake 2: Drill

Choose the answer that produces the most effective, clear, and exact sentence. Answers are on page 161.

1. Although her first business, a health food store, went bank-rupt, <u>but she eventually launched a successful mail-order business</u>.

   (A) but she eventually launched a successful mail-order business

   (B) a successful mail-order business was eventually launched

   (C) and eventually launched a successful mail-order business

   (D) a successful mail-order business, successfully launched

   (E) she eventually launched a successful mail-order business

2. Because the carpenter would not do the work exactly as
   Edda wanted it done, <u>so she refused</u> to pay him.

   (A) so she refused

   (B) but she was refusing

   (C) she refused

   (D) and this led to her refusing

   (E) and she refused

3. <u>Because her sons believed in the power of print advertising</u>,
   pictures of Lydia Pinkham appeared with her vegetable
   compound in newspapers across America in the late
   nineteenth century.

   (A) Because her sons believed in the power of print
       advertising

   (B) Her sons believed that print advertising was powerful

   (C) Being as her sons believed in the power of print
       advertising

   (D) That her sons believed in the power of print
       advertising, they put

   (E) Although her sons believed that print advertising was
       powerful

4. Yeats eventually created a unique voice in his <u>poetry, but he
   was</u> able to shake off the restricting influences of the British
   literary tradition.

   (A) poetry, but he was

   (B) poetry; however, he was

   (C) poetry because he was

   (D) poetry that was

   (E) poetry only while being

Common Mistake 3: Sentence Fragments

The Writing section usually includes one or two sentence fragments. Sentence fragments are
parts of sentences that have no independent clauses. What looks like a sentence on the Writing
section may actually be a mere fragment. Take a look at this example:

> While many office managers are growing more and more depen-
> dent on facsimile machines, others resisting this latest technological
> breakthrough.

This just sounds wrong, doesn't it? Here's why: this is a sentence fragment because it has no
independent clause. The first clause begins with the subordinating conjunction *while*, and the

phrase following the comma contains the incomplete verb form *resisting*. A sentence should always have at least one clause that could stand alone, and here neither of the clauses can do that. The easiest way to repair this sentence is to insert the helping verb *are*:

> While many office managers are growing more and more dependent on facsimile machines, others are resisting this latest technological breakthrough.

Here's another sentence fragment:

> In the summertime, the kindergarten students who play on the rope swing beneath the crooked oak tree.

Once again, neither of the sentence clauses can stand alone. Here we have a fragment not because something is missing, but because something is included that makes a clause dependent. The word *who* makes everything after the comma a dependent clause; one that cannot stand alone. Simply remove the word *who*, and look at what you get:

> In the summertime, the kindergarten students play on the rope swing beneath the crooked oak tree.

Now you have a grammatically complete sentence that is shorter than the fragment.

Common Mistake 3: Drill

Choose the answer that produces the most effective, clear, and exact sentence. Answers are page 161.

1. It would appear that no significant portion of the electorate <u>troubled by doubts</u> substantial enough to result in the defeat of the incumbent.

   (A) troubled by doubts
   (B) is troubled by doubts
   (C) troubled by doubts which are
   (D) are troubled with doubts, these are
   (E) being troubled with doubts that are

2. Most students enter college right after high school, <u>while a few waiting a year or two before seeking admission</u>.

   (A) while a few waiting a year or two before seeking admission
   (B) and a few, waiting a year or two before seeking admission
   (C) but a few wait a year or two before seeking admission
   (D) but a wait of a year or two is sought by a few
   (E) though a few will have begun to wait a year or two before seeking admission

3. Mysteriously beautiful, the Nepalese shrine <u>inlaid with semiprecious stones</u> rare enough to honor the spiritual essence of the Buddha.

    (A) inlaid with semiprecious stones

    (B) inlaid with semiprecious stones which are

    (C) being inlaid with semiprecious stones that are

    (D) is inlaid with semiprecious stones

    (E) is inlaid with semiprecious stones, these are

4. The general increase in salaries <u>surprised and delighted the employees</u>.

    (A) surprised and delighted the employees

    (B) surprised the employees, delighting them

    (C) surprised the employees and they were delighted

    (D) was a surprise and caused delight among the employees

    (E) was surprising to the employees, delighting them

5. For reasons not fully understood, nearly all children on the island <u>gifted with musical ability</u> so strong they can master any instrument within hours.

    (A) gifted with musical ability

    (B) gifted with musical ability which is

    (C) are gifted with musical ability

    (D) being gifted with musical ability that is

    (E) are gifted with musical abilities, these are

6. <u>That many people believe him to be</u> the most competent and well-informed of all the candidates currently listed on the ballot.

    (A) That many people believe him to be

    (B) That many people believe he is

    (C) Because many people believe him to be

    (D) Many people believe him to be

    (E) That many people believe him

Common Mistake 4: Misplaced Modifiers

A modifier is a word or group of words that gives the reader more information about a noun or verb in the sentence. To be grammatically correct, the modifier must be positioned so that it is clear which word is being modified. Here is an example of a misplaced modifier like those you may see on the Writing section:

> Flying for the first time, the roar of the jet engines intimidated the small child, and he grew frightened as the plane roared down the runway.

The modifying phrase above is found at the beginning of the sentence: *Flying for the first time*. A modifying phrase that begins a sentence should relate to the sentence's subject. Usually, this kind of introductory modifier is set off by a comma, and then the subject immediately follows the comma.

Logically, in this example, you know that what is flying for the first time is *the small child*. But the grammatical structure of the sentence indicates that *flying for the first time* is modifying *roar*, which doesn't make sense. The sentence needs to be revised:

> Flying for the first time, the small child was intimidated by the roar of the jet engines and grew frightened as the plane roared down the runway.

Here's an example of a sentence with a misplaced modifying clause:

> An advertisement was withdrawn by the producer of the local news program that was considered too sensational by members of the community.

Grammatically, the clause *that was considered too sensational* refers to the nearest noun, *the local news program*. Is that what the writer means? Is it the local news program or the advertisement that was considered sensational by members of the community? Grammatically, the above sentence is correct only if the writer means to say that the local news program was too sensational. However, if the writer means to say that the advertisement was deemed sensational, he or she should rewrite the sentence this way:

> The producer of the local news program withdrew an advertisement that was considered too sensational by members of the community.

In this sentence too, a misplaced modifier makes things confusing:

> The despondent little girl found her missing doll playing in the back yard under the swing.

The position of the modifying phrase *playing in the back yard under the swing* suggests that the phrase modifies *her missing doll*. It's unlikely that the missing doll was doing the playing. It is more likely that the writer intended the phrase to modify *the despondent little girl*. If so, the sentence should instead read:

> Playing in the back yard under the swing, the despondent little girl found her missing doll.

Common Mistake 4: Drill

Choose the answer that produces the most effective, clear, and exact sentence. Answers are on page 161.

1. <u>A familiar marketing strategy was reintroduced by a former client that</u> had served the company dependably in the past.

    (A) A familiar marketing strategy was reintroduced by a former client that

    (B) By reintroducing a familiar marketing strategy, the former client that

    (C) Reintroduced by a former client, a familiar marketing strategy that

    (D) A former client reintroduced a familiar marketing strategy that

    (E) A former client, by reintroducing a familiar marketing strategy

2. <u>After practicing for months, auditions went much more smoothly for the young actor.</u>

    (A) After practicing for months, auditions went much more smoothly for the young actor.

    (B) Auditions, after practicing for months, went much more smoothly for the young actor.

    (C) The young actor having practiced for auditions for months, auditions went much more smoothly for him.

    (D) The young actor presenting auditions after months of practice, they went much more smoothly.

    (E) After practicing for months, the young actor found auditions to go much more smoothly.

3. To ensure that a novel will sell well, <u>it should appeal to currently popular tastes</u>.

    (A) it should appeal to currently popular tastes

    (B) a novel should be appealing to currently popular tastes

    (C) a writer should appeal to currently popular tastes

    (D) currently popular tastes should be appealed to

    (E) currently popular tastes should be appealed to by the novel

4. Hoping to receive a promotion, <u>the letter he received instead informed the employee</u> that he had been fired.

    (A) the letter he received instead informed the employee

    (B) the letter having been received, instead informing the employee

    (C) the employee instead received a letter informing him

    (D) information from the received letter instead told the employee

    (E) the employee, instead informed by the letter he received

5. <u>A cornerstone of the community since 1925, the fund-raising drive did not generate enough revenue to keep the recreational center operating another year.</u>

    (A) A cornerstone of the community since 1925, the fund-raising drive did not generate enough revenue to keep the recreational center operating another year.

    (B) The fund-raising drive did not generate enough revenue to keep the recreational center, a cornerstone of the community since 1925, operating another year.

    (C) The fund-raising drive did not generate enough revenue, a cornerstone of the community since 1925, to keep the recreational center operating another year.

    (D) A cornerstone of the community since 1925, the recreational center did not generate enough revenue to keep the fund-raising drive operating another year.

    (E) The fund-raising drive, a cornerstone of the community since 1925, did not generate enough revenue to keep the recreational center operating another year.

Common Mistake 5: Faulty Parallelism

This class of errors covers a wide range of faulty sentence constructions. A certain set of words in a sentence or the general design of a sentence often requires a parallel construction. If this construction is off balance, then parallelism in the sentence is faulty.

There are generally two situations in which the Writing section tests your ability to spot errors in parallel construction. The first occurs in sentences with pairs of connective words that require parallelism. Here is a list of connective words that demand parallel constructions:

> neither…nor
>
> either…or
>
> both…and
>
> the better…the better
>
> the more…the more (or less)
>
> not only…but also

In the sentence below, look at that first pair of words, *neither…nor*, and the phrases that follow both words:

> Nineteenth-century nihilists were concerned with neither the ori-
> gins of philosophical thought nor *how societal laws developed.*

The phrases following the words *neither* and *nor* must be parallel in grammatical structure. That is, if a noun phrase follows *neither*, then a noun phrase must follow *nor*, too.

If the phrase after a first paired connective word is adverbial, the phrase after the second connective word must also be adverbial. In this sentence, the words that follow *neither* are *the origins of philosophical thought*; this is a noun phrase, composed of a noun followed by a prepositional phrase. But what follows *nor* is *how societal laws developed*, which is a dependent clause. These two parts of the sentence are not grammatically parallel.

The dependent clause, the italicized part of the sentence, must be changed to be parallel to the first phrase; it must be revised into a noun phrase. The sentence can be rewritten as follows:

> Nineteenth-century nihilists were concerned with neither the ori-
> gins of philosophical thought nor *the development of societal laws.*

In this revision, both phrases following the connective words consist of a noun followed by a prepositional phrase. In other words, both are noun phrases, so the sentence now has a proper parallel construction.

The second common way in which the use of parallel grammatical structure is tested on the Writing section is when a sentence consists of a list of two or more items. That list can include two or more nouns or noun phrases, verbs or verb phrases, or dependent clauses. Any kind of list calls for grammatically parallel items. Look for the faulty parallelism in the sentence below:

> To run for a seat in the United States Senate, a candidate must be an adult at least 30 years of age, a citizen of the United States, and *is to reside in the state* to be represented.

This sentence ends with three listed phrases. The first two phrases in the list, *an adult at least 30 years of age* and *a citizen of the United States*, are both nouns modified by prepositional phrases.

The third phrase in the list is *is to reside in the state*. This is a verb phrase including the present tense form *is* plus the infinitive form *to reside*. The two noun phrases plus one verb phrase cause faulty parallelism!

To correct this error, transform the italicized verb phrase into a noun phrase. If a person is to live in a state in order to be elected to the Senate, he or she must be a resident of the state. The revised sentence should be:

> To run for a seat in the United States Senate, a candidate must be an adult at least 30 years of age, a citizen of the United States, and *a resident of the state* to be represented.

Common Mistake 5: Drill

Choose the answer that produces the most effective, clear, and exact sentence. Answers are on page 161.

1. The great wastes of the southeast quadrant of Saudi Arabia are at once forbiddingly empty, climatically harsh, <u>and the beauty of them is haunting</u>.

    (A) and the beauty of them is haunting

    (B) with haunting beauties

    (C) while their beauties are haunting

    (D) and hauntingly beautiful

    (E) but their beauty is haunting

2. When the artist first began sketching, she discovered that it is important both <u>to be attentive to the line of the figure and studying</u> the relationship of one volume to another.

   (A) to be attentive to the line of the figure and studying

   (B) being attentive to the line of the figure, and studying

   (C) be attentive to the line of the figure as well as studying

   (D) being attentive to the line of the figure and that one study

   (E) to be attentive to the line of the figure and to study

3. After the doctor warned her that she was in poor health, the chairwoman resolved to go on a diet, stop smoking, <u>and exercising every day</u>.

   (A) and exercising every day

   (B) and exercise every day

   (C) and be exercising every day

   (D) and therefore exercise every day

   (E) as well as exercising every day

CHAPTER 7 SUMMARY

Improving Sentences questions test a small number of grammar issues. You have to *fix* the mistakes, not just spot them.

Follow Kaplan's Four-Step Method for Improving Sentences:

Step 1. Read the sentence carefully, listening for a mistake.

Step 2. Identify the error(s).

Step 3. Predict a correction.

Step 4. Check the choices for a match that doesn't introduce a new error.

There are five sentence mistakes the SAT tests repeatedly:

1. Run-on sentences
2. Faulty coordination/subordination
3. Sentence fragments
4. Misplaced modifiers
5. Faulty parallelism

CHAPTER SEVEN DRILLS: ANSWERS AND EXPLANATIONS

Common Mistake 1: Drill

l. B 2. C 3. E 4. D

Common Mistake 2: Drill

l. E 2. C 3. A 4. C

Common Mistake 3: Drill

l. B 2. C 3. D 4. A 5. C 6. D

Common Mistake 4: Drill

l. D 2. E 3. C 4. C 5. B

Common Mistake 5: Drill

l. D 2. E 3. B

Sharpen Your Skills

Now use what you have learned in this chapter on this Improving Sentences Practice Quiz. These questions are just like the ones that will be on the SAT. For the questions you get wrong or have trouble with on this Practice Quiz, reread the part of this chapter about the specific mistake that was being tested. Make sure you fully understand what the mistake was, and why you missed it.

IMPROVING SENTENCES PRACTICE QUIZ

Directions: The following sentences test correctness and effectiveness of expression. In choosing answers, follow the requirements of standard written English; that is, pay attention to grammar, choice of words, sentence construction, and punctuation.

In each of the following sentences, part of the sentence or the entire sentence is underlined. Beneath each sentence, you will find five ways of phrasing the underlined part. Choice (A) repeats the original; the other four are different.

Choose the answer that best expresses the meaning of the original sentence. If you think the original is better than any of the alternatives, choose it; otherwise, choose one of the others. Your choice should produce the most effective sentence—clear and precise, without awkwardness or ambiguity.

1. Although the candidate received crucial votes from rural precincts, <u>but he was defeated by</u> his opponent's broad base of political support.

   (A) but he was defeated by
   (B) defeating him by
   (C) and what made his defeat possible
   (D) he was defeated by
   (E) and he was defeated by

2. Most wholesale dealers are reluctant to reveal either how much they pay for their goods or <u>their profit margin per item sold</u>.

   (A) their profit margin per item sold
   (B) how great a profit margin per item sold
   (C) how great a profit they receive per item sold
   (D) if their profit margin per item sold
   (E) how great the margin of profit

3. Exposed to the extremely long and severe cold spell, <u>frost soon killed the buds of the citrus trees and they did not produce fruit that season</u>.

   (A) frost soon killed the buds of the citrus trees and they did not produce fruit that season
   (B) soon the buds of the citrus trees were killed by frost, and therefore not producing fruit that season
   (C) the buds of the citrus trees were soon killed by frost, they did not produce fruit that season
   (D) fruit was not produced by the citrus trees that season because their buds had been killed by frost
   (E) the buds of the citrus trees were soon killed by frost, and the trees did not produce fruit that season

4. This group of artists, masters of the short brush stroke developed by the Impressionists in the nineteenth century, did not believe in selling works of art; however, <u>some giving paintings away</u>.

   (A) some giving paintings away
   (B) giving some paintings away
   (C) paintings were given away by some of them
   (D) some having given paintings away
   (E) some gave paintings away

5. <u>Credulous people believe</u> in the existence of extra-terrestrial beings, most scientists and other informed students of nature do not.

   (A) Credulous people believe
   (B) While credulous people believe
   (C) Credulous people are always believing
   (D) Since credulous people believe
   (E) Credulous people tend to believe

6. In the closing decades of the eighteenth century, it was believed that young women should not only <u>be obedient and soft-spoken but also master</u> such skills as needlepoint.

   (A) be obedient and soft-spoken but also master
   (B) being obedient and soft-spoken but also mastering
   (C) obey and speak softly but also to master
   (D) be obedient and soft-spoken but also to master
   (E) obeying and speaking softly but also mastering

7. Few of us have seen war, but <u>most of us fearing it</u>.

   (A) most of us fearing it
   (B) most of us fear it
   (C) it is feared by most of us
   (D) it has been feared
   (E) it is being feared by most of us

8. Learning the rules of musical harmony is one <u>thing, but applying</u> them with inspired, creative zest is another.

   (A) thing, but applying
   (B) thing and applying
   (C) thing; to apply
   (D) thing, but to apply
   (E) thing, that you apply

9. Saint Bernard dogs are fabled to have rescued many a stranded <u>traveler, such displays of valor</u> have endeared these dogs to many pet owners.

   (A) traveler, such displays of valor
   (B) traveler, displays of such valor
   (C) traveler and therefore, such displays of valor
   (D) traveler; such displays of valor
   (E) traveler but such displays of valor

10. Environmental scientists are very concerned <u>about dangerous fluorocarbons, found in pressurized aerosol cans which quicken the erosion of the ozone layer</u>.

   (A) about dangerous fluorocarbons, found in pressurized aerosol cans which quicken the erosion of the ozone layer
   (B) that, while emitting dangerous fluorocarbons, pressurized aerosol cans quicken the erosion of the ozone layer
   (C) about the erosion of the ozone layer caused by pressurized aerosol cans emitting dangerous fluorocarbons
   (D) that pressurized aerosol cans emit dangerous fluorocarbons, which quicken the erosion of the ozone layer
   (E) when, quickening the erosion of the ozone layer, pressurized aerosol cans emit dangerous fluorocarbons

11. The last of the world's leaders to do so, the Prime Minister admits that terrorist threats <u>credible enough to warrant</u> the imposition of stringent security measures.

   (A) credible enough to warrant
   (B) credible enough warrant
   (C) are credible enough to warrant
   (D) credible enough, warranting
   (E) are credible enough to be warranted

12. The characteristics of a typical Avery canvas are a purposely limited palette, a distinctive use of color for perspective, <u>and it employs obvious brush strokes for effect</u>.

   (A) and it employs obvious brush strokes for effect

   (B) and an employment of obvious brush strokes for effect

   (C) but it employs obvious brush strokes for effect

   (D) whereby, for effect, it employs obvious brush strokes

   (E) it employs obvious brush strokes for effect

13. According to Aristotle, a catastrophe <u>is when the action of a tragic drama turns toward its disastrous conclusion</u>.

   (A) is when the action of a tragic drama turns toward its disastrous conclusion

   (B) is where a tragic drama turns the action toward its disastrous conclusion

   (C) occurs where, toward its disastrous conclusion, the action of a tragic drama is turning

   (D) approaches when the action of a tragic drama has turned toward its disastrous conclusion

   (E) is the turning point at which the action of a tragic drama approaches its disastrous conclusion

14. Abhorring rampant commercialism, the neighborhood theater group <u>has always attempted to try to</u> produce original work by worthy, if unknown, playwrights.

   (A) has always attempted to try to

   (B) has always tried to

   (C) tries and attempts to

   (D) makes an attempt at

   (E) attempts to try to

15. Emerging from the jungle to surrender decades after the war ended, <u>the last Japanese soldier still in World War II uniform was hailed as</u> a symbol of steadfastness.

   (A) the last Japanese soldier still in World War II uniform was hailed as

   (B) they called the last Japanese soldier still in World War II uniform

   (C) was the last Japanese soldier still in World War II uniform hailed as

   (D) the last Japanese soldier still in World War II uniform hailed as

   (E) popular opinion refers to the Japanese soldier still in World War II uniform as

16. Women are not rejecting the idea of raising children, but <u>many taking jobs</u> as well.

   (A) many taking jobs

   (B) many are taking jobs

   (C) jobs are taken by many of them

   (D) jobs are being taken

   (E) many having taken jobs

17. Changing over from a military to a peacetime economy means producing tractors rather than tanks, radios rather than rifles, and <u>to producing running shoes rather than combat boots</u>.

    (A) to producing running shoes rather than combat boots
    (B) to the production of running shoes rather than combat boots
    (C) running shoes rather than combat boots
    (D) replacing combat boots with running shoes
    (E) to running shoes rather combat boots

18. The protest movement's impact will depend on both how many people it touches and <u>its durability</u>.

    (A) its durability
    (B) is it going to endure
    (C) if it has durability
    (D) how long it endures
    (E) the movement's ability to endure

IMPROVING SENTENCES PRACTICE QUIZ ANSWERS AND EXPLANATIONS

1. D

The original sentence contains both a dependent and an independent clause, but it uses two connecting words when only one is needed. Choice (D) creates an independent clause with no unnecessary connecting word joining the two clauses.

2. C

The given sentence has faulty parallelism. With coordinating words like *either…or*, word order and sentence structure following the two coordinating words should be parallel. Here, a dependent clause follows the word *either*: *how much they pay for their goods*. Choice (C) contains a dependent clause and makes the wording after *or* parallel to the wording after *either*.

3. E

This sentence contains a misplaced modifier. The introductory phrase should modify the noun immediately following the comma. In choices (E) and (C), the modified noun, *the buds*, is in the correct position following the introductory modifying phrase. But notice that choice (C) introduces a new error when it links the second clause to the first with only a comma. Only choice (E) corrects the original problem without adding a new one.

4. E

The semicolon requires an independent clause. Choice (C) is an independent clause, but the passive verb, *were given (away)*, makes it wordy. Only choice (E) gives the proper grammatical structure concisely.

5. B

The given sentence is a run-on; two independent clauses are joined only by a comma, with no proper conjunction. The run-on can be corrected by turning the first clause into a dependent clause. Only choice (B) creates a clause, which solves the run-on problem and expresses the logical relation of the two clauses.

6. A

The sentence is correct as written. Word order is parallel after the correlative words *not only…but also*.

7. B

The phrase following the comma should be a second clause with word order parallel to that of the first clause. Choice (B) correctly supplies a main or indicative verb, *fear*, for the subject, *most of us*, and converts the phrase to a clause. The word order and active verb of this second clause also follow the active construction of the first clause.

8. A

The sentence is correct as written. The subjects of the two clauses, *learning* and *applying*, are in parallel gerund form.

9. D

This is another run-on sentence. The semicolon in choice (D) correctly separates the two independent clauses.

10. D

This sentence contains a misplaced modifier, *which quicken the erosion of the ozone layer*. Choice (D) correctly places the modifier immediately following the noun it modifies, that is, *fluorocarbons*.

11. C

The second clause of the given sentence lacks a main verb. Choice (C) provides the verb *are* for the subject *threats* so that the second dependent clause is complete and the sentence is correct.

12. B

This sentence has faulty parallelism. The underlined portion of the sentence is a clause. But to be parallel with the two preceding noun phrases, the underlined part should also be a noun phrase.

13. E

The problem with this sentence is faulty logic, rather than a grammatical error. A *catastrophe*, a noun, cannot actually be *when…*, though it could occur *when…* Only choice (E) solves the original problem without introducing a new one. A *catastrophe can be*, and *is*, a *turning point*.

14. B

The underlined phrase contains a redundant verb because *to attempt* and *to try to* are synonymous. Choice (B) simply removes one of the two synonyms from an otherwise grammatically correct sentence.

15. A

This sentence is correct as written.

16. B

This sentence uses a *not…but…* word pair, so it requires parallel blocks of words around each half of the pair. The first block is *are not rejecting,* so the second block must be *are taking*. Don't be misled because *are* and *rejecting* are separated by the word *not*. *Are* is still a helping verb that works together with *rejecting*.

17. C

This sentence presents a list of comparisons. All items in a list must have parallel construction. Only choice (C) gives the last comparison an appearance parallel to the previous two comparisons. The word *producing* could have been repeated in all three comparisons. But since it wasn't repeated in the second comparison, it can't be repeated in the third one either.

18. D

This sentence uses a *both…and…* pair, so it requires parallel blocks of words following each half of the pair. Only choice (D) has a second block of words, *how long it endures,* similar to the first block, *how many people it touches*.

Chapter Eight: **Improving Paragraphs**

You're almost done! In this chapter, we'll discuss the third multiple-choice question type on the Writing section. As in the Identifying Sentence Errors and Improving Sentences chapters, we've included lots of sample questions and practice drills to help you develop a fairly good idea of what to expect on the Improving Paragraphs portion of the Writing section.

WHAT ARE IMPROVING PARAGRAPHS QUESTIONS?

Improving Paragraphs questions are based on short essays (three to five paragraphs long). The essays can be about any topic; you do not need any prior knowledge about the topic in order to answer the questions.

The most important thing to keep in mind when working on these questions is the importance of *context*. Most Improving Paragraphs questions ask you to revise or combine sentences. Specifically, you'll need to clean up sentences that are awkward or ambiguous. That's where context comes in: you can't determine the best way to repair poor or unclear sentences without knowing what comes before and after them.

A few Improving Paragraphs questions will also ask you about the overall organization of the essay. Again, context is critical. You can't, for example, decide which of five sentences best concludes an essay without having a strong sense of what the essay is all about.

So essays generally have three to five short paragraphs and are followed by three to five questions.

The Kaplan Five-Step Method for Improving Paragraphs

Step 1. Read the passage quickly for the overall idea and tone.

Step 2. Read the question.

Step 3. Reread the relevant portion and its context.

Step 4. Predict the correction.

Step 5. Check the choices for a match that doesn't introduce a new error.

Step 1: Read the Passage

Read the entire essay quickly. Get a sense of the essay's overall main idea, as well as the main idea of each paragraph. This will come in handy when you're asked to answer questions about the essay as a whole.

Step 2: Read the Question

Now read the question closely. Make sure that you understand exactly what you're asked to do. Questions that require you to revise or combine sentences will supply you with the sentence numbers. Questions that ask about the entire essay generally won't refer to specific sentences.

Step 3: Reread the Relevant Portion of the Essay and Consider Context

Go back and reread the sentence or two that the question is about. But don't stop there: *It is important that you also reread the sentences before and after the target sentence(s)!* Rereading the lines around the target sentence(s) will provide you with its context. Context helps you to choose the best construction from among the answer choices.

Note: For those questions about the essay as a whole, skim quickly over the entire essay to refamiliarize yourself with its contents.

Step 4: Predict the Correction

Say in your head what you think the correct sentence structure should be.

Step 5: Find the Best Match That Doesn't Introduce a New Error

Go to the answer choices and pick the choice that best matches the sentence in your head. Make sure the one you pick doesn't introduce a new mistake into the sentence.

Let's see how it works, shall we?

THE THREE KINDS OF IMPROVING PARAGRAPHS QUESTIONS

There are three basic types of Improving Paragraphs questions:

1. General Organization questions

2. Revising Sentences questions

3. Combining Sentences questions

In this chapter, we'll cover each question type. Answers to all of the practice questions and the Improving Paragraphs Practice Quiz are at the end of the chapter starting on page 176.

1. General Organization

If you've got a firm grasp of the essay after you first read through it, you should jump right to the General Organization questions first. Do these questions while the essay is fresh in your mind.

On the other hand, if your grasp of the essay is a bit shaky, work on General Organization questions last. Start with questions that ask you to revise or combine sentences: doing so should improve your grasp of the overall essay, making it easier for you to tackle the General Organization questions later.

General Organization Drill

Read the following essay excerpt and answer the questions that follow. For each question, pick the best answer choice among those given. Answers are on page 176.

(1) At the Battle of Gettysburg in July 1863, 75,000 Confederate troops faced 90,000 Union soldiers in one of the largest battles of the American Civil War. **(2)** For two days, both armies suffered heavy casualties in constant fighting, without either gaining a clear advantage. **(3)** On the third and final day of the battle, Confederate forces mounted one last effort to penetrate Union lines. **(4)** But the attempt ended in complete failure, forcing Confederate troops to withdraw to the south.

(5) Gettysburg was a turning point in the Civil War. **(6)** Before the battle, Confederate forces had defeated their Union counterparts in a string of major engagements. **(7)** After the battle, however, Union forces took the initiative, finally defeating the Confederacy less than two years later. **(8)** By invading Union territory, the Confederate leadership sought to shatter the Union's will to continue the war and to convince European nations to recognize the Confederacy as an independent nation.

1. Which sentence most appropriately follows sentence 8?

(A) The Confederacy lost the war because it lacked the industrial capacity of the Union.

(B) Gettysburg is considered by military experts to be the bloodiest battle of the Civil War.

(C) France and Great Britain refused to provide the Confederacy with military assistance.

(D) When President Lincoln issued the Emancipation Proclamation, which ended slavery in the United States, the Confederacy's international position was weakened.

(E) Instead, the Union's willingness to fight was strengthened and the Confederacy squandered its last chance for foreign support.

2. In the essay, the author does all of the following EXCEPT

   (A) describe a specific example

   (B) criticize an opposing viewpoint

   (C) explain the importance of an event

   (D) analyze the results of a historical event

   (E) discuss what happened on a particular day

2. Revising Sentences

Take a look at the following paragraph and question. The question focuses on a single word in one sentence, but in order to answer this typical example of a revision question, you'll need to reread the entire paragraph.

> **(1)** The Spanish-American War was one of the shortest and most decisive wars ever fought. **(2)** The postwar settlement, the Treaty of Paris, reflected the results of the fighting. **(3)** Under its terms, Spain was compelled to cede large territories in North America and the Pacific. **(4)** The United States gained control over some of these territories, including Puerto Rico and Guam. **(5)** It was reduced in status from a major to a minor power. **(6)** The United States, in contrast, emerged from the war as a world power and would soon go on to become a major participant in Asian and European affairs.

In context, which is the best version of the underlined part of sentence 5 (reproduced below)?

It was reduced in status from a major to a minor power.

   (A) (As it is now)

   (B) Spain was reduced

   (C) The war caused Spain to be reduced

   (D) As a result of the war, it had been reduced

   (E) It had now been reduced

Sentence 5 refers to Spain's status. That much should have been clear to you by reading sentences 2, 3, 4, and 6. The pronoun *it*, however, makes sentence 5 ambiguous. What does *it* refer to? To make this sentence less ambiguous, *it* should be changed to the noun *Spain*. That leaves (B) and (C) as possible correct answers. Since (B) is a more concise and less awkward construction, it is correct.

Revising Sentences Drill

For each question, pick the choice that creates the clearest sentence in the context of the paragraph. Answers are on page 176.

(1) Marine mammals like seals, sea lions, and whales would be in danger of freezing to death if not for their natural defenses against the cold. (2) Their principal defense consists of several types of insulation. (3) Body hair traps air, which is then heated by the body, creating a warm air mass around the animal. (4) More important than hair is a layer of body fat (or blubber) that lies between the skin and muscle. (5) Commonly known as blubber, it has a freezing temperature well below that of water. (6) Thus, it prevents the body's heat from flowing into colder surroundings.

1. In context, which is the best version of sentence 5 (reproduced below)?

   Commonly known as blubber, it has a freezing temperature well below that of water.

   (A) (As it is now)

   (B) Known as blubber, it has a freezing temperature well below that of water.

   (C) It has a freezing temperature well below that of water.

   (D) Water has a freezing temperature well below that of blubber.

   (E) The freezing temperature of blubber is well below the freezing temperature of water.

(1) The archaeopteryx, a prehistoric bird that lived in the Jurassic period 150 million years ago, is a perfect example of a transitional form in the evolution of modern birds from reptiles. (2) Despite its birdlike appearance, the bone structure of archaeopteryx suggests that it could not fly particularly well. (3) The absence of a sternum indicates that it had not fully developed the strong pectoral muscles that modern birds require for flight.

2. In context, which is the best version of the underlined part of sentence 2 (reproduced below)?

   Despite its birdlike appearance, the bone structure of archae-opteryx suggests that it could not fly particularly well.

   (A) (As it is now)

   (B) Because of its birdlike appearance

   (C) Due to its birdlike appearance

   (D) In spite of archaeopteryx's birdlike appearance

   (E) In contrast to its birdlike appearance

(1) The earliest colonists in America were not very concerned with creating a formal legal system. (2) Solutions to problems were based on common sense rather than abstract principles. (3) Once England strengthened its hold over the American colonies, however, this informal system was gradually displaced by a formal legal system of laws, courts, and judges. (4) Even though it eventually rejected its political domination, its legal system rests heavily on the English model.

3. In context, which is the best version of the underlined part of sentence 4 (reproduced below)?

Even though it eventually rejected its political domination, its legal system rests heavily on the English model.

(A) (As it is now)

(B) Despite its rejection of its political domination

(C) Although America rejected its political domination

(D) Its rejection of its political domination notwithstanding

(E) Even though the United States eventually rejected English political domination

3. Combining Sentences

Take a look at the following paragraph and question.

(1) Albert Einstein was a great physicist. (2) He won a Nobel Prize in Physics. (3) He got the prize for his research into the photoelectric effect. (4) Later physicists demonstrated the validity of Einstein's ideas.

Which of the following is the best way to combine sentences 2 and 3 (reproduced below)?

He won a Nobel Prize in Physics. He got the prize for his research into the photoelectric effect.

(A) The Nobel Prize in Physics that he won was for his research into the photoelectric effect.

(B) Having researched the photoelectric effect, he won a Nobel Prize in Physics.

(C) He won a Nobel Prize in Physics for his research into the photoelectric effect.

(D) He got the prize in physics, the Noble Prize in Physics, for his research into the photoelectric effect.

(E) Because of his research into the photoelectric effect he got the Nobel Prize in Physics.

Did you choose (C)? It's the best written and most economical of the choices. Whether you're asked to revise or combine sentences, the correct answer will often (but not always) be the shortest answer. Good writing is concise.

Combining Sentences Drill

Combine each pair of sentences into a single sentence that conforms to the rules of standard written English on the lines that follow. There is no single correct way to combine the sentences. Just try to make your sentences concise and straightforward. Answers are on page 176.

1. Marsha went to the grocery store. At the grocery store, she bought cheese, eggs, and milk.

   _____

   _____

2. I attended a lecture at the university. My wife, on the other hand, decided to watch a movie.

   _____

   _____

3. Napoleon won many great military victories. He was eventually defeated and dethroned.

   _____

   _____

4. Interstellar travel is far beyond the limits of today's rockets. Their engines are not powerful enough to reach even the closest star.

   _____

   _____

5. The first function of tariffs is to protect local industry. And the second function of tariffs is to raise money for the national government.

   _____

   _____

CHAPTER 8 SUMMARY

The most important thing to keep in mind when it comes to doing well on Improving Paragraphs questions is the importance of *context*.

There are three basic types of Improving Paragraphs questions:
- General organization sentences
- Revising sentences questions
- Combining sentences questions

Kaplan has a "predict the correction" method that works for every kind of Improving Paragraphs question. This Kaplan Five-Step Method is as follows:

Step 1. Read the passage quickly for the overall idea and tone.

Step 2. Read the question.

Step 3. Reread the relevant portion and its context.

Step 4. Predict the correction.

Step 5. Check the choices for a match that doesn't introduce a new error.

CHAPTER EIGHT DRILLS: ANSWERS AND EXPLANATIONS

General Organization Drill

1. E

The second paragraph of the essay assesses the results of Gettysburg. Collectively, sentences 5–7 indicate that the Confederacy's fortunes went downhill after the battle. Sentence 8 reveals what the Confederacy sought to gain from the battle. Hence, the following sentence should contrast the Confederacy's high hopes with reality. (E) does exactly that by pointing out that Gettysburg both strengthened the Union's will to fight and ended the Confederacy's chances for international recognition. (A), (B), and (D) raise issues that aren't even addressed in the essay. While (C) touches on the results of Gettysburg, it's a much less relevant choice than (E).

2. B

What opposing viewpoint? This essay provides only the author's perspective on Gettysburg. The first paragraph describes the Battle of Gettysburg, including what happened on specific days, while the second paragraph evaluates the importance of the battle to the final outcome of the Civil War. Thus, choices (A), (C), (D), and (E) are eliminated.

Revising Sentences Drill

1. C

Since the layer of body fat is identified as blubber in sentence 4, there's no need to identify it again in sentence 5. Thus, the sentence in (C) is clearly the best fit in the context of the paragraph.

2.   A

This choice creates the necessary contrast with the second part of sentence 2. (D), too, creates the necessary contrast, but it isn't as concise and smooth as (A).

3.   E

What do *it* and *its* in sentence 4 refer to? The antecedents of these pronouns aren't clear from the larger context. Choice (E)'s substitution of *the United States* for *it* and *English* for *its* clarifies the sentence's meaning in the larger context of the paragraph.

Combining Sentences Drill

 1. Marsha bought cheese, eggs, and milk at the grocery store.

 2. While I attended a lecture at the university, my wife watched a movie.

 3. Although Napoleon won many great military victories, he was eventually defeated and dethroned.

 4. Interstellar travel is far beyond the limits of today's rockets, whose engines are not powerful enough to reach even the closest star.

 5. Tariffs have two functions: to protect local industry and to raise money for the national government.

Sharpen Your Skills

Now use everything you have learned about combining sentences, revising sentences, and answering "big picture" questions on the following Improving Paragraphs Practice Quiz. These questions are just like the ones that will be on the SAT. For the questions you get wrong or have trouble with on this Practice Quiz, reread the part of this chapter that addresses them. Make sure you fully understand what the mistake was and why you missed it.

IMPROVING PARAGRAPHS PRACTICE QUIZ

Directions: The passage below is an early draft of an essay. Parts of the passage need to be rewritten.

Read the passage and answer the questions that follow. Some questions are about individual sentences or parts of sentences; in these questions, you are asked to select the choice that will improve sentence structure and word choice. Other questions refer to parts of the essay or the entire essay and ask you to consider the organization and development of the essay. You should follow the conventions of standard written English in answering the questions. After you have chosen your answer, fill in the corresponding oval on your answer sheet.

Questions 1–6 are based on the following essay.

(1) When I was younger, I thought to myself, "Why do baseball players get paid so much for swinging a bat?" (2) Baseball, basketball, or football games they would have seemed like a real waste of money to me. (3) I would watch a game for about ten minutes without seeing a single hit and wonder why these athletes got so much money.

(4) I recently joined the Little-League home-team. (5) Before this time, sports was just recreation to me like wiffleball with my friends. (6) Once I began Little League, though, I went through all sorts of drills, like catch and batting practice. (7) I started to understand what it felt like to become an athlete. (8) Sure, natural talent helped. (9) I realized hard work and practice were just as important. (10) Because of my experience, I was able to appreciate professional sports more because I finally understood the strong commitment to the game that every professional athlete has to have.

(11) There is only a small group of great athletes. (12) Because of intense competition, hardly any of them in this group make it to the pros. (13) And the ones who want to make it have to dedicate all their energies to perfecting their skills so they can be the best. (14) People feel that professional athletes get paid too much for too little. (15) I'm convinced our sports heroes are receiving a fair salary for displaying and maintaining their hard-won skills.

1. Which of the following revisions of the underlined portion of sentence 2 (reproduced below) is clearest?

   Baseball, basketball, or football games they would have seemed like a real waste of money to me.

   (A) (As it is now)
   (B) Baseball, basketball, or football games seemed
   (C) Baseball, basketball, or football games will have seemed
   (D) Games of baseball, basketball, or football would have seemed
   (E) Games of baseball, basketball, or, football would be seeming

2. Which sentence listed below, if placed after sentence 3, would best tie in the first paragraph with the rest of the essay?

   (A) I have kept my point of view about the salaries of sports stars for a long time.
   (B) Still, my school coaches defended the excessive salaries of their favorite players.
   (C) My friends could never convince me to go to a local sporting event with them.
   (D) However, I ended up changing my mind about whether famous athletes deserve all the money they make.
   (E) Usually, sports personalities don't even work a full year.

3. Which of the following options is the best edit for the underlined portions of sentences 8 and 9 (reproduced below) so that the two sentences are combined into one?

    Sure, natural talent <u>helped. I realized</u> hard work and practice were just as important.

    (A) helped, and I realized
    (B) helped, so I realized
    (C) helped, so I was realizing
    (D) helped, but I realize
    (E) helped, but I realized

4. Which of the following words or phrases best replaces *And* at the beginning of sentence 13 (reproduced below)?

    <u>And</u> the ones who want to make it have to dedicate all their energies to perfecting their skills so they can be the best.

    (A) Therefore,
    (B) Besides this,
    (C) Nevertheless,
    (D) Moreover,
    (E) Including this,

5. In the context of the preceding paragraphs, which of the following would be the best way to combine the underlined portions of sentences 14 and 15 (reproduced below)?

    <u>People feel that professional athletes get paid too much for too little. I'm convinced our sports heroes are receiving</u> a fair salary for displaying and maintaining their hard-won skills.

    (A) While some people feel that professional athletes get paid too much for too little, I've been convinced that our sports heroes are receiving
    (B) In relation to people who feel that professional athletes get paid too much for too little, I will be convinced that they receive
    (C) Unlike some people who feel that professional athletes get paid too much for too little, I'm now convinced our sports heroes are receiving
    (D) People feel that professional athletes get paid too much for too little, and I am different because I'm convinced our sports heroes receive
    (E) People were feeling that professional athletes get paid too much for too little, I was convinced our sports heroes were receiving

6. All of the following strategies are used by the writer of the passage EXCEPT

    (A) referring to personal experience in order to illustrate an idea
    (B) quoting those whose opinions concur with his
    (C) using a narrative to develop a point
    (D) articulating a change of opinion from an original position stated in the first paragraph
    (E) supporting conclusions by evidence or example

Questions 7–12 are based on the following essay.

(1) Recently a report came out in a science magazine that claimed the earth's protective ozone layer was being steadily depleted. (2) It named several companies that produced chemicals responsible for this situation, and consumers were advised by it to boycott these businesses. (3) An editorial in a business magazine insisted that this report was faulty. (4) It stated that there could be other, less dangerous reasons for the changes in climate that we've been experiencing. (5) However, I believe that the scientists are right, we should all consider the effect we can have on making sure the ozone layer is not harmed more than it already has been.

(6) In the past few decades, the ozone layer has been steadily depleted. (7) This means harmful ultraviolet rays get through to our atmosphere. (8) People who do these bad things which contribute to this situation should know that their actions could harm future generations. (9) Not buying products that are harmful to the ozone layer means our children's children will be more secure. (10) Consumers can choose to purchase any kind of product they desire. (11) They should be aware of what happens when they make their choices. (12) If they don't boycott companies that produce harmful substances, our atmosphere will steadily worsen.

7. Considering the essay as a whole, which is the best edit for the underlined section of sentence 2 (reproduced below)?

   It named several companies that produced chemicals responsible for this situation, and consumers were advised by it to boycott these businesses.

   (A) (As it is now)

   (B) It names several companies that produced chemicals responsible for this situation and advises consumers

   (C) Naming several companies that produce chemicals responsible for this situation, consumers are advised by the report

   (D) It is naming several companies that produce chemicals responsible for this situation and advising consumers

   (E) The report named several companies that produced chemicals responsible for this situation and advised consumers

8. Considering the essay as a whole, which is the best way to edit and link the underlined portions of sentences 3 and 4 (reproduced below)?

   An editorial in a business magazine insisted that this report was faulty. It stated that there could be other, less dangerous reasons for the changes in climate that we've been experiencing.

   (A) The report was faulty, an editorial in a business magazine insisted, it stated

   (B) An editorial in a business magazine insisted that this report was faulty, stating

   (C) In an editorial in a business magazine was the insistence that the report was faulty and

   (D) The editorial in a business magazine insists that the consumers were faulty,

   (E) Insisting that the report was faulty, an editorial in a business magazine states

9. The phrase *do these bad things* in sentence 8 can be made clearer in relation to the content of the essay if it is edited as

(A) exacerbate the situations

(B) don't participate in events

(C) are in need of services

(D) use the types of chemicals

(E) consider options

10. Which is the best version of the underlined portions of sentences 10 and 11 (reproduced below)?

Consumers can choose to purchase any kind of product they desire. They should be aware of what happens when they make their choices.

(A) (As it is now)

(B) Evidently, consumers can choose to purchase any kind of product they desire. If they would just be aware

(C) Consumers can definitely choose to purchase any kind of product they desire, in spite

(D) Consumers can definitely choose to purchase any kind of product they desire, but they should be aware

(E) While consumers can choose to purchase any kind of product they desire, they are also aware

11. Which of the following words or phrases best replaces the word *they* in sentence 12?

(A) workers

(B) future generations

(C) consumers

(D) chemical industries

(E) editors

12. What sentence most clearly represents the main idea of the writer?

(A) I understand now how the scientists who wrote the report are right.

(B) From now on, consumers must refuse to buy products that threaten the ozone layer and the health and safety of us all.

(C) In conclusion, we all have to watch out for each other.

(D) All of us have to find ways to maintain integrity in our economic choices.

(E) Businesses are responsible for the safety of their products.

IMPROVING PARAGRAPHS PRACTICE QUIZ: ANSWERS AND EXPLANATIONS

1. B

Choice (B) is the only one that is consistent in tense with the rest of the paragraph. Also, *they* in the original sentence is unnecessary.

2. D

This choice introduces the idea of a change of opinion that is articulated and explained in the remainder of the essay.

3. E

The coordinating conjunction *but* emphasizes how the author's thoughts developed from seeing the role of natural talent as important to recognizing that hard work and practice were just as important. The word *and* in choice (A) lacks the emphasis that shows development in thought. The tense in choice (D) is inconsistent with the rest of the sentence.

4. A

Therefore logically introduces the idea that because of intense competition, the ones who want to make it have to dedicate all their energies to perfecting their skills so they can be the best.

5. C

Unlike contrasts the author with the people who feel athletes are overpaid. Additionally, the phrase *I'm now* indicates how the author's original position has changed from the position stated in the first paragraph. The phrase *I've been* in choice (A) is more ambiguous than choice (C)—that is, the author might have been convinced in the past, but it is not clear that he is convinced now. Choice (D) is grammatically awkward and its tense is inconsistent with the rest of the paragraph.

6. B

The author does not actually quote anyone else's opinion in this essay, though he does refer to other people.

7. E

The word *It* does not clearly refer to the report, so choices (A), (B), and (D) are incorrect. Only choice (E) includes the phrase *The report*. Furthermore, the rest of this sentence is grammatically consistent with the paragraph as a whole.

8. B

Choices (B) and (E) are the only ones that clearly maintain that the editorial, as opposed to the magazine itself, was stating that there could be other, less dangerous reasons for the changes in climate that we've been experiencing. However, choice (E) is in the present tense, whereas the rest of the information surrounding the discussion of the report and the editorial is in the past tense. Therefore, choice (B) is correct.

9. D

The types of products that contribute to the destruction of the ozone layer are certain types of chemicals; therefore, choice (D) is the most logical and specific answer.

10. D

The essay serves to dissuade from using harmful chemicals. Therefore, the word *but* following the first independent clause in choice (D)—*Consumers can definitely choose to purchase any kind of product they desire*—consistently carries on the tone and meaning of the essay by suggesting that consumers should be aware of the results of their choices.

11. C

Since the author is talking about the choices that consumers make and how their choices affect the ozone layer, choice (C) is best.

12. B

Again, the essay tends to focus on the responsibility consumers have in regard to the condition of the ozone layer, so choice (B) is best. Choices (C) and (D) are too vague in terms of the people and actions they refer to. Though the author would agree with choice (A), this is not the main idea of the essay.

Practice Tests and Explanations

Before taking these Practice Tests, find a quiet room where you can work uninterrupted for 60 minutes. Make sure you have a comfortable desk and several No. 2 pencils. Use the answer sheets provided to record your answers. (You can tear them out or photocopy them.)

Once you start each Practice Test, do not stop until you have finished. Remember, you may review any questions within a section, but you may not go back or forward a section.

When you have finished taking a Practice Test, go on to the Compute Your Score section to see how you did.

Good luck.

SAT Practice Test A
Answer Sheet

Remove (or photocopy) this answer sheet and use it to complete the Practice Test. See the answer key following the test when finished. The Compute Your Score section at the back of the book will show you how to find your score.

Section 2

1. Ⓐ Ⓑ Ⓒ Ⓓ Ⓔ	11. Ⓐ Ⓑ Ⓒ Ⓓ Ⓔ	21. Ⓐ Ⓑ Ⓒ Ⓓ Ⓔ	31. Ⓐ Ⓑ Ⓒ Ⓓ Ⓔ
2. Ⓐ Ⓑ Ⓒ Ⓓ Ⓔ	12. Ⓐ Ⓑ Ⓒ Ⓓ Ⓔ	22. Ⓐ Ⓑ Ⓒ Ⓓ Ⓔ	32. Ⓐ Ⓑ Ⓒ Ⓓ Ⓔ
3. Ⓐ Ⓑ Ⓒ Ⓓ Ⓔ	13. Ⓐ Ⓑ Ⓒ Ⓓ Ⓔ	23. Ⓐ Ⓑ Ⓒ Ⓓ Ⓔ	33. Ⓐ Ⓑ Ⓒ Ⓓ Ⓔ
4. Ⓐ Ⓑ Ⓒ Ⓓ Ⓔ	14. Ⓐ Ⓑ Ⓒ Ⓓ Ⓔ	24. Ⓐ Ⓑ Ⓒ Ⓓ Ⓔ	34. Ⓐ Ⓑ Ⓒ Ⓓ Ⓔ
5. Ⓐ Ⓑ Ⓒ Ⓓ Ⓔ	15. Ⓐ Ⓑ Ⓒ Ⓓ Ⓔ	25. Ⓐ Ⓑ Ⓒ Ⓓ Ⓔ	35. Ⓐ Ⓑ Ⓒ Ⓓ Ⓔ
6. Ⓐ Ⓑ Ⓒ Ⓓ Ⓔ	16. Ⓐ Ⓑ Ⓒ Ⓓ Ⓔ	26. Ⓐ Ⓑ Ⓒ Ⓓ Ⓔ	
7. Ⓐ Ⓑ Ⓒ Ⓓ Ⓔ	17. Ⓐ Ⓑ Ⓒ Ⓓ Ⓔ	27. Ⓐ Ⓑ Ⓒ Ⓓ Ⓔ	
8. Ⓐ Ⓑ Ⓒ Ⓓ Ⓔ	18. Ⓐ Ⓑ Ⓒ Ⓓ Ⓔ	28. Ⓐ Ⓑ Ⓒ Ⓓ Ⓔ	
9. Ⓐ Ⓑ Ⓒ Ⓓ Ⓔ	19. Ⓐ Ⓑ Ⓒ Ⓓ Ⓔ	29. Ⓐ Ⓑ Ⓒ Ⓓ Ⓔ	
10. Ⓐ Ⓑ Ⓒ Ⓓ Ⓔ	20. Ⓐ Ⓑ Ⓒ Ⓓ Ⓔ	30. Ⓐ Ⓑ Ⓒ Ⓓ Ⓔ	

right

wrong

Section 3

1. Ⓐ Ⓑ Ⓒ Ⓓ Ⓔ	11. Ⓐ Ⓑ Ⓒ Ⓓ Ⓔ
2. Ⓐ Ⓑ Ⓒ Ⓓ Ⓔ	12. Ⓐ Ⓑ Ⓒ Ⓓ Ⓔ
3. Ⓐ Ⓑ Ⓒ Ⓓ Ⓔ	13. Ⓐ Ⓑ Ⓒ Ⓓ Ⓔ
4. Ⓐ Ⓑ Ⓒ Ⓓ Ⓔ	14. Ⓐ Ⓑ Ⓒ Ⓓ Ⓔ
5. Ⓐ Ⓑ Ⓒ Ⓓ Ⓔ	
6. Ⓐ Ⓑ Ⓒ Ⓓ Ⓔ	
7. Ⓐ Ⓑ Ⓒ Ⓓ Ⓔ	
8. Ⓐ Ⓑ Ⓒ Ⓓ Ⓔ	
9. Ⓐ Ⓑ Ⓒ Ⓓ Ⓔ	
10. Ⓐ Ⓑ Ⓒ Ⓓ Ⓔ	

right

wrong

KAPLAN

Practice Test A

Section 1

Essay
Time—25 Minutes (1 Question)

You will have 25 minutes to write your essay in your test booklet (two pages).

Directions: Consider carefully the following statement(s) and the assignment below it.

"The greatest griefs are those we cause ourselves."

—Sophocles

Assignment: What do you think of the view that the worst sorrows are those for which we are responsible? In an essay, support your position by discussing an example (or examples) from literature, science and technology, the arts, current events, or your own experience or observation.

SAT Practice Test A: **Answer Sheet**

ESSAY. Begin your composition on this side. If you need more space, you may continue on the following page.

_____

_____

_____

_____

_____

_____

_____

_____

_____

_____

_____

_____

_____

_____

_____

_____

_____

_____

_____

SAT Practice Test A: **Answer Sheet**

Continuation of ESSAY from previous page. If you need more space, you may continue on the reverse side.

Continuation of ESSAY from reverse side. Write below if you need more space.

Section 2
Time—25 Minutes (35 Questions)

Directions: The following sentences test correctness and effectiveness of expression. In choosing answers, follow the requirements of standard written English; that is, pay attention to grammar, choice of words, sentence construction, and punctuation.

In each of the following sentences, part of the sentence or the entire sentence is underlined. Beneath each sentence, you will find five ways of phrasing the underlined part. Choice (A) repeats the original; the other four are different.

Choose the answer that best expresses the meaning of the original sentence. If you think the original is better than any of the alternatives, choose it; otherwise, choose one of the others. Your choice should produce the most effective sentence—clear and precise, without awkwardness or ambiguity.

1. After depositing and burying her eggs, the female sea turtle returns to the water, <u>never to view or nurture the offspring that she is leaving behind.</u>

   (A) never to view or nurture the offspring that she is leaving behind

   (B) never to view or nurture the offspring which she had left behind

   (C) never to view nor nurture the offspring that are being left behind

   (D) never to view or nurture the offspring she has left behind

   (E) never to view or nurture the offspring who she has left behind

2. Congress was in no doubt <u>about who would take credit</u> for winning the war on inflation.

   (A) about who would take credit

   (B) about who takes credit

   (C) about whom would take credit

   (D) of who would take credit

   (E) over who would take credit

3. In *War and Peace*, Tolstoy presented his theories on history and <u>illustrated them</u> with a slanted account of actual historical events.

   (A) illustrated them

   (B) also illustrating them

   (C) he also was illustrating these ideas

   (D) then illustrated the theories also

   (E) then he went about illustrating them

4. Laval, the first bishop of Quebec, exemplified aristocratic vigor and concern <u>on account of his giving up his substantial inheritance to become an ecclesiastic</u> and to help shape Canadian politics and education.

   (A) on account of his giving up his substantial inheritance to become an ecclesiastic

   (B) since he gave up his substantial inheritance to become an ecclesiastic

   (C) since giving up his substantial inheritance to become an ecclesiastic

   (D) because of his having given up his substantial inheritance for the purpose of becoming an ecclesiastic

   (E) as a result of becoming an ecclesiastic through giving up his substantial inheritance

5. In the United States, an increasing number of commuters <u>that believe their families to be</u> immune from the perils of city life.

   (A) that believe their families to be

   (B) that believe their families are

   (C) believes their families are

   (D) who believe their families to be

   (E) believe their families to be

GO ON TO THE NEXT PAGE

KAPLAN

6. <u>Developed by a scientific team at his university,</u> the president informed the reporters that the new process would facilitate the diagnosing of certain congenital diseases.

   (A) Developed by a scientific team at his university

   (B) Having been developed by a scientific team at his university

   (C) Speaking of the discovery made by a scientific team at his university

   (D) Describing the developments of a scientific team at his university

   (E) As it had been developed by a scientific team at his university

7. The Equal Rights Amendment to Islandia's constitution is dying a lingering political death, <u>many dedicated groups and individuals have attempted</u> to prevent its demise.

   (A) many dedicated groups and individuals have attempted

   (B) although many dedicated groups and individuals have attempted

   (C) many dedicated groups and persons has attempted

   (D) despite many dedications of groups and individuals to attempt

   (E) however, many dedicated groups and individuals have attempted

8. One ecological rule of thumb states that there is opportunity for the accumulation of underground water reservoirs <u>but in regions where vegetation remains undisturbed.</u>

   (A) but in regions where vegetation remains undisturbed

   (B) unless vegetation being left undisturbed in some regions

   (C) only where undisturbed vegetation is in regions

   (D) except for vegetation remaining undisturbed in some regions

   (E) only in regions where vegetation remains undisturbed

9. The ancient Chinese were convinced that air was composed of two kinds of particles, <u>one inactive and one active, the latter of which they called yin and which we today call oxygen</u>.

   (A) one inactive and one active, the latter of which they called yin and which we today call oxygen

   (B) an inactive and an active one called yin, now known as oxygen

   (C) an inactive type and the active type they called yin we now know to be oxygen

   (D) inactive and active; while they called the active type yin, today we call it oxygen

   (E) contrasting the inactive type with the active ones they named yin and we call oxygen

10. There are several rules <u>which must be followed by whomever</u> wants to be admitted to this academy.

   (A) which must be followed by whomever

   (B) that must be followed by whomever

   (C) which must get followed by whom

   (D) that must be followed by whoever

   (E) which must be followed by those who

11. Developing a suitable environment for houseplants <u>is in many ways like when you are managing</u> soil fertilization for city parks.

   (A) is in many ways like when you are managing

   (B) is in many ways similar to when you are managing

   (C) in many ways is on a par with managing your

   (D) is in many ways similar to the managing of

   (E) is in many ways like managing

GO ON TO THE NEXT PAGE ⟩

Directions: The following sentences test your knowledge of grammar, usage, diction (choice of words), and idiom.

Some sentences are correct.
No sentence contains more than one error.

You will find that the error, if there is one, is underlined and lettered. Elements of the sentence that are not underlined will not be changed. In choosing answers, follow the requirements of standard written English.

If there is an error, select the one underlined part that must be changed to make the sentence correct, and fill in the corresponding oval on your answer sheet.

If there is no error, fill in answer oval E.

12. Before <u>the advent of</u> modern surgical
       A
    techniques, <u>bleeding patients</u> with leeches
                      B
    <u>were considered</u> <u>therapeutically effective</u>.
          C   D
    <u>No error</u>
       E

13. The <u>recent</u> establishment <u>of</u> "Crime Busters,"
          A   B
    officially sanctioned neighborhood block-

    watching groups, <u>have</u> dramatically improved
                        C
    relations <u>between</u> citizens and police. <u>No error</u>
                 D   E

14. The masterpiece auctioned so <u>successfully</u>
                                        A
    today depicts a Biblical <u>scene in which</u> the
                                 B
    king is on his throne with his <u>counselors</u>
                                       C
    standing <u>respectively</u> below. <u>No error</u>
                 D   E

15. During the election campaign, the major

    political parties agreed that minorities must be

    given the opportunity <u>to advance</u>, <u>to seek</u>
                              A   B
    justice, and <u>to the kinds</u> of special treatment
                     C
    that might compensate <u>in part</u> for historical
                              D
    inequities. <u>No error</u>
                    E

16. Most of the delegates <u>which</u> attended the conven-
                             A
    tion <u>felt</u> the resolution was <u>too strongly</u> worded,
           B   C
    and the majority voted <u>against</u> it. <u>No error</u>
                               D   E

17. <u>Lost in the forest</u> on a cold night, the hunters
       A
    <u>built</u> a fire <u>to keep themselves</u> warm and
       B   C
    <u>to frighten away</u> the wolves. <u>No error</u>
       D   E

18. The effort <u>to create appropriate</u> theatrical effects
                  A
    <u>often result</u> in settings that cannot be <u>effective</u>
       B   C
    without an imaginative <u>lighting</u> crew. <u>No error</u>
                              D   E

GO ON TO THE NEXT PAGE

KAPLAN

19. Every one of the shops in the town <u>were closed</u>
                                          A
on Thursday <u>because</u> of the <u>ten-inch</u> rainfall
                  B   C
that <u>had fallen</u> during the day. <u>No error</u>
        D   E

20. <u>According</u> to the directions on the package, the
     A
contents <u>are</u> intended for external use <u>only</u> and
          B   C
<u>should not be</u> swallowed, even in small
     D
quantities. <u>No error</u>
              E

21. <u>The late president's numerous memoirs</u>, now
                      A
<u>about to be published</u>, <u>promises</u> to be of special
        B   C
<u>historical</u> interest. <u>No error</u>
     D   E

22. Mr. Webster's paper is <u>highly imaginary</u> and
                              A
<u>very creative</u>, <u>but</u> <u>lacking in</u> cogency. <u>No error</u>
     B   C   D   E

23. The point at issue <u>was whether</u> the dock
                          A
workers, <u>which</u> were <u>an extremely vocal group</u>,
          B   C
<u>would decide to return</u> to work. <u>No error</u>
     D   E

24. <u>Raising</u> living costs, <u>together</u> with escalating
     A   B
taxes, <u>have</u> proved to be a burden for
        C
<u>everyone</u>. <u>No error</u>
     D   E

25. The more scientists learn about subatomic
particles, <u>the more closely</u> they come
              A
<u>to being able</u> to describe <u>the ways in which</u> the
     B   C
universe <u>operates</u>. <u>No error</u>
          D   E

26. To have <u>reached a verdict</u> <u>so quickly</u>, the
              A   B
members of the <u>jury would have to make up</u>
                  C
<u>their minds</u> before leaving the courtroom.
     D
<u>No error</u>
     E

27. <u>Drinking carbonated beverages</u> and eating
              A
food <u>that</u> <u>contain</u> chemical preservatives can
      B   C
be unhealthy <u>when indulged in excess</u>.
                  D
<u>No error</u>
     E

28. Albert Schweitzer <u>was</u> not only
                        A
<u>an accomplished doctor</u> but also
        B
<u>a talented musician</u> <u>as well</u>. <u>No error</u>
     C   D   E

29. Harley Goodsleuth, private detective, <u>found</u>
                                            A
the <u>incriminating</u> evidence <u>where</u> the murderer
     B   C
<u>had left</u> it. <u>No error</u>
     D   E

GO ON TO THE NEXT PAGE ▷

KAPLAN

Directions: The passage below is an early draft of an essay. Parts of the passage need to be rewritten.

Read the passage and answer the questions that follow. Some questions are about individual sentences or parts of sentences; in these questions, you are asked to select the choice that will improve sentence structure and word choice. Other questions refer to parts of the essay or the entire essay and ask you to consider the organization and development of the essay. You should follow the conventions of standard written English in answering the questions. After you have chosen your answer, fill in the corresponding oval on your answer sheet.

Questions 30–35 are based on the following essay.

(1) Last year, my social studies class attended a talk given by a young woman who worked in a factory in Central America making shirts for a popular U.S. retail chain. (2) The working conditions she described were horrific. (3) She spoke of being forced to work 14-hour days and even longer on weekends. (4) The supervisors often hit her and the other women, most of whom were teenagers, to get them to work faster. (5) He gave them contaminated water to drink and were only allowed to go to the bathroom twice a day. (6) She urged us to boycott the retail chain and to inform consumers about the conditions in their factories.

(7) A group of us decided to meet with a representative of the chain and we would discuss our concerns and would announce our plans to boycott. (8) The representative said that low wages were necessary to keep costs down. (9) And she was claiming a boycott would never work because it would be impossible to stop people from shopping at such a popular store. (10) "Nobody is going to listen to a bunch of teenagers," she said. (11) We decided to prove her wrong.

(12) First, we calculated that the workers' wages accounted for less than one percent of the price people paid for the shirts in the United States. (13) We argued that if the chain were willing to make slightly lower profits, it could afford to pay the workers more without raising prices. (14) And when we began informing people about the conditions under which the shirts they bought were made, they were horrified. (15) Many were agreeing to shop there no longer, they even wrote letters to the president of the chain in which he was urged to do something about the conditions in the factories. (16) Even local politicians got involved. (17) The winner of that year's City Council election pledged to change the conditions in the factories or shut the store down once and for all. (18) Finally, with business almost at a standstill, the store agreed to consumers' demands.

30. In context, which is the best version of the underlined portion of sentence 5 (reproduced below)?

He gave them contaminated water to drink and were only allowed to go to the bathroom twice a day.

(A) (As it is now)
(B) and were only allowing them to go
(C) and only allowed them to go
(D) and they were only given permission to go
(E) and were allowed to only go

31. In context, which of the following best replaces the word "their" in sentence 6?

(A) the consumers'
(B) its
(C) the conditions'
(D) the supervisors'
(E) the students'

GO ON TO THE NEXT PAGE

KAPLAN

32. In context, which of the following is the best way to revise the underlined wording in sentence 7 (reproduced below)?

    A group of us decided to meet with a representative of the chain <u>and we would discuss our concerns and would announce our plans to boycott</u>.

    (A) (As it is now)

    (B) to discuss our concerns and announce our plan to boycott

    (C) for discussing our concerns and in order to announce to them our plans for a boycott

    (D) who would discuss our concerns and our plans to boycott

    (E) and we would discuss our concerns and would announce our plans and would boycott

33. In context, which of the following is the best way to revise the underlined wording in order to combine sentences 8 and 9?

    The representative said that low wages were necessary to keep costs <u>down. And she was claiming that a boycott would never work</u> because it would be impossible to stop people from shopping at such a popular store.

    (A) down because a boycott would never work

    (B) down, and she was claiming that a boycott would never work

    (C) down and claimed that a boycott would never work

    (D) down; she was claiming that a boycott would never work

    (E) down so that a boycott could work

34. In context, which of the following is the best way to revise the underlined portion of sentence 15 (reproduced below)?

    <u>Many were agreeing to shop there no longer, they even wrote letters to the president of the chain in which he was urged</u> to do something about the conditions in the factories.

    (A) (As it is now)

    (B) Many were agreeing to no longer shop there and even writing letters to the president of the chain in order that he be urged

    (C) Many agreed to shop there no longer and even wrote letters to the president of the chain urging him

    (D) Many agreed to no longer shop there and also to urge the president of the chain by writing letters in which they asked him

    (E) Shopping there no longer, many agreed to write letters to the president of the chain and also to urge him

35. Which sentence would most appropriately follow sentence 18?

    (A) Despite the boycott, people were not willing to pay more for clothing.

    (B) Unfortunately, people rarely do things for selfless reasons.

    (C) Simply informing others is not enough; a plan of action must be devised.

    (D) We should have listened to the young factory worker in the first place.

    (E) We had proven the representative wrong; people had listened to "a bunch of teenagers."

IF YOU FINISH BEFORE TIME IS CALLED, YOU MAY CHECK YOUR WORK ON THIS SECTION ONLY. DO NOT TURN TO ANY OTHER SECTION IN THE TEST. **STOP**

Section 3
Time—10 Minutes (14 Questions)

Directions: The following sentences test correctness and effectiveness of expression. In choosing answers, follow the requirements of standard written English; that is, pay attention to grammar, choice of words, sentence construction, and punctuation.

In each of the following sentences, part of the sentence or the entire sentence is underlined. Beneath each sentence, you will find five ways of phrasing the underlined part. Choice (A) repeats the original; the other four are different.

Choose the answer that best expresses the meaning of the original sentence. If you think the original is better than any of the alternatives, choose it; otherwise, choose one of the others. Your choice should produce the most effective sentence—clear and precise, without awkwardness or ambiguity.

1. In addition to her volunteer work with the elementary school girls' track team, assistance is given by Tasha to seniors from the Parkview Apartments for their weekly shopping trip.

   (A) assistance is given by Tasha to seniors from the Parkview Apartments for their weekly shopping trip

   (B) seniors from the Parkview Apartments receiving assistance from Tasha with their weekly shopping trip

   (C) Tasha's assistance was also given to seniors from the Parkview Apartments for their weekly shopping trip

   (D) and while Tasha assisted seniors from the Parkview Apartments with their weekly shopping trip

   (E) Tasha assists seniors from the Parkview Apartments with their weekly shopping trip

2. After his exam was completed, Liam had to remain in the room for another hour because of the proctor's enforcing strictly the rules.

   (A) because of the proctor's enforcing strictly the rules

   (B) because the enforcement of the rules by the proctor had been strict

   (C) because of the proctor's strict enforcement of the rules

   (D) because the proctor strictly was enforcing the rules

   (E) because of the rules that were being strictly enforced by the proctor

3. To be eligible for the junior swim team, a student should be able both to tread water for five minutes and her exhaling when underwater should be normal.

   (A) and her exhaling when underwater should be normal

   (B) while her exhaling underwater is normal

   (C) and her exhaling underwater being normal

   (D) with exhaling normally underwater

   (E) and to exhale normally underwater

GO ON TO THE NEXT PAGE

KAPLAN

4. Jason's article was pulled from the weekly paper because it claimed <u>not only that he was not being compensated fairly but the paper's editors were holding a grudge against him</u>.

   (A) not only that he was not being compensated fairly but the paper's editors were holding a grudge against him

   (B) not only that that he was not being compensated fairly and also the paper's editors were holding a grudge against him as well

   (C) that he was not being compensated fairly but in addition that the paper's editors were holding a grudge against him as well

   (D) that he was not being compensated fairly and that the paper's editors were holding a grudge against him

   (E) that he was not being compensated fairly and he also believed that the paper's editors were holding a grudge against him

5. Vision loss caused by a head injury often lasts for only a few days, <u>and this is not true of vision loss caused by a progressive disease, which is often</u> permanent.

   (A) and this is not true of vision loss caused by a progressive disease, which is often

   (B) not true of vision loss caused by a progressive disease, which is often

   (C) as opposed to vision loss caused by a progressive disease

   (D) vision loss caused by a progressive disease being often

   (E) but vision loss caused by a progressive disease is often

6. The skyrocketing price of Midwest Financial's insurance policies, especially for drivers under 30, <u>have angered many customers and threatened to change companies</u>.

   (A) have angered many customers and threatened to change companies

   (B) has angered many customers and caused them to threaten to change companies

   (C) have angered many customers, and a change in companies is threatened

   (D) has angered many customers, which caused threatening to change companies

   (E) has angered many customers to threaten to change companies

7. When you see a block filled with New Orleans' wrought-iron balconies <u>for the first time, one may think</u> of the delicate lace of an old-fashioned dress.

   (A) for the first time, one may think

   (B) for the first time, people may be thinking

   (C) for the first time, you may think

   (D) viewed for the first time, one may be thinking

   (E) initially, one's thoughts are

8. Although he claimed to have considered each interview candidate equally, <u>Brian based his choice on the candidates' qualifications less than what he did on</u> their business connections.

   (A) Brian based his choice on the candidates' qualifications less than what he did on

   (B) Brian's choice is based less on the candidates' qualifications than it was on

   (C) Brian based his choice less on the candidates' qualifications than on

   (D) Brian made his choice, and this choice being based less on the candidates' qualifications than on

   (E) Brian making a choice based on the candidates' qualifications less than

GO ON TO THE NEXT PAGE

9. Charging much less than her competitors do for the same service, <u>over half of our neighbors' lawns are now landscaped by Harmony</u>.

   (A) over half of our neighbors' lawns are now landscaped by Harmony

   (B) of our neighbors' lawns, over half are now landscaped by Harmony

   (C) over half of our neighbors now have their lawns landscaped by Harmony

   (D) Harmony now landscapes over half of our neighbors' lawns

   (E) our neighbors' lawns now are landscaped over half by Harmony

10. Alexander Ramsey was the first governor of the territory of <u>Minnesota, his house, built</u> in 1872, is now a museum.

    (A) Minnesota, his house, built

    (B) Minnesota, however, his house, built

    (C) Minnesota, yet his house, having been built

    (D) Minnesota; his house, built

    (E) Minnesota; but his house, built

11. As little as 20 minutes of activity each day, <u>many fitness experts believe, may have</u> significant health benefits for people of all ages.

    (A) many fitness experts believe, may have

    (B) which, many fitness experts believe, may have

    (C) having possibly, in the belief of many fitness experts,

    (D) there are many fitness experts believing that it may have

    (E) fitness experts believing it may have

12. The earliest midwives received <u>no formal training and left no records of their work other than</u> letters, diaries, and other personal papers.

    (A) no formal training and left no records of their work other than

    (B) no formal training, and leaving no records of their work besides

    (C) no other formal training or records of their work excepting

    (D) no formal training nor left any records of their work other than

    (E) neither formal training nor records of their work except for

13. <u>One important cause of the medication shortage is when</u> healthy people, attempting to build up immunity, take medications that are intended to treat illnesses.

    (A) One important cause of the medication shortage is when

    (B) One important cause of the medication shortage is that

    (C) Most medication shortages result from when

    (D) Most medication shortages are the result of that

    (E) Most medication shortages are due to the fact that when

14. <u>Unlike them on the East Coast, the beaches of the West Coast</u> are graced with palm trees, white sand, and clear blue water that reflects the sky.

    (A) Unlike them on the East Coast, the beaches of the West Coast

    (B) The beaches of the West Coast, when contrasted to them on the East Coast,

    (C) The beaches of the West Coast, when in contrast to those of the East Coast,

    (D) The beaches of the West Coast, in contrast to those of the East Coast,

    (E) The beaches of the West Coast contrast to those of the East Coast in that they

IF YOU FINISH BEFORE TIME IS CALLED, YOU MAY CHECK YOUR WORK ON THIS SECTION ONLY. DO NOT TURN TO ANY OTHER SECTION IN THE TEST. **STOP**

Answers and Explanations

SECTION 1
The Essay

This section contains sample essays for the essay topic in Practice Test A. Use these sample essays as benchmarks to help you grade your own essay on the same topic. Does your essay sound more like the grade 5 essay or the grade 3 essay?

Sample Grade 5 Essay

It was a crisp weekend morning in early spring. The sun shone through the still chilly air and the crocus buds were pushing their way through the thawing earth. My team-mates and I had just arrived at Dellville High's lacrosse field, where the final game of the season would be played. Tension hung heavy in the air: we were tied for first place in Girls' Division 3.

But no one felt tenser than me. Our team had never done as well as it was doing that season, and as captain of the team our success had earned me the admiration of my classmates. Everyone envied me and wanted to be my friend. Little did they know how much pressure I was under, how much I feared a fall from grace.

Dellville turned out to be a worthy opponent. With only five minutes left, we were tied 4-4. My chest ached from running and my legs were sore. Suddenly, one of my teammates passed the ball to me. Like a dog trained to respond unthinking-ly to certain stimuli, I began charging down the field, and with my aching arms I flung the hard rubber sphere into the goalie's cage. Instead of the cheers I expect-ed, there was nothing but silence. I looked around me and with horror realized I had scored a goal for the other team!

On the bus ride home, I sat alone. No one would talk to me. But the rejection by others did not wound nearly as much as my own overwhelming feeling that I had done this and that I had no one to blame but myself. This is why I agree with the statement, "The greatest griefs are those we cause ourselves." The grief one feels is compounded by an awful sense of guilt; knowing you could have prevented your unhappiness emphasizes it even more.

Grader's comments: This essay solidly fulfills the writing assignment. It is logically organized, uses vocabulary well, and mixes sentence structure well. The evidence provided clearly supports the writer's ideas. There are occasional flaws ("no one felt tenser than me," and "as captain of the team our success…"), but they do not detract from the overall effectiveness of the writing.

Sample Grade 3 Essay

Someone once said that "The greatest griefs are those we cause ourselves," but I for one do not agree. I think that if your greif results from some tragedy you did not cause, it can be even worse because you feel no sense of control over your life. My cousin dying of cancer when she was only 28 was this way. We did not cause her cancer, but we felt great greif. Can you say that our greif would of been greater if we had caused her to die?

Likewise, in The Scarlet Letter Hester Prynne is made to suffer and were an A on her chest because of having a baby out of wedlock. So she suffers, but Hawthorn makes it clear his heroin did not cause her own suffering. It is Puritannical society which is hypocritical and punishes Hester while letting the minister that's the father of her baby get off. So Hester does not cause her greif, it is the society she lived in who caused it. If they didn't have such a repressive attitude about sex outside of marriage, she wouldn't have suffered as much. On the other hand, you could say Hester caused her own suffering because she got involved with a minister, which she must have known was not such a good idea back in her day and age. But the minister is responsable too, so shouldn't he take some of the blame?

Grader's comments: This essay demonstrates limited competence. There are numerous errors in grammar, diction, and sentence structure that detract from its quality. Moreover, the essay's organization is inadequate. Although the evidence about the cousin supports the writer's argument, the evidence from *The Scarlet Letter* is confused. The writer makes conflicting statements about Hester Prynne's innocence or guilt and is not clear about the overall point being made.

Sample Grade 1 Essay

I agree with the statement, "The greatest greifs are those we cause ourselves." If I do something to myself, it's much worse. Like the time my dog got run over because I didn't leave him tied up in the yard. It is true I didn't drive the car (it was Mrs. Savini from next door), but I could of prevented the acident so I felt really bad. Of course it depends on the situatian. When my grandfather died I had nothing to do with it but I still got sad from his deth. I guess I would of felt worse if I had made him die. So in general I agree but their may be excepitons to the rule. Trying to make up your mind about something like this is tough to do when you only have 20 minutes total for thinking about it and

Grader's comments: This essay is deficient. First, it's very poorly organized. Second, its ideas are inadequately developed. Finally, the many and serious errors in usage and syntax somewhat obscure the writer's intended meaning.

The Multiple-Choice Section

Answer Key

Section 2				Section 3	
1.	D	18.	B	1.	E
2.	A	19.	A	2.	C
3.	A	20.	E	3.	E
4.	B	21.	C	4.	D
5.	E	22.	A	5.	E
6.	D	23.	B	6.	B
7.	B	24.	A	7.	C
8.	E	25.	A	8.	C
9.	D	26.	C	9.	D
10.	D	27.	C	10.	D
11.	E	28.	D	11.	A
12.	C	29.	E	12.	A
13.	C	30.	C	13.	B
14.	D	31.	B	14.	D
15.	C	32.	B		
16.	A	33.	C		
17.	E	34.	C		
		35.	E		

Section 2

1. D

The present perfect *has left* makes the sequence of events clearer than the present progressive *is leaving*. Note that *nor* in (C) is wrong.

2. A

The original sentence is best.

3. A

The original sentence is best.

4. B

Since he gave up is clearer and more concise than *on account of his giving up* or any of the other choices. Note also that *to help shape* must be paired with another infinitive.

5. E

In the original form of the sentence, the word *that* forms a dependent clause and leaves the sentence without a main verb. The main verb should be *believe*, which is plural because its subject is *commuters*.

6. D

The introductory clause has to describe the nearest noun, *the president.* This is not the case in the original sentence. (D) is preferable to (C) because it maintains the same word, *development*, as in the original sentence. (D) is also more concise and direct than the passive voice construction in (C).

7. B

This sentence contains a comma splice: two independent clauses joined only by a comma. Choice (B) corrects the sentence by adding the conjunction *although* to make the second clause dependent.

8. E

But is used incorrectly in this sentence; the correct word to use here is *only*.

9. D

This sentence contains a great deal of information. Choice (D) is the most successful in conveying that information clearly, logically, and directly.

10. D

Whomever is the subject of the verb *wants*, so it should be in the subjective form, *whoever*. Choice (E) uses the right case, but the wrong number: *wants* is singular, but *those* is plural.

11. E

Things being compared should be in the same grammatical form; *developing* should be compared with *managing*. (E) is the simplest and clearest choice.

12. C

Note that *patients* is not the subject of this sentence, *bleeding* is (it's a gerund, the *-ing* form of a verb used as a noun). *Bleeding* is singular, so *were* should be changed to *was*.

13. C

The subject of the sentence is *establishment*, which is singular; so the main verb should be *has*, not *have*.

14. D

Respectively means "with respect to each in order." One might say, "Their names were John, Paul, and George, respectively." *Respectively* doesn't make any sense in this context. The word that's probably intended is *respectfully*.

15. C

Items in a list should always be in parallel grammatical form. *To advance* and *to seek* are infinitive verbs. But *to the kinds* is a noun preceded by a preposition. It should be changed to something like *to get the kinds*.

16. A

The word *which* should not be used to refer to people. In this sentence, it needs to be corrected to *who*.

17. E

There is no error in this sentence.

18. B

The subject of this sentence is the singular noun *effort*. The main verb should therefore be *results*, rather than the plural *result*.

19. A

Every one is singular. *Were closed* is plural. It should be corrected to *was closed*.

20. E

There is no error in this sentence.

21. C

The subject of the sentence is *memoirs*, which is plural. The main verb is *promises*, which is singular. It should be *promise*.

22. A

If the paper were imaginary, it wouldn't exist. The correct word is *imaginative*, an approximate synonym of *creative*.

23. B

The pronoun *which* should never be used to refer to people. *Which* should be changed to *who*.

24. A

Raise is a transitive verb: one thing *raises* another thing, but something that is getting higher on its own, with no specified cause, isn't described as *raising*. The correct word here is *rising*.

25. A

Since the word *closely* modifies *they*, not *come*, it should be in the adjectival form, *close*. The comparative form of *close* is *closer*.

26. C

The sentence forms the conditional mood incorrectly. Instead, it should read *would have to have made up,...*

27. C

The subject of *contain* is *food*, which is singular. So the sentence should say *contains*.

28. D

To say both *also* and *as well* is redundant. Since *as well* is underlined, it should be deleted.

29. E

With *found* in the past tense, *had left* is correct, indicating that the leaving took place before the finding.

30. C

In sentence 5, the shift to the passive voice makes it sound as if it was the supervisor whose bathroom visits were restricted. Only (C) fixes this error. In addition to the other choices' incorrect use of the passive voice, (B) is inconsistent in tense, (D) is unnecessarily wordy and needlessly substitutes *given permission* for *allowed*, and (E) splits an infinitive.

31. B

From the context, it is clear that the author means that the factories belong to the retail chain, but the use of the word *their* incorrectly conveys the idea that they belong to the consumers. Substituting *its* for *their* fixes this problem.

32. B

The sentence is wordy and rambling; (B) tightens it up without losing any of the meaning. (C) is still wordy and lacks parallel structure. (D) changes the meaning of the sentence. (E) is even wordier than the original.

33. C

In the original, the verbs aren't in parallel form, so simply combining the two sentences with a comma, choice (B), or a semicolon, (D), doesn't work. (C) clearly and concisely captures both ideas in parallel form. (A) uses the wrong connecting word; there is no causal relationship between these two ideas. (E) confuses the logic of the sentence.

34. C

As written, the sentence incorrectly connects two clauses with a comma and is inconsistent in tense; it also contains a misplaced modifier (which appears to refer to the chain when it should refer to the letter) and an unnecessary shift to the passive voice *(he was urged)*. (C) fixes these errors. (B) is incorrect in context; the use of the past progressive *(were agreeing)* changes the meaning of the sentence. (D), too, changes the meaning: consumers agreed to stop patronizing the store, not to write letters to the president. (E) likewise changes the original meaning and is repetitive and awkward.

35. E

Choice (E) works well as a concluding sentence because it provides a nice summary of the author's main point and ties the second and third paragraphs together with the reference to *a bunch of teenagers.* Choice (A) does not logically follow from the essay; it is never stated whether consumers were willing to pay more. (B) comes out of left field, and choices (C) and (D) are just wrong: the students did devise a plan of action (boycotting), and they did listen to the factory worker.

Section 3

1. E

The first part of this sentence provides a clue to the correct answer. The words *in addition to* can help you think of what to look for: in addition to one thing (volunteering), Tasha does another thing. That's the simplest rephrasing of this sentence; it is unnecessarily wordy as written. (B) uses

an incorrect verb form. (C), like (A), is cumbersome and obscures the meaning of the sentence. (D) creates a sentence fragment; there's no reason for the use of *and* here. (E) provides the answer we're looking for: in addition to volunteering, Tasha assists the seniors with their shopping.

2. C

This wordy sentence simply needs to be rewritten in the clearest way possible. You can move through the choices, considering which one conveys the message of the sentence without any extra words or punctuation. (B) is wordy and also changes verb tense, implying that the enforcement of the rules happened prior to Liam finishing his exam. (C) is the best choice: The reason Liam couldn't leave was the proctor's strict enforcement of the rules. (D) contains a misplaced modifier (the correct phrasing would be *was strictly enforcing*). (E) is misleading; the problem is not the rules themselves, but the fact that the proctor was enforcing them so strictly.

3. E

The non-underlined section of the sentence can provide a clue about how to correct the underlined section. The structure of the first part of the sentence tells us that the student should be able to do two things. The first thing is *to tread water*. In order to make this sentence parallel, the second thing should be in the same form: the student should be able *both* to tread water *and* to do another thing. The use of *while* in (B) is redundant, since the sentence already contains *both*. (C) joins the two parts of the sentence correctly, but the verb tense here is inconsistent with the first half of the sentence. (D) also introduces an incorrect verb tense. (E) uses *and* to join the actions correctly and keeps the verb tense consistent within the sentence.

4. D

This question includes a parallel construction: the two parts of the sentence that come after the verb (*claimed*) need to *match up* in order for the sentence to be correct. Taking a look at the underlined portion of the sentence, you can see that there are two statements here: Jason claims that he's not being compensated fairly, and he also claims that the editors are holding a grudge. All of the answer choices contain these two statements, so you will be looking for the choice that avoids wordiness and includes a parallel construction. Choice (A) is not parallel; *not only that* would need to be followed by *but that*. (B) is incorrect for the same reason and is redundant as well. (C) is wordy and redundant, using both *but in addition* and *as well* where one phrase would suffice. (D) contains the parallel construction we're seeking: Jason claimed *that he was not* being paid enough *and that* the editors had a grudge. (E) is not parallel, using the unnecessary phrase *he also believed*.

5. E

Your ability to choose the correct answer here hinges on understanding that the sentence is making a comparison. The correct choice will show a distinction between the two parts of he sentence. Choice (A) does this to a degree, but is unnecessarily wordy. (B) lacks a verb that is necessary to make this sentence complete. (C) looks correct initially, but when you fit it into the sentence, you can see that it, too, is missing a verb before *permanent*. (D) is cumbersome and unnecessarily introduces a new verb tense into the sentence. (E) is the correct choice: it's simply worded, shows a contrast between the two parts of the sentence, and links them together without any errors.

6. B

To find the correct choice, you will need to determine where the subject in the sentence lies. When you're looking for a subject, find the verb first. Then ask, *Who or what ____?* In this case, who or what has angered the customers? It's the price, not the policies, so you will look for a singular verb to match the singular subject. (B) provides the correct form, *has*, and phrases the second part of the sentence simply and correctly. (C) uses a plural verb form and is therefore incorrect. (D) and (E) use the correct form of *has*, but provide unnecessarily complicated versions of the second part of the sentence: (D) uses an incorrect tense of *threaten*, and (E) omits the necessary *and* between the two actions.

7. C

Keep an eye out for pronouns. If you didn't read this sentence carefully, you might miss the error and be tempted to choose an answer that rewords without fixing the problem. The issue here is that the sentence switches from *you*, to *one*. That's why (A) is incorrect, and (B) does nothing to remedy the problem. (C) is the correct choice; it makes the pronoun usage consistent. (D) and (E) attempt to distract you by rewriting the underlined phrase in a more complicated way, but neither corrects the error.

8. C

This question tests your ability to distinguish between verb tenses and to choose the correct one that completes a thought.

Getting to the answer: The inclusion of *what* in the underlined phrase is unnecessary and clutters up the sentence. (B) initially looks like an improvement, but introduces a verb tense change with *was*. (C) is the simplest and best choice; it keeps the verbs of the sentence in the same tense and avoids adding extra words. (D) and (E) introduce new verb tenses that confuse the meaning of the sentence.

9. D

The unclear use of a modifier is a favorite of SAT test makers. As this question is written, the modifier (*Charging much less than her competitors…*) isn't followed by the thing it's modifying (*Harmony*). In fact, it's followed by a different noun altogether (*neighbors*). The correct answer will fix this error. (B), (C), and (E) simply rearrange the order of (A), not addressing the modifier issue at all. (D) provides the simplest restatement of the underlined phrase and restores the correct order between the modifier and subject.

10. D

This sentence is a classic run-on, joining two separate ideas with a comma. Your key to finding the correct answer will be your ability to recognize the independent clauses within the sentence: Ramsey was the first governor, and his house is now a museum. If each clause would be able to stand as its own sentence, then the clauses need to be separated with a semicolon. (B) and (C) are incorrect because, like (A), they use a comma to separate the two independent clauses. (D) is the correct answer, joining the two ideas with a semicolon. A conjunction like *but* is not used after a semicolon that joins two ideas, so (E) is incorrect.

11. A

As you evaluate the answer choices, insert each one into the sentence and confirm that it does not create a fragment. Choice (A) is the only option that does not create a sentence fragment. Choices (B) and (C) each create a fragment with a subject but no predicate. (D) also creates a fragment and is unnecessarily wordy. (E) does not create a complete sentence.

12. A

If verb tense changes within a sentence, be certain that there's a good reason for the switch. Choice (A) is the only answer that maintains a consistent verb tense and joins the two parts of the sentence in a simple, clear way. (B) incorrectly switches from the past (*received*) to present (*leaving*) tense. Choices (C) and (E) imply that the midwives *received* records of their work, rather than *leaving* them, and are therefore incorrect. (D) uses *nor* without the antecedent *neither*, creating a choppy and confusing sentence.

13. B

Finding the correct answer here will require you to choose the correct conjunction. The word *when* should be used if a time element is present, for example, in the sentence *One important time of day is when we back up the computer system.* In this case, however, there is no issue of time, but one of causation. It may help to simplify the sentence in your head: "The cause is *when*" versus "The cause is *that*." (B) is correct in this context. Choices (C), (D), and (E) make a shift from *the medicine shortage* to *most medicine shortages*, which changes the meaning of the original sentence. Additionally, (D) creates a phrase that is not idiomatic.

14. D

This question requires you to clarify a comparison between two things. The sentence is giving us a description of the features of West Coast beaches and telling us that beaches on the East Coast do not possess these features. Choices (A) and (B) use the incorrect pronoun *them* to refer to the beaches of the East Coast. (C) is redundant (*when* is unnecessary before *in contrast*). (D) offers the simplest restatement of the sentence and uses pronouns and *in contrast* correctly. (E) includes a nonstandard use of *contrast*; a better word choice here would be *differ from*.

SAT Practice Test B
Answer Sheet

Remove (or photocopy) this answer sheet and use it to complete the Practice Test. See the answer key following the test when finished. The Compute Your Score section at the back of the book will show you how to find your score.

Section 2

1. Ⓐ Ⓑ Ⓒ Ⓓ Ⓔ	11. Ⓐ Ⓑ Ⓒ Ⓓ Ⓔ	21. Ⓐ Ⓑ Ⓒ Ⓓ Ⓔ	31. Ⓐ Ⓑ Ⓒ Ⓓ Ⓔ
2. Ⓐ Ⓑ Ⓒ Ⓓ Ⓔ	12. Ⓐ Ⓑ Ⓒ Ⓓ Ⓔ	22. Ⓐ Ⓑ Ⓒ Ⓓ Ⓔ	32. Ⓐ Ⓑ Ⓒ Ⓓ Ⓔ
3. Ⓐ Ⓑ Ⓒ Ⓓ Ⓔ	13. Ⓐ Ⓑ Ⓒ Ⓓ Ⓔ	23. Ⓐ Ⓑ Ⓒ Ⓓ Ⓔ	33. Ⓐ Ⓑ Ⓒ Ⓓ Ⓔ
4. Ⓐ Ⓑ Ⓒ Ⓓ Ⓔ	14. Ⓐ Ⓑ Ⓒ Ⓓ Ⓔ	24. Ⓐ Ⓑ Ⓒ Ⓓ Ⓔ	34. Ⓐ Ⓑ Ⓒ Ⓓ Ⓔ
5. Ⓐ Ⓑ Ⓒ Ⓓ Ⓔ	15. Ⓐ Ⓑ Ⓒ Ⓓ Ⓔ	25. Ⓐ Ⓑ Ⓒ Ⓓ Ⓔ	35. Ⓐ Ⓑ Ⓒ Ⓓ Ⓔ
6. Ⓐ Ⓑ Ⓒ Ⓓ Ⓔ	16. Ⓐ Ⓑ Ⓒ Ⓓ Ⓔ	26. Ⓐ Ⓑ Ⓒ Ⓓ Ⓔ	
7. Ⓐ Ⓑ Ⓒ Ⓓ Ⓔ	17. Ⓐ Ⓑ Ⓒ Ⓓ Ⓔ	27. Ⓐ Ⓑ Ⓒ Ⓓ Ⓔ	
8. Ⓐ Ⓑ Ⓒ Ⓓ Ⓔ	18. Ⓐ Ⓑ Ⓒ Ⓓ Ⓔ	28. Ⓐ Ⓑ Ⓒ Ⓓ Ⓔ	
9. Ⓐ Ⓑ Ⓒ Ⓓ Ⓔ	19. Ⓐ Ⓑ Ⓒ Ⓓ Ⓔ	29. Ⓐ Ⓑ Ⓒ Ⓓ Ⓔ	
10. Ⓐ Ⓑ Ⓒ Ⓓ Ⓔ	20. Ⓐ Ⓑ Ⓒ Ⓓ Ⓔ	30. Ⓐ Ⓑ Ⓒ Ⓓ Ⓔ	

right

wrong

Section 3

1. Ⓐ Ⓑ Ⓒ Ⓓ Ⓔ	11. Ⓐ Ⓑ Ⓒ Ⓓ Ⓔ
2. Ⓐ Ⓑ Ⓒ Ⓓ Ⓔ	12. Ⓐ Ⓑ Ⓒ Ⓓ Ⓔ
3. Ⓐ Ⓑ Ⓒ Ⓓ Ⓔ	13. Ⓐ Ⓑ Ⓒ Ⓓ Ⓔ
4. Ⓐ Ⓑ Ⓒ Ⓓ Ⓔ	14. Ⓐ Ⓑ Ⓒ Ⓓ Ⓔ
5. Ⓐ Ⓑ Ⓒ Ⓓ Ⓔ	
6. Ⓐ Ⓑ Ⓒ Ⓓ Ⓔ	
7. Ⓐ Ⓑ Ⓒ Ⓓ Ⓔ	
8. Ⓐ Ⓑ Ⓒ Ⓓ Ⓔ	
9. Ⓐ Ⓑ Ⓒ Ⓓ Ⓔ	
10. Ⓐ Ⓑ Ⓒ Ⓓ Ⓔ	

right

wrong

Practice Test B

Section 1

Essay
Time—25 Minutes (1 Question)

You will have 25 minutes to write your essay in your test booklet (two pages).

Directions: Consider carefully the following statement(s) and the assignment below it.

> "I would rather be able to appreciate things I cannot have than to have things I am not able to appreciate."
>
> —Elbert Hubbard

Assignment: Do you agree that it is important not to take things for granted? In an essay, support your position by discussing an example (or examples) from literature, science and technology, the arts, current events, or your own experience or observation.

SAT Practice Test B: **Answer Sheet**

ESSAY. Begin your composition on this side. If you need more space, you may continue on the following page.

_____

_____

_____

_____

_____

_____

_____

_____

_____

_____

_____

_____

_____

_____

_____

_____

_____

_____

_____

_____

SAT Practice Test B: **Answer Sheet**

Continuation of ESSAY from previous page. If you need more space, you may continue on the reverse side.

_____

_____

_____

_____

_____

_____

_____

_____

_____

_____

_____

_____

_____

_____

_____

_____

_____

_____

KAPLAN

Continuation of ESSAY from reverse side. Write below if you need more space.

Section 2
Time—25 Minutes (35 Questions)

Directions: The following sentences test correctness and effectiveness of expression. In choosing answers, follow the requirements of standard written English; that is, pay attention to grammar, choice of words, sentence construction, and punctuation.

In each of the following sentences, part of the sentence or the entire sentence is underlined. Beneath each sentence you will find five ways of phrasing the underlined part. Choice (A) repeats the original; the other four are different.

Choose the answer that best expresses the meaning of the original sentence. If you think the original is better than any of the alternatives, choose it; otherwise, choose one of the others. Your choice should produce the most effective sentence—clear and precise, without awkwardness or ambiguity.

---

1. The poet Oscar Wilde was known for his aphoristic wit and brilliant conversation, he wrote a number of memorable literary essays including "The Critic as Artist."

   (A) The poet Oscar Wilde was known for his aphoristic wit and brilliant conversation, he

   (B) The poet Oscar Wilde, known for his aphoristic wit and brilliant conversation; he

   (C) Known for his aphoristic wit and brilliant conversation, the poet Oscar Wilde

   (D) The poet Oscar Wilde was known for his aphoristic wit and brilliant conversation, however he

   (E) Oscar Wilde, the poet, known for his aphoristic wit and brilliant conversation, and he

2. According to Westin's book, the typical Victorian family was more interested in maintaining the appearance of propriety than in securing happiness for its individual members.

   (A) the typical Victorian family was more interested in maintaining the appearance of propriety than in

   (B) the appearance of propriety was more interesting to the typical Victorian family than

   (C) the typical Victorian family, more interested in maintaining the appearance of propriety than it was in

   (D) for a Victorian family it was typical that they would be more interested in maintaining the appearance of propriety than in

   (E) the typical Victorian family was more interested in the appearance of propriety than in

GO ON TO THE NEXT PAGE

KAPLAN

3. Once an enclave of privileged white males, the Wodehouse Club's directors have now decided to adopt a more inclusive membership policy.

   (A) Once an enclave of privileged white males, the Wodehouse Club's directors have

   (B) The directors of the Wodehouse Club, which was once an enclave of privileged white males, have

   (C) Though once an enclave of privileged white males, the Wodehouse Club's directors

   (D) Once an enclave of privileged white males, the Wodehouse Club's directors having

   (E) The directors of the enclave of privileged white males, the Wodehouse Club, has

4. Supporters of the Eighteenth Amendment thought that banning alcohol would improve citizens' morals and enhance their quality of life by removing the temptation to drink; national prohibition ushered in 13 years of bootlegging, speakeasies, and violent gangster crime.

   (A) national prohibition

   (B) in fact, national prohibition

   (C) furthermore, national prohibition

   (D) but national prohibition

   (E) consequently, national prohibition

5. Though multimedia presentations have their place in the school curriculum, it is ridiculous to claim, as some do, that children learn as much from watching a one-hour video as a book.

   (A) that children learn as much from watching a one-hour video as a book

   (B) that children will learn as much from watching a one-hour video as they did from a book

   (C) that children learn as much from watching a one-hour video as they do from reading a book

   (D) that a one-hour video teaches more to children than book-reading

   (E) that children watching a one-hour video learn as much as reading a book

6. Finland's national epic, the *Kalevala*, based on an oral tradition that the Balto-Finnish people preserved for some 2,500 years despite the upheavals of history and the pressures of foreign domination.

   (A) based on an oral tradition that

   (B) being based on an oral tradition that

   (C) is based on an oral tradition; this

   (D) basing itself on an oral tradition which

   (E) is based on an oral tradition that

7. The island of Santa Ynez was once a playground for wealthy American tourists; in recent years, however, civil unrest and a series of natural disasters have made it so that it is not nearly as appealing as a vacation spot.

   (A) have made it so that it is not nearly as appealing

   (B) are causing it to be made less appealing

   (C) greatly reducing its appeal

   (D) have greatly lessened its appeal

   (E) have not nearly made it as appealing

8. In retrospect, one can see the folly of trying to unite a region containing some 400 distinct ethnic groups, each with its own language, laws, and traditions.

   (A) each with its own language, laws, and traditions

   (B) each of them has its own language, laws, and traditions

   (C) each with their own language, laws, and traditions

   (D) and each of them having its own language, laws, and traditions

   (E) when they each have their own language, laws, and traditions

GO ON TO THE NEXT PAGE ▷

9. Proponents of campaign finance reform point out that people who make large donations to politicians expect to be rewarded with special favors <u>and gaining easy access</u> to the corridors of power.

(A) and gaining easy access

(B) and they gain easy access

(C) and easy access

(D) as well as gaining easy access

(E) and to be rewarded with easy access

10. <u>Had Churchill sent planes to defend Coventry</u> from the German air raid, the Nazis would have realized that their secret code had been broken by the Allies.

(A) Had Churchill sent planes to defend Coventry

(B) If Churchill would have sent planes to defend Coventry

(C) Churchill having sent planes to defend Coventry

(D) If Churchill sent planes to defend Coventry

(E) Churchill, by sending planes to Coventry to defend it

11. <u>Television shows such as *M*A*S*H* and *All in the Family* took</u> months or even years to build a large audience, most new series today never get that chance.

(A) Television shows such as *M*A*S*H* and *All in the Family* took

(B) Although television shows such as *M*A*S*H* and *All in the Family* took

(C) With television shows such as *M*A*S*H* and *All in the Family* taking

(D) Such television shows as *M*A*S*H* and *All in the Family* took

(E) When television shows such as *M*A*S*H* and *All in the Family* took

GO ON TO THE NEXT PAGE ⟹

KAPLAN

Directions: The following sentences test your knowledge of grammar, usage, diction (choice of words), and idiom.

Some sentences are correct.
No sentence contains more than one error.

You will find that the error, if there is one, is underlined and lettered. Elements of the sentence that are not underlined will not be changed. In choosing answers, follow the requirements of standard written English.

If there is an error, select the one underlined part that must be changed to make the sentence correct, and fill in the corresponding oval on your answer sheet.

If there is no error, darken in answer oval E.

---

12. <u>As</u> a college student, Delaney was hesitant
    A
    <u>to participate</u> <u>in any</u> rallies or demonstrations
         B   C
    because he hoped <u>for having</u> a political career
                          D
    someday. <u>No error</u>
              E

13. The castaways' situation was <u>beginning</u> to look
                                     A
    <u>desperate</u>: they had <u>drank</u> the last of their water
        B   C
    the night <u>before</u>, and there was only one
               D
    flare left in the emergency kit. <u>No error</u>
                                     E

14. <u>Among</u> the many factors contributing to the
      A
    revival of the medieval economy <u>was</u> the
                                      B
    <u>cessation</u> of Viking raids and the <u>development</u>
        C   D
    of the heavy plow. <u>No error</u>
                        E

15. Raoul gave Frederick very little warning before

    <u>striking</u> a match and setting fire <u>to his</u> entire
        A   B
    collection of documents, <u>which</u> had been
                               C
    <u>painstakingly</u> compiled over the course of
        D
    several decades. <u>No error</u>
                     E

16. Native <u>to</u> New Zealand, the kiwi <u>has few</u>
              A   B
    natural predators but <u>is</u> currently endangered
                           C
    <u>by</u> deforestation and human encroachment.
     D
    <u>No error</u>
     E

17. Diabetes can strike anyone, <u>irregardless</u> of age;
                                     A
    <u>nevertheless</u>, many people <u>still make</u> the
        B   C
    mistake <u>of considering</u> it a geriatric disease.
              D
    <u>No error</u>
     E

GO ON TO THE NEXT PAGE

KAPLAN

18. The <u>much-publicized</u> study was <u>deemed</u>
         A   B
    unscientific because it failed to take <u>into</u>
                                    C
    account such variables <u>as</u> heredity and income.
                          D
    <u>No error</u>
      E

19. The early Egyptian monks <u>sought</u> complete
                            A
    solitude so <u>that</u> they <u>might</u> pray without
             B   C
    distraction, pursue an ideal of perfection, and

    <u>to attain</u> a higher level of religious experience.
      D
    <u>No error</u>
      E

20. Perhaps the coach was remembered <u>so fondly</u>
                               A
    because he was <u>always</u> less interested in
                B
    winning than in <u>making sure</u> that avll the boys
                C
    participated <u>with</u> the game. <u>No error</u>
          D   E

21. Thirty years ago, one could say that those <u>who</u>
                            A
    the president nominated to <u>serve</u> on the
                    B
    Supreme Court were <u>chosen not</u> because of
                C
    their political leanings, <u>but because</u> of their
                   D
    fine legal minds and their judicial expertise.

    <u>No error</u>
      E

22. <u>Even</u> today, there are many who <u>would</u> say
      A   B
    that the old tribal practice of <u>paying</u> blood-
                        C
    money to families of murder victims <u>are more</u>
                            D
    just than our modern system of trial and

    punishment. <u>No error</u>
               E

23. In a move <u>that</u> distressed the clergy as much as
              A
    <u>it</u> delighted the barons, King Arnulf <u>named</u>
     B   C
    one of his illegitimate sons <u>as</u> heir and
                      D
    successor to the throne. <u>No error</u>
                    E

24. <u>Hopefully</u>, it is not <u>too</u> late to reverse the
      A   B
    damage <u>that years of</u> neglect and harsh
               C
    weather <u>have wrought on</u> the beautiful old
               D
    mansion. <u>No error</u>
            E

25. As <u>soon</u> as the employees realized <u>that</u>
        A   B
    management would never accede <u>with</u> their
                       C
    demands for a shorter work week, a strike

    became <u>inevitable</u>. <u>No error</u>
           D   E

26. <u>Lacking</u> an objective standard <u>by which</u> to
      A   B
    judge the contestants, the sponsors of the

    pageant <u>finally</u> resorted <u>to drawing a</u>
            C   D
    name at random from a hat. <u>No error</u>
                    E

GO ON TO THE NEXT PAGE →

KAPLAN

27. The aurora borealis is a dazzling <u>phenomena</u>
                                            A
     that <u>occurs when the</u> earth's magnetic field inter-
               B
     acts <u>with</u> the solar wind, <u>producing</u> ionized atoms
             C   D
     and molecules. <u>No error</u>
                        E

28. So <u>great was</u> John Lennon's fame <u>as</u> he
            A   B
     <u>could scarcely</u> walk out his door without <u>being</u>
          C   D
     accosted by fans and photographers. <u>No error</u>
                                            E

29. <u>At</u> the counseling center, <u>a person</u> should feel
       A   B
     <u>free to</u> express their true emotions without fear
        C
     <u>of</u> ridicule or reprisal. <u>No error</u>
      D   E

GO ON TO THE NEXT PAGE

KAPLAN

Directions: The passage below is an early draft of an essay. Parts of the passage need to be rewritten.

Read the passage and answer the questions that follow. Some questions are about individual sentences or parts of sentences; in these questions, you are asked to select the choice that will improve sentence structure and word choice. Other questions refer to parts of the essay or the entire essay and ask you to consider the organization and development of the essay. You should follow the conventions of standard written English in answering the questions. After you have chosen your answer, fill in the corresponding oval on your answer sheet.

Questions 30–35 are based on the following essay.

(1) There is no way I expected to enjoy summer camp this year. (2) All of my friends were being sent to fashionable camps in the Berkshires and Vermont. (3) Not only did these camps specialize in sports that I've always wanted to try (tennis, canoeing, and white water rafting are examples). (4) Additionally everyone I knew got to go with their best friends.

(5) Was this what my parents did? (6) Instead, Dad decided to send me to a camp in New Hampshire where he'd gone as a kid. (7) Old Deer Head Falls, NH, twenty miles from the nearest sign of human habitation. (8) The camp's main and primary activity was hiking in the rocky, rainy trails of the nearby White Mountains. (9) Thanks a lot, Dad. (10) Regarded as one of the least fit students in my class, this summer had all the hallmarks of a disaster for me. (11) It took a couple of hikes, participation in a handful of camp fire sing-alongs, and bursting many a blister on my feet to change my mind. (12) The scenery in the mountains was a major factor. (13) Another was that (even though I am a self-confessed couch potato) I actually found the exercise enjoyable. (14) I made new friends, and to my surprise I liked the camp counselors a lot. (15) There were counselors from all over the world. (16) The debates at rest stops got pretty interesting. (17) After a summer above the treeline, I think I returned to school with better stories than my friends who went to "fashionable" resorts!

30. Which of the following is the best way to revise the underlined portions of sentences 3 and 4 (reproduced below) so that the two sentences are combined into one?

Not only did these camps specialize in sports that I've always wanted to <u>try (tennis, canoeing, and white water rafting are examples). Additionally everyone</u> I knew got to go with their best friends.

(A) try, examples being tennis, canoeing, and white water rafting; additionally everyone

(B) try, such as tennis, canoeing, and white water rafting, but all the people

(C) try: tennis, canoeing, and white water rafting for example, plus they all

(D) try (tennis, canoeing, white water rafting, for example), furthermore all the people

(E) try, such as tennis canoeing, and white water rafting, and everyone

31. Which of the following sentences, if inserted in place of sentence 5, would provide the best transition between the first paragraph and the rest of the essay?

(A) However, my parents chose not to send me to a "fashionable" camp.

(B) Unlike my friends, my parents chose something else altogether.

(C) Rather than being sent to a "fashionable camp," Dad chose otherwise.

(D) Unfortunately, this situation was not the case with my parents.

(E) You might have expected that my parents would have been doing the same.

GO ON TO THE NEXT PAGE ⟩

32. What is the best way to deal with sentence 8 (reproduced below)?

    The camp's main and primary activity was hiking in the rocky, rainy trails of the nearby White Mountains.

    (A) Leave it as it is.

    (B) Switch its position with that of sentence 12.

    (C) Change *was* to *were*.

    (D) Delete *main and* and replace *in* with *on*.

    (E) Remove the comma and insert *and*.

33. In the context of the second paragraph, which of the following is the best version of the underlined portion of sentence 10 (reproduced below)?

    Regarded as one of the least fit students in my class, this summer had all the hallmarks of a disaster for me.

    (A) (As it is now)

    (B) I predicted that this summer would be a disaster for me

    (C) this summer was beginning to look disastrous for me

    (D) and for me, this summer had all the hallmarks of a disaster

    (E) so this summer had all the hallmarks of a disaster for me

34. Which of the following versions of the underlined portion of sentence 11 (reproduced below) is clearest?

    It took a couple of hikes, participation in a handful of camp fire sing-alongs, and bursting many a blister on my feet to change my mind.

    (A) (As it is now)

    (B) a handful of camp fire sing-alongs, and bursting many blisters

    (C) the participation in some camp fire sing-alongs, and the bursting of many a blister

    (D) a handful of camp fire sing-alongs, and many a burst blister

    (E) my participating in a handful of camp fire sing-alongs, and my bursting many a blister

35. In context, which is the best way to combine the underlined wording in sentences 14, 15, and 16 (reproduced below)?

    I made new friends, and to my surprise I liked the camp counselors a lot. There were counselors from all over the world. The debates at rest stops got pretty interesting.

    (A) and I liked the camp counselors and they came from all over the world and the debates at rest stops got

    (B) but I liked the camp counselors; they came from all over the world and made the debates at the rest stops

    (C) therefore I liked the camp counselors, who came from all over the world, making the debates at rest stops

    (D) and to my surprise I liked the camp counselors, who came from all over the world, making the debates at rest stops

    (E) and I liked the camp counselors, coming from all over the world to my surprise, and the debates at rest stops were

IF YOU FINISH BEFORE TIME IS CALLED, YOU MAY CHECK YOUR WORK ON THIS SECTION ONLY. DO NOT TURN TO ANY OTHER SECTION IN THE TEST.

STOP

Section 3
Time—10 Minutes (14 Questions)

Directions: The following sentences test correctness and effectiveness of expression. In choosing answers, follow the requirements of standard written English; that is, pay attention to grammar, choice of words, sentence construction, and punctuation.

In each of the following sentences, part of the sentence or the entire sentence is underlined. Beneath each sentence, you will find five ways of phrasing the underlined part. Choice (A) repeats the original; the other four are different.

Choose the answer that best expresses the meaning of the original sentence. If you think the original is better than any of the alternatives, choose it; otherwise, choose one of the others. Your choice should produce the most effective sentence—clear and precise, without awkwardness or ambiguity.

1. Police response times to emergency calls have decreased dramatically with the introduction of new technologies—<u>in some neighborhoods by as much as 40 percent in the last six months</u>.

    (A) in some neighborhoods by as much as 40 percent in the last six months

    (B) in some neighborhoods having 40 percent in the last six months

    (C) in some neighborhoods decreasing about 40 percent in the last six months semiannually

    (D) decreasing the equivalent of 40 percent in the last six months in some neighborhoods

    (E) which, in some neighborhoods, the decrease amounts to 40 percent in the last six months

2. <u>Known for its educational excellence, parents will place their young children on the long waiting list for Valley Crest Prep rather than settling for a neighborhood public school.</u>

    (A) Known for its educational excellence, parents will place their young children on the long waiting list for Valley Crest Prep rather than settling for a neighborhood public school.

    (B) Known as educationally excellent, parents will place their young children on the long waiting list for Valley Crest Prep rather than settling for a neighborhood public school.

    (C) Known for its educational excellence, Valley Crest Prep has a long waiting list of young children whose parents are unwilling to settle for a neighborhood school.

    (D) As known, Valley Crest Prep, which is educationally excellent, has a long waiting list of young children whose parents are unwilling to settle for a neighborhood school.

    (E) Valley Crest Prep known for its educational excellence by parents who will place their young children on a waiting list but not to settle for a neighborhood public school.

GO ON TO THE NEXT PAGE

KAPLAN

3. Feedback from test audiences and focus groups <u>show movie patrons tend to go to films</u> more frequently during the winter months.

   (A) show movie patrons tend to go to films
   (B) show movie patrons that tend to go to films
   (C) is showing movie patrons tends to go to films
   (D) shows that movie patrons tend to go to films
   (E) shows movie patrons tends to go

4. Passing the baton as they ran alongside each other, Emily and Lorin were aiming <u>to be the quickest pairs</u> to finish the race.

   (A) to be the quickest pairs
   (B) to be the quickest pair
   (C) at having been the quickest pair
   (D) at being the quickest of the pair
   (E) to being the quickest pair

5. <u>In order to focus before an important game, Mia runs laps at the track, Angel sleeps late and eats a healthy breakfast.</u>

   (A) In order to focus before an important game, Mia runs laps at the track, Angel sleeps late and eats a healthy breakfast.
   (B) Mia runs laps at the track in order to focus before an important game, and Angel, she sleeps late and eats a healthy breakfast.
   (C) In order to focus before an important game, Mia runs laps at the track; Angel sleeps late and eats a healthy breakfast.
   (D) Angel sleeps late and eats a healthy breakfast with Mia running laps at the track in order to focus before an important game.
   (E) In order to focus before an important game, Mia runs laps at the track; Angel sleeps late and eating a healthy breakfast.

6. <u>Mr. Freeman, the head of Accounting, has a reputation for awarding the Employee of the Month honors to a member of his own department, and</u> this month he presented the award to Jean Everly in Customer Service.

   (A) Mr. Freeman, the head of Accounting, has a reputation for awarding the Employee of the Month honors to a member of his own department, and
   (B) Mr. Freeman, the head of Accounting, has a reputation for awarding the Employee of the Month honors to a member of his own department,
   (C) While Mr. Freeman, the head of Accounting, has a reputation for awarding the Employee of the Month honors to a member of his own department, however,
   (D) Although Mr. Freeman, the head of Accounting, has a reputation for awarding the Employee of the Month honors to a member of his own department,
   (E) As Mr. Freeman, the head of Accounting, has a reputation for awarding the Employee of the Month honors to a member of his own department, and

7. Last year, more of Western University's English graduates entered master's degree programs in literature than <u>creative writing</u>.

   (A) creative writing
   (B) creative writing did
   (C) those compared to creative writing
   (D) creative writing ones
   (E) in creative writing

GO ON TO THE NEXT PAGE ⟶

8. Marie, an experienced graphic designer, has completed a proposal for <u>Clearview Media, they produce</u> corporate catalogs and brochures.

   (A) Clearview Media, they produce
   (B) Clearview Media, which produces
   (C) Clearview Media is producing
   (D) Clearview Media, it produces
   (E) Clearview Media; for the producing of

9. The collection I saw at Mrs. Kowalski's shop does not contain as many figurines <u>as does my grandmother</u>.

   (A) as does my grandmother
   (B) as does my grandmother's collection
   (C) compared to what my grandmother does
   (D) like my grandmother's collection does
   (E) like the one at my grandmother's do

10. The ballet teacher reported at the conference that she found Jeannette to be both a challenge because of her high energy level <u>but her natural ability made her a pleasure to have in class</u>.

    (A) but her natural ability made her a pleasure to have in class
    (B) although she is a pleasure to have in class due to her natural ability
    (C) and her natural ability makes class a pleasure when she is in it
    (D) while having such a natural ability as to be a delight
    (E) and a pleasure to have in class because of her natural ability

11. Having worked on the piece for over a year, <u>that the journal rejected her article disappointed Professor Hill deeply</u>.

    (A) that the journal rejected her article disappointed Professor Hill deeply
    (B) Professor Hill's deep disappointment resulted from the journal rejecting her article
    (C) Professor Hill's disappointment at the journal's rejecting her article was deep
    (D) Professor Hill was deeply disappointed by the journal's rejection of her article
    (E) the journal's rejecting her article was a deep disappointment to Professor Hill

12. The main points Senator Gutierrez made during his speech to the conventioneers <u>was that he had supported measures to improve health care for the working class and would introduce</u> a bill to fund a new bus route.

    (A) was that he had supported measures to improve health care for the working class and introduced
    (B) was supporting measures to improve health care for the working class and he introduced
    (C) were that he had supported measures to improve health care for the working class and that he would introduce
    (D) was that he had supported measures to improve health care and introducing
    (E) were support measures to improve health care, in addition to introduce

GO ON TO THE NEXT PAGE

KAPLAN

13. The Agricultural Board reports that this year's crop, <u>which is 300 percent greater than projected and 450 percent greater than</u> last year's, is expected to produce record earnings.

    (A) which is 300 percent greater than projected and 450 percent greater than

    (B) is 300 percent greater than projected while also 450 percent greater than

    (C) with a yield 300 percent greater than the one that was projected, as well as being 450 percent greater

    (D) 300 percent greater than projected, and it yields a crop 450 percent greater than

    (E) which is 300 percent greater than projected and 450 percent as great when compared with

14. <u>Styling her hair the next morning, the new cut looked much less flattering to Frances</u> than it had when she was at the salon the day before.

    (A) Styling her hair the next morning, the new cut looked much less flattering to Frances

    (B) Having styled her new haircut the next morning, it looks much less flattering to Frances

    (C) Styling her hair, it looked the next morning to be much less flattering to her

    (D) Frances styled her hair the next morning, the new cut looked much less flattering

    (E) Styling her hair the next morning, Frances realized that the new cut looked much less flattering to her

IF YOU FINISH BEFORE TIME IS CALLED, YOU MAY CHECK YOUR WORK ON THIS SECTION ONLY. DO NOT TURN TO ANY OTHER SECTION IN THE TEST. STOP

Answers and Explanations

SECTION 1

The Essay

This section contains sample essays for the essay topic in Practice Test B. Use these sample essays as benchmarks to help you grade your own essay on the same topic. Does your essay sound more like the grade 5 essay or the grade 3 essay?

Sample Grade 5 Essay

Running for the bus was one of those things that seem like a good idea at the time. Our school is located on the edge of town, five miles from my house. Miss the school bus, and you have a long wait ahead of you. And so when I saw that the rear of that yellow vehicle disappearing past the gymnasium, I automatically burst into a sprint across the parking lot to try and catch it. This seemed like a very good idea until I tripped and turned into the human torpedo, pitching head-long into the concrete and breaking my right arm in the process.

My broken arm taught me the importance of not taking anything for grant-ed—especially my right arm! As a junior, many exams were looming in front of me which I needed to be able to write for. Not only did I have classes that I wanted to do well in. I had the PSAT coming up, and I couldn't even scrawl my name. At least, not in a form that people could read. Teachers were kind enough to let me borrow notes from other students, but I was definitely concerned about keeping up.

Of course, academic studies weren't the only area of my life effected by my broken arm. I had all these commitments to sports teams (football, basketball, etc.) that now had to play on without me. Boy was I concerned about that! There were some benefits to this however; I still wanted to stay involved while I got bet-ter, so I travelled with the teams and helped out organizationally. I was impatient to play again, but I realized that there is more to sports than putting on the num-ber 19 jersey.

Breaking my arm definitely helped me value the use of my right arm, and my health in general. As the old saying goes, you don't know what you've got until you lose it so you're better off appreciating what you've got and not taking even basic things for granted. Next time I have a bright idea like running for the bus, I'll have another think coming!

Grader's comments: This essay fulfills the writing assignment with a degree of competence. It shows an original approach to the topic and a solid grasp of structure. The writer picks good examples to support the argument, and occasional grammatical flaws and digressions do not detract from its overall effectiveness.

Sample Grade 3 Essay

I agree you shouldn't take things for granted, and one thing I will never take for granted is my favorite bands. Music has a major impact on people's lives. Almost everyone listens to it—for pleasure, relaxation and to be entertained. And yet, music is more than just popcorn for the ears. You can learn things from it. Some of the best bands have lyrics that are pretty intelligent—they tell a story or make a political statement. At its best, they can be almost as good as poetry.

My favorite example of a good songwriter is Sting, formerly in the Police. For years, Sting was an English teacher. Then he realized his dream to be a pop star with one of the biggest groups of the 1980s. His music was not like all the other groups—he didn't only write fluffy songs about falling in love. He had lyrics about the Cold War, un-employment and the rainforest. Additionally to the lyrics, he always used musicians of the highest calibber. Some of the best jazz musicians in New York ended up in his solo band producing sophisticated music indeed.

A lot of adults and learned people think that only classical music, opera and jazz are "art." I don't necessarily agree. I think that Sting's music shows that "pop" music can just as complicated and meaningful than so-called "art" forms. While many people take things for granted in life, I think music contributes heavily to our understanding of the world. For this reason, I'll never take pop music for granted, I always appreciate it.

Grader's comments: This essay demonstrates limited competence. In the first paragraph, the author's argument lacks some coherence. The author chooses good examples to illustrate points in paragraphs 2 and 3, but there are many lapses in grammar and logic.

Sample Grade 1 Essay

I definitely take a lot of things for granted. Movies, computer games and TV dinners are examples that spring to mind. Plenty of people globally don't have access to these. And we take them for granted—just like that! How would it be if someone came to our neighborhood and took all our convenience away? People would be in a sorry state, let me tell you. Immigrants show you that you can't take stuff for granted for a minute they come over here and work all hours of the day feeding their families. I think that plenty of people forgot that they where in the same position. That's the problem with the country today—too many people sitting on they're butts and not enough action. If I was elected mayor, this would be the first thing I'd fix and fast.

Grader's comments: This essay is deficient. First, it answers the basic question in a roundabout and convoluted way. Second, the author's ideas are not adequately developed. Third, there are many errors in usage and syntax.

The Multiple-Choice Section

Answer Key

Section 2				Section 3	
1.	C	18.	E	1.	A
2.	A	19.	D	2.	C
3.	B	20.	D	3.	D
4.	B	21.	A	4.	B
5.	C	22.	D	5.	C
6.	E	23.	E	6.	D
7.	D	24.	A	7.	E
8.	A	25.	C	8.	B
9.	C	26.	E	9.	B
10.	A	27.	A	10.	E
11.	B	28.	B	11.	D
12.	D	29.	B	12.	C
13.	C	30.	B	13.	A
14.	B	31.	A	14.	E
15.	B	32.	D		
16.	E	33.	B		
17.	A	34.	D		
		35.	D		

Section 2

1. C

(C) is the only choice that corrects this run-on sentence in a logical way: *Known for his aphoristic wit and brilliant conversation* introduces Oscar Wilde; the rest of the sentence provides additional information about him. (B) contains a fragment, (D) is a run-on that presents an illogical contrast between Wilde's wit and his writing, and (E) is extremely garbled.

2. A

The sentence is correct: *maintaining* and *securing* are in the proper parallel form (both gerunds). (B) is convoluted and slightly alters the meaning of the sentence. (C) is a fragment. (D) is verbose and tangled. (E) has sacrificed correct parallel structure for the sake of brevity, comparing *the appearance* (a noun) to *securing* (a gerund).

3. B

The sentence contains a misplaced modifier: *Once an enclave of privileged white males* refers to *the Wodehouse Club*, not to its *directors*. Choice (B) correctly places the modifying phrase right next to the thing it's describing. (C) and (D) do not correct the misplaced modifier, and (D) is a fragment. (E) is poorly worded, and the verb *has* does not agree with the subject, *directors*.

4. B

What actually occurred when alcohol was banned turned out to be the opposite of what the prohibitionists had envisioned. Drinking continued (illegally) and crime actually increased. Therefore, you're looking for words that will express this ironic contrast between the idea and the reality. *In fact* is the best choice. Although *but* expresses a contrast, it also creates a fragment (*but* must follow a comma, not a semicolon), so (D) is wrong. Choices (A), (C), and (E) fail to express the logical contrast between the two halves of the sentence.

5. C

What is being compared here? You can't compare an action (*watching* a video) to an object (*a book*)—it's not logical and it violates the rules of parallelism. (C) corrects the sentence by putting the two activities in parallel form. (B) fails to fix the parallelism problem, and it introduces strange and unnecessary changes in verb tense. (D) is awkwardly phrased (would you say "book-reading"?), and (E) also fails to fix the parallelism problem, creating a somewhat confusing comparison.

6. E

To correct this sentence fragment, all you need to do is insert the helping verb *is* before the participle *based*. *Based*, *being based*, and *basing* are all verb forms that cannot stand on their own as a sentence's main verb.

7. D

The underlined portion of the sentence is wordy and awkward. (D) expresses the same thought in a clearer, more concise way. (B) and (E) are just as convoluted as the original sentence, and (C) is a fragment.

8. A

The sentence is fine as it is. (B) is a run-on. (C) and (E) contain plural pronouns that don't agree with their singular antecedents, and (D) makes no sense grammatically.

9. C

The donors expect to be rewarded with two things: *special favors* and *easy access.* For the sake of parallelism, both these things should be expressed in the same grammatical form: adjective + noun. (A), (B), and (D) are wordy and lack parallel structure; (E) is redundant.

10. A

The first clause of the sentence correctly sets up a condition that was not fulfilled: Churchill did not send planes to defend Coventry, and hence the Nazis did not realize the Allies had broken their code. Choice (A) is another way of saying *If Churchill had sent planes to defend Coventry.* (B) is grammatically unsound: *if he would have* is a very common error. Watch out for it! (C) and (E) are fragments, and (D) uses a wrong verb tense (*sent* for the past perfect *had sent*).

11. B

The conjunction *although* correctly expresses the contrast that is implied here: television shows were formerly given time to build up an audience, but now they are not. Choices (A) and (D) are run-on sentences, and (C) and (E) are illogical.

12. D

An idiom error—watch out for those little connecting words on test day. The sentence should read *he hoped to have,* not *he hoped for having.*

13. C

The past participle of *drink* is *drunk,* so the sentence should read *they had drunk* the last of the water. *Drank* is the simple past tense: "They drank the water."

14. B

This is a tricky one, since the subject follows the verb: *the cessation…and the development* is a compound subject requiring the plural verb *were.*

15. B

Whose collection of documents was it? It is not clear from the sentence whether *his* refers to Raoul or to Frederick; hence, this is a case of vague pronoun reference.

16. E

The sentence contains no error.

17. A

There is no such word as *irregardless.* People who make this mistake are probably conflating *irrespective* and *regardless,* either of which would be correct here.

18. E

The sentence contains no error.

19. D

Because the third verb in this list of monastic goals is in a different form from the other two verbs, it ruins the parallelism of the sentence. The sentence should read *so that they might pray…pursue…and attain.*

20. D

Another idiom problem here. *Participate* takes the preposition *in,* not *with.*

21. A

The pronoun should be *whom* rather than *who,* because it is the object of the verb *nominated.Who* should only be used when the pronoun is the verb's subject. If in doubt about whether to use *who* or *whom,* try reversing the sentence: you'd say the president nominated *him,* not the president nominated *he.*

22. D

If a verb is underlined, always check that it agrees with the subject. Here, the second verb should be *is* to agree with its singular subject, *practice.*

23. E

The sentence contains no error.

24. A

In standard written English, it is unacceptable to use *hopefully* as a shorthand substitute for *I hope*, even though we frequently use it this way in casual conversation. *Hopefully* should only be used as an adverb (e.g., *She smiled hopefully*).

25. C

Another idiom error: The sentence should read *accede to* (meaning "agree to"), not *accede with*.

26. E

The sentence contains no error.

27. A

Phenomena is the plural form of *phenomenon*, which would be the correct word here. Other plural nouns commonly mistaken for singulars include *alumni* (plural of *alumnus*), *media* (plural of *medium*), and *criteria* (plural of *criterion*).

28. B

So great should be followed by *that*, not *as*.

29. B

The subject should be the plural noun *people* in order to agree in number with the pronoun *their*.

30. B

Remember that the phrase *not only* needs to be followed by *but* or *but also*. B completes the thought begun with the *not only* clause, and it also uses *such as* to introduce the examples, which is less wordy and more graceful than the phrasing of the original sentence. The other answer choices are wordy and awkward, and they do not introduce the second clause with the required *but*. (Note, too, that *everyone* has been changed to a plural noun to agree with the plural pronoun *their*.)

31. A

You're looking for a sentence that sums up the actions of other kids' parents (i.e., sending their kids to fashionable resorts) to set up a contrast with the author's father's decision. Choice (A) expresses this idea. Choice (B) sets up an illogical comparison—between the choices of friends and

the choices of parents. Choice (C) has a misplaced modifier—Dad wasn't being sent to a camp. (D) has a vague linking phrase—it's not clear from the preceding sentence what *this situation* might refer to. (E) is also too vague a transition (*doing the same as what?*). Since the previous sentence refers to students, you need a linking sentence that focuses on parents' decisions, as (A) does.

32. D

In the original sentence, *main and primary* is redundant—one word or the other is sufficient. And we don't hike *in* trails, we hike *on* them. So (D) corrects the errors. Switching with sentence 12, (B), would make no sense in the context. The verb is correctly singular; *main and primary* are not separate parts of a compound subject, but two adjectives modifying the singular subject *activity*. (E) is an unnecessary change that makes the sentence slightly wordier.

33. B

Regarded as one of the least fit students in my class describes the author, not the summer. All the other choices contain misplaced modifiers, and (D) and (E) are not complete sentences.

34. D

You have a list of three things, all of which should be in parallel grammatical form. The first item in the list (which you can't change) sets the pattern that the other two must follow: *a [quantity] of [plural noun]*. Only choice (D) puts the other two list items in this form: *a handful of camp fire sing-alongs, and many a burst blister*. It is also concise rather than wordy (notice that it's the shortest answer choice).

35. D

Determine the relationship among the ideas in these sentences before trying to combine them. The writer liked the counselors because they came from different places and that made conversation interesting. (D) uses a relative pronoun clause and a modifying phrase to make these relationships clearest. Choice (A) merely strings the ideas together without clarifying the relationships. (B) and (C) misrepresent the relationship between the first and second clauses. (E) confuses some of the meaning and doesn't clarify the relationship between the last clause and the rest of the sentence.

Section 3

1. A

The dash correctly introduces additional information explaining how dramatically response times have decreased. In the correct choice, the additional information will read correctly with *decreased*. Choice (A) does this. (B) is not idiomatic English. (C) adds *semiannually*—which changes the meaning. (D) needlessly repeats *decreasing* and adds *the equivalent of*, making it wordy. (E) is not idiomatic English.

2. C

An introductory modifying phrase should be followed closely by the thing that it modifies. (B) does not fix the modifier problem. (D) corrects the problem but misplaces another modifier, separating *known all over the state* from *for educational excellence.* This confuses the meaning of the sentence. (E) omits the main verb *is*, creating a fragment.

3. D

Although the subject and verb are separated by the phrase *from test audiences and focus groups*, they must still agree in number. The correct form is *Feedback…shows*, and adding *that* makes the sentence clearer. (B) doesn't correct the problems and distorts the meaning. (C) needlessly changes to the progressive form *is showing* and introduces a new agreement problem, pairing the plural *patrons* with the singular *tends*. (E) also pairs a plural noun with a singular verb.

4. B

Emily and Lorin together constitute one pair, not several pairs. (C) incorrectly uses the modifier form *having been*. (D) completes the idiom *aims to* incorrectly with the awkward *aiming at being*. (E) uses the wrong form of the verb *to be.*

5. C

This run-on sentence needs punctuation or a conjunction, or one of the clauses must be made dependent. (C) uses the correctly placed semicolon to fix the problem. (B) is redundant, using two subjects (*Angel* and *she*) where only one is necessary. (D) distorts the meaning of the sentence. (E) uses the semicolon correctly, but uses the wrong form of *eats.*

6. D

The issue in this sentence is one of contrast. The sentence is saying that while Mr. Freeman usually does one thing, this time he did another. The original conjunction *and* does not express this contrast. (B), with no conjunction at all, creates a run-on sentence. (C) is redundant, using both *while* and *however* where either one would be sufficient. (E) uses *as* to express contrast, but also uses a conjunction, making the sentence redundant.

7. E

The two parts of this comparison need to match up: *more…in* one area *than in* another. (B) uses a verb incorrectly, implying that the creative writing itself entered a master's degree program. (C) confuses the meaning of the sentence. (D) doesn't correct the problem and uses the unnecessary *ones*.

8. B

This run-on consists of two separate thoughts joined incorrectly with a comma. (C) muddles the meaning. (D) simply substitutes a better pronoun (*it* to refer to Clearview Media), but without fixing the run-on. (E) uses the semicolon, but by eliminating the verb, results in a clause fragment after the semicolon.

9. B

This sentence compares one collection and, presumably, a second collection, using the idiom *as many…as*. Choices (A) and (C) fail to show correctly which items are being compared, implying that the grandmother, not her collection, holds the figurines. Choices (D) and (E) create the phrase *as many…like*, which is not idiomatic. Additionally, (E) contains a subject and verb that disagree.

10. E

The use of *both* implies that two things will follow, joined by *and*—both one thing and another. The two phrases that follow should be similar in structure. The only choices here that use *and* are (C) and (E). Choices (A), (B), and (D) do not follow the *both…and* pattern. (B) uses the unnecessary *although*. (C) is in the present tense; the sentence is in the past tense. (D) is awkwardly worded and does not complete the *both…and* construction.

11. D

Since it is Professor Hill who had worked on the article, her name needs to follow the modifier. Choices (A), (B), and (C) imply that Professor Hill's disappointment had worked on the article, not Professor Hill herself! (E) rearranges the sentence without correcting the modifier placement issue.

12. C

The subject *main points* requires a plural verb—*were*, not *was*. This eliminates choices (A), (B), and (D). Choices (B) and (D) also contain discrepancies in verb tense. (E) uses the correct form of *were* but incorrect forms of the other two verbs in the sentence.

13. A

The underlined clause serves to provide more information about the subject, *this year's crop*. As it's written, it serves this purpose without interfering with the flow of the sentence. (B) lacks a pronoun to connect the subject and verb and uses the awkward *while also* where *and* would suffice. (C) is unnecessarily wordy and doesn't include the necessary *than* at the end of the phrase. (D) omits the verb *is*, creating a fragment, and then introduces an unnecessary verb, *yields*. (E) is wordy and uses *when* incorrectly.

14. E

As the sentence is set up, the beginning modifier *Styling her hair* needs to be followed by the subject it's modifying. This eliminates choices (A) and (C). Choice (B) rephrases the modifier but does not correct the problem. (B) also uses the present tense incorrectly; the sentence is in the past tense. (C) also misplaces the modifier *the next morning*, confusing the sentence's meaning. (D) creates a run-on sentence.

SAT Practice Test C
Answer Sheet

Remove (or photocopy) this answer sheet and use it to complete the Practice Test. See the answer key following the test when finished. The Compute Your Score section at the back of the book will show you how to find your score.

Section 2

1. Ⓐ Ⓑ Ⓒ Ⓓ Ⓔ
2. Ⓐ Ⓑ Ⓒ Ⓓ Ⓔ
3. Ⓐ Ⓑ Ⓒ Ⓓ Ⓔ
4. Ⓐ Ⓑ Ⓒ Ⓓ Ⓔ
5. Ⓐ Ⓑ Ⓒ Ⓓ Ⓔ
6. Ⓐ Ⓑ Ⓒ Ⓓ Ⓔ
7. Ⓐ Ⓑ Ⓒ Ⓓ Ⓔ
8. Ⓐ Ⓑ Ⓒ Ⓓ Ⓔ
9. Ⓐ Ⓑ Ⓒ Ⓓ Ⓔ
10. Ⓐ Ⓑ Ⓒ Ⓓ Ⓔ

11. Ⓐ Ⓑ Ⓒ Ⓓ Ⓔ
12. Ⓐ Ⓑ Ⓒ Ⓓ Ⓔ
13. Ⓐ Ⓑ Ⓒ Ⓓ Ⓔ
14. Ⓐ Ⓑ Ⓒ Ⓓ Ⓔ
15. Ⓐ Ⓑ Ⓒ Ⓓ Ⓔ
16. Ⓐ Ⓑ Ⓒ Ⓓ Ⓔ
17. Ⓐ Ⓑ Ⓒ Ⓓ Ⓔ
18. Ⓐ Ⓑ Ⓒ Ⓓ Ⓔ
19. Ⓐ Ⓑ Ⓒ Ⓓ Ⓔ
20. Ⓐ Ⓑ Ⓒ Ⓓ Ⓔ

21. Ⓐ Ⓑ Ⓒ Ⓓ Ⓔ
22. Ⓐ Ⓑ Ⓒ Ⓓ Ⓔ
23. Ⓐ Ⓑ Ⓒ Ⓓ Ⓔ
24. Ⓐ Ⓑ Ⓒ Ⓓ Ⓔ
25. Ⓐ Ⓑ Ⓒ Ⓓ Ⓔ
26. Ⓐ Ⓑ Ⓒ Ⓓ Ⓔ
27. Ⓐ Ⓑ Ⓒ Ⓓ Ⓔ
28. Ⓐ Ⓑ Ⓒ Ⓓ Ⓔ
29. Ⓐ Ⓑ Ⓒ Ⓓ Ⓔ
30. Ⓐ Ⓑ Ⓒ Ⓓ Ⓔ

31. Ⓐ Ⓑ Ⓒ Ⓓ Ⓔ
32. Ⓐ Ⓑ Ⓒ Ⓓ Ⓔ
33. Ⓐ Ⓑ Ⓒ Ⓓ Ⓔ
34. Ⓐ Ⓑ Ⓒ Ⓓ Ⓔ
35. Ⓐ Ⓑ Ⓒ Ⓓ Ⓔ

☐ # right

☐ # wrong

Section 3

1. Ⓐ Ⓑ Ⓒ Ⓓ Ⓔ
2. Ⓐ Ⓑ Ⓒ Ⓓ Ⓔ
3. Ⓐ Ⓑ Ⓒ Ⓓ Ⓔ
4. Ⓐ Ⓑ Ⓒ Ⓓ Ⓔ
5. Ⓐ Ⓑ Ⓒ Ⓓ Ⓔ
6. Ⓐ Ⓑ Ⓒ Ⓓ Ⓔ
7. Ⓐ Ⓑ Ⓒ Ⓓ Ⓔ
8. Ⓐ Ⓑ Ⓒ Ⓓ Ⓔ
9. Ⓐ Ⓑ Ⓒ Ⓓ Ⓔ
10. Ⓐ Ⓑ Ⓒ Ⓓ Ⓔ

11. Ⓐ Ⓑ Ⓒ Ⓓ Ⓔ
12. Ⓐ Ⓑ Ⓒ Ⓓ Ⓔ
13. Ⓐ Ⓑ Ⓒ Ⓓ Ⓔ
14. Ⓐ Ⓑ Ⓒ Ⓓ Ⓔ

☐ # right

☐ # wrong

KAPLAN

Practice Test C

Section 1

Essay
Time—25 Minutes (1 Question)

You will have 25 minutes to write your essay in your test booklet (two pages).

Directions: Consider carefully the following statement(s) and the assignment below it.

"The most important days of our lives are those in which we learn something new about ourselves."

—Jesse Pharios

"It's exhilarating to be alive in a time of awakening consciousness; it can also be confusing, disorienting, and painful."

—Adrienne Rich

Assignment: Is it true that the most memorable days of our lives are those in which we underwent some personal transformation or awakening? In an essay, support your position by discussing an example (or examples) from literature, science and technology, the arts, current events, or your own experience or observation.

SAT Practice Test C: **Answer Sheet**

ESSAY. Begin your composition on this side. If you need more space, you may continue on the following page.

SAT Practice Test C: **Answer Sheet**

Continuation of ESSAY from previous page. If you need more space, you may continue on the reverse side.

Continuation of ESSAY from reverse side. Write below if you need more space.

Section 2
Time—25 Minutes (35 Questions)

Directions: The following sentences test correctness and effectiveness of expression. In choosing answers, follow the requirements of standard written English; that is, pay attention to grammar, choice of words, sentence construction, and punctuation.

In each of the following sentences, part of the sentence or the entire sentence is underlined. Beneath each sentence, you will find five ways of phrasing the underlined part. Choice (A) repeats the original; the other four are different.

Choose the answer that best expresses the meaning of the original sentence. If you think the original is better than any of the alternatives, choose it; otherwise, choose one of the others. Your choice should produce the most effective sentence—clear and precise, without awkwardness or ambiguity.

1. Mary Cassatt, an American painter strongly influenced by French <u>impressionism, she also responded</u> to Japanese paintings exhibited in Paris in the 1890s.

   (A) impressionism, she also responded

   (B) impressionism, also responded

   (C) impressionism, also responding

   (D) impressionism, nevertheless, she responded

   (E) impressionism before responding

2. The choreographer Katherine Dunham <u>having trained as an anthropologist, she studied</u> dance in Jamaica, Haiti, and Senegal and developed a distinctive dance method.

   (A) having trained as an anthropologist, she studied

   (B) was also a trained anthropologist, having studied

   (C) was also a trained anthropologist and a student of

   (D) was also a trained anthropologist who studied

   (E) training as an anthropologist, she studied

3. The few surviving writings of Greek philosophers before Plato <u>are not only brief and obscure, but also figurative</u> at times.

   (A) are not only brief and obscure, but also figurative

   (B) are not only brief and obscure, they can be figurative too,

   (C) not only are brief and obscure, but also figurative

   (D) while not only brief and obscure, they also are figurative

   (E) being not only brief and obscure, are also figurative

GO ON TO THE NEXT PAGE

KAPLAN

4. <u>Because its glazed finish resembles a seashell's sur-</u>
<u>face is why porcelain china derives its name from</u>
<u>the French word for the cowrie shell.</u>

   (A) Because its glazed finish resembles a seashell's
        surface is why porcelain china derives its
        name from the French word for the cowrie
        shell.

   (B) Its glazed finish resembling a seashell's sur-
        face, therefore, porcelain china derives its
        name from the French word for the cowrie
        shell.

   (C) Resembling a seashell's surface in its glazed
        finish, that is why porcelain china derives its
        name from the French word for the cowrie
        shell.

   (D) The French word for the cowrie shell gives its
        name to porcelain china because, with its
        glazed finish, its resemblance to a seashell's
        surface.

   (E) Because its glazed finish resembles a seashell's
        surface, porcelain china derives its name from
        the French word for the cowrie shell.

5. <u>In 1891, the Chace Copyright Act began protect-</u>
<u>ing British authors, until then</u> American publish-
ers could reprint British books without paying
their writers.

   (A) In 1891, the Chace Copyright Act began pro-
        tecting British authors, until then

   (B) The Chace Copyright Act began, in 1891,
        protecting British authors, whom, until then

   (C) Although the Chace Copyright Act began
        to protect British authors in 1891, until
        which time

   (D) Before 1891, when the Chace Copyright Act
        began protecting British authors,

   (E) Finally, the Chace Copyright Act began pro-
        tecting British authors in 1891, however,
        until then

6. Theorists of extraterrestrial intelligence depend on
astronomical observations, chemical research, <u>and</u>
<u>they draw inferences about nonhuman biology</u>.

   (A) and they draw inferences about nonhuman
        biology

   (B) while they infer biologically about nonhuman
        life

   (C) and biologically infer about nonhuman life

   (D) as well as drawing inferences biologically
        about nonhuman life

   (E) and biological inferences about nonhuman
        life

7. Even after becoming blind, <u>the poet John Milton's</u>
<u>daughters took dictation of his epic poem</u> *Paradise*
Lost.

   (A) the poet John Milton's daughters took dicta-
        tion of his epic poem *Paradise Lost*

   (B) the poet John Milton's daughters taking dicta-
        tion, his epic poem *Paradise Lost* was written

   (C) the epic poem *Paradise Lost* was dictated by
        the poet John Milton to his daughters

   (D) the epic poem *Paradise Lost* was dictated to
        his daughters by the poet John Milton

   (E) the poet John Milton dictated his epic poem
        Paradise Lost to his daughters

GO ON TO THE NEXT PAGE

8. Initiated in 1975, <u>sandhill cranes must unwittingly cooperate in the conservationists' project to raise</u> endangered whooping crane chicks.

   (A) sandhill cranes must unwittingly cooperate in the conservationists' project to raise

   (B) sandhill cranes' unwitting cooperation is required in the conservationists' project to raise

   (C) the conservationists require that sandhill cranes unwittingly cooperate in their project of raising

   (D) the conservationists require sandhill cranes to cooperate unwittingly in their project to raise

   (E) the conservationists' project requires the unwitting cooperation of sandhill cranes in raising

9. <u>The journalist lived and conversed with the guerrilla rebels and he</u> was finally accepted as an informed interpreter of their cause.

   (A) The journalist lived and conversed with the guerrilla rebels and he

   (B) The journalist living and conversing with the guerrilla rebels, and he

   (C) The journalist, who lived and conversed with the guerrilla rebels,

   (D) The journalist's having lived and conversed with the guerrilla rebels,

   (E) While living and conversing with the guerrilla rebels, the journalist

10. Modern dance and classical ballet help strengthen concentration, tone muscles, <u>and for creating a sense of poise</u>.

    (A) and for creating a sense of poise

    (B) thereby creating a sense of poise

    (C) and the creation of a sense of poise

    (D) and create a sense of poise

    (E) so that a sense of poise is created

11. Historians of literacy encounter a fundamental <u>obstacle, no one can know for certain</u> how many people could read in earlier centuries.

    (A) obstacle, no one can know for certain

    (B) obstacle; no one can know for certain

    (C) obstacle; no one being able to know for certain

    (D) obstacle; none of whom can know with certainty

    (E) obstacle and no one can know for certain

GO ON TO THE NEXT PAGE

Directions: The following sentences test your knowledge of grammar, usage, diction (choice of words), and idiom.

Some sentences are correct.
No sentence contains more than one error.

You will find that the error, if there is one, is underlined and lettered. Elements of the sentence that are not underlined will not be changed. In choosing answers, follow the requirements of standard written English.

If there is an error, select the one underlined part that must be changed to make the sentence correct and fill in the corresponding oval on your answer sheet.

If there is no error, fill in answer oval E.

---

12. <u>Virtually</u> all of the members <u>who</u> attended the
    A   B
    meeting <u>agreed to</u> the president's viewpoint on
            C
    <u>the issue</u> of budgetary restraints. <u>No error</u>
    D   E

13. <u>Fewer</u> U.S. citizens are visiting
    A
    Europe <u>as</u> American currency dwindles in
           B
    exchange value and prices <u>raise</u> <u>in</u> several
                               C   D
    European countries. <u>No error</u>
                         E

14. The first public school in North America,

    Boston Latin School, <u>begun</u> <u>teaching</u> <u>its</u>
                          A   B

    classical curriculum in 1635, one year <u>before</u>
                                            C
    Harvard University <u>was founded</u>. <u>No error</u>
                        D   E

15. <u>Of all</u> the disasters that occurred during the
    A
    movie's production, the death of the two stars

    <u>who</u> performed their own stunts <u>were</u> surely
    B   C
    <u>the worst</u>. <u>No error</u>
    D   E

16. There is no sense <u>in continuing</u> the research, now
                       A
    that the assumptions <u>on which</u> it
                          B
    <u>was based</u> <u>had been</u> disproved. <u>No error</u>
    C   D   E

17. The councilwoman could not understand how

    the mayor <u>could declare</u> that the city
               A
    <u>is thriving</u> <u>when</u> the number of firms declaring
    B   C
    bankruptcy <u>increase</u> every month. <u>No error</u>
                D   E

18. Arthur Rubinstein was long ranked <u>among</u> the
                                       A
    world's finest pianists, <u>although</u> he was sometimes
                              B
    known <u>as playing</u> several wrong notes
           C
    <u>in a single</u> performance. <u>No error</u>
    D   E

19. The new office complex is beautiful, but <u>nearly</u>
                                              A
    two hundred longtime residents <u>were forced</u>
                                    B
    to move when <u>they</u> <u>tore down</u> the old
                  C   D
    apartment buildings. <u>No error</u>
                          E

GO ON TO THE NEXT PAGE ▷

20. Neither the singers <u>on stage</u> <u>or</u> the announcer
                        A   B
    in the wings <u>could be heard</u> <u>over</u> the noise of
                      C   D
    the crowd. <u>No error</u>
                   E

21. The delegates <u>among which</u> the candidates
                      A
    circulated <u>became</u> <u>gradually less</u> receptive and
                   B   C
    more determined <u>to elicit</u> candid responses.
                        D
    <u>No error</u>
       E

22. None of this injury <u>to life</u> and damage to property
                            A
    <u>wouldn't have</u> happened if the amateur
        B
    pilot <u>had only</u> heeded the weather forecasts
              C
    and <u>stayed</u> on the ground. <u>No error</u>
            D   E

23. The doctor recommended that young athletes

    <u>with a history</u> of severe asthma <u>take</u> <u>particular</u>
        A   B   C
    care <u>not to exercise</u> alone. <u>No error</u>
             D   E

24. The piano, although <u>considerably less</u> capable
                            A
    of expressive nuance <u>than many other</u> musical
                             B
    instruments, <u>are</u> <u>marvelously dramatic</u>.
                    C   D
    <u>No error</u>
       E

25. <u>Fewer buildings</u> with granite facades are
        A
    <u>being erected</u> as skilled stonecarvers die out
        B
    and <u>as</u> the cost of granite <u>will soar</u>. <u>No error</u>
           C   D   E

26. However strong the desires for freedom and

    independence, there <u>are</u> <u>invariably</u> a conflicting
                            A   B
    urge <u>toward</u> security, <u>as well as</u> an emotional
             C   D
    need for stability. <u>No error</u>
                            E

27. Hiking along mountain trails <u>is</u> a less expensive
                                    A
    but <u>considerably</u> <u>more demanding</u>
            B   C
    vacation activity than <u>to cruise</u> in the Bahamas.
                               D
    <u>No error</u>
       E

28. <u>Among</u> divergent schools of psychology,
        A
    differences of opinion <u>about</u> human motivation
                               B
    <u>have led</u> to <u>widely different</u> methods of treatment
        C   D
    and research. <u>No error</u>
                      E

29. Even though <u>their</u> commissions <u>are paid</u> by the
                    A   B
    musicians, the <u>typical</u> booking agent represents
                       C
    the interests <u>of</u> the nightclub owners and
                     D
    managers. <u>No error</u>
                  E

GO ON TO THE NEXT PAGE

KAPLAN

Directions: The passage below is an early draft of an essay. Parts of the passage need to be rewritten.

Read the passage and answer the questions that follow. Some questions are about individual sentences or parts of sentences; in these questions, you are asked to select the choice that will improve sentence structure and word choice. Other questions refer to parts of the essay or the entire essay and ask you to consider the organization and development of the essay. You should follow the conventions of standard written English in answering the questions. After you have chosen your answer, fill in the corresponding oval on your answer sheet.

Questions 30–35 are based on the following essay, which was written in response to an assignment to write a letter to the editor of a local newspaper.

(1) I agree with the school board's recent decision to require high school students to complete a community service requirement before graduating. (2) As a student who has both worked and volunteered, my volunteer experience has truly enriched me as a person. (3) When I worked at a hamburger joint all I cared about was the money. (4) Tutoring disadvantaged children taught me to appreciate how much I have.

(5) Volunteering teaches you different lessons than working for pay does. (6) Your paycheck is not your motivation but something higher. (7) In today's consumer-oriented society, it is especially important that students learn to value something other than material things. (8) Taking care of elderly patients at a hospital can teach them respect for age. (9) Getting together with a nonprofit group to clean up abandoned neighborhoods can teach them the importance of teamwork and of doing good for others. (10) There is simply no way they can get so many good lessons out of the types of paying jobs available to them. (11) This is why I support the school board's decision. (12) Furthermore, it is feasible for low-income students, despite what critics have said.

30. Which of the following is the best way to revise the underlined portion of sentence 2 (reproduced below)?

As a student who has both worked and volunteered, my volunteer experience has truly enriched me as a person.

(A) my experience as a volunteer has been the thing that has truly enriched me as a person

(B) I have truly been enriched by my volunteer experience

(C) it is by volunteering that I have truly become an enriched person

(D) I will have truly been enriched by my volunteer experience

(E) that which has truly enriched me as a person is my volunteer experience

GO ON TO THE NEXT PAGE

31. In context, which is the best way to revise and combine the underlined portions of sentences 3 and 4 (reproduced below)?

    When I worked at a hamburger joint, all I was caring about was the money. Tutoring disadvantaged children taught me to appreciate how much I have.

    (A) Working at a hamburger joint, it was only the money that mattered to me, and tutoring disadvantaged children

    (B) While working at a hamburger joint, all I was caring about was the money, until tutoring disadvantaged children

    (C) Although the money was the only thing that mattered to me while working at a hamburger joint, when I tutored disadvantaged children

    (D) Despite working at the hamburger joint, where all I was caring about was the money, by contrast when I was tutoring disadvantaged children

    (E) When I worked at a hamburger joint, all I cared about was the money, but tutoring disadvantaged children

32. In context, which version of sentence 6 (reproduced below) is the clearest?

    Your paycheck is not your motivation but something higher.

    (A) (As it is now)

    (B) Your paycheck is not what motivates you but it is something higher.

    (C) You are motivated not by your paycheck but by something higher.

    (D) Your paycheck is not what you are being motivated by but something higher.

    (E) Not your paycheck, something higher, is your motivation.

33. Which of the following best describes the relationship between sentences 7 and 8?

    (A) Sentence 8 adds to the informatin reported in sentence 7.

    (B) Sentence 8 introduces a new source that confirms the claims made in sentence 7.

    (C) Sentence 8 provides an example to illustrate an idea presented in sentence 7.

    (D) Sentence 8 concludes that the theory mentioned in sentence 7 is wrong.

    (E) Sentence 8 poses an argument that contradicts the point made in sentence 7.

34. In context, which of the following would be best to add at the beginning of sentence 9?

    (A) Then

    (B) Similarly,

    (C) On the other hand,

    (D) Therefore,

    (E) In fact,

35. The author could best improve sentence 12 by

    (A) explaining how the requirement is feasible for low-income students.

    (B) including a definition of "low income."

    (C) outlining other criticisms of the proposal.

    (D) providing examples of volunteer opportunities.

    (E) acknowledging the opinions of high school students.

IF YOU FINISH BEFORE TIME IS CALLED, YOU MAY CHECK YOUR WORK ON THIS SECTION ONLY. DO NOT TURN TO ANY OTHER SECTION IN THE TEST.   STOP

Section 3
Time—10 Minutes (14 Questions)

Directions: The following sentences test correctness and effectiveness of expression. In choosing answers, follow the requirements of standard written English; that is, pay attention to grammar, choice of words, sentence construction, and punctuation.

In each of the following sentences, part of the sentence or the entire sentence is underlined. Beneath each sentence, you will find five ways of phrasing the underlined part. Choice (A) repeats the original; the other four are different.

Choose the answer that best expresses the meaning of the original sentence. If you think the original is better than any of the alternatives, choose it; otherwise, choose one of the others. Your choice should produce the most effective sentence—clear and precise, without awkwardness or ambiguity.

1. Learning that the drama department was in danger of losing its funding, <u>a petition was circulated by the junior class president to persuade school officials</u> to save the program.

   (A) a petition was circulated by the junior class president to persuade school officials

   (B) a petition to persuade school officials was circulated by the junior class president

   (C) school officials were persuaded because of a petition circulated by the junior class president

   (D) the junior class president circulated a petition to persuade school officials

   (E) the junior class president, by way of a petition having been circulated, had persuaded school officials

2. One of the most common mistakes that Algebra I students make is attempting to divide by <u>zero, another error that is often made</u> is failing to change the sign when multiplying by a negative number.

   (A) zero, another error that is often made

   (B) zero; another error that is often made

   (C) zero, the other error, and it is made often

   (D) zero; another error which is often being made

   (E) zero and also an error being made often

3. Genevieve worked overtime to ensure that the center would open on time but refused to have her name <u>be included in the program nor otherwise being acknowledged for her</u> hard work.

   (A) be included in the program nor otherwise being acknowledged for

   (B) included in the program nor otherwise was she acknowledged for

   (C) have been included in the program or otherwise to have been acknowledged for

   (D) included in the program or otherwise acknowledging

   (E) included in the program or to be otherwise acknowledged

4. Having completed two graduate programs, Randall is <u>almost as talented a designer as he is an architect</u>.

   (A) almost as talented a designer as he is an architect

   (B) of almost an equal talent, whether as a designer or an architect

   (C) of the same talent as a designer and as an architect, almost

   (D) a talented designer, with almost as much skill in architecture

   (E) talented as a designer and almost so talented in architecture

GO ON TO THE NEXT PAGE

5. If one attempts to examine the conclusion of the play, the main character's increasing fear of death may be said to mirror the playwright's own struggle with mortality at the end of her life.

   (A) If one attempts to examine the conclusion of the play
   (B) In the conclusion of the play
   (C) When the play's conclusion is looked at
   (D) Considering its conclusion
   (E) Looking at the conclusion during the play

6. Many students refuse to comply with the dress code, in other respects they present no discipline problems, however.

   (A) Many students refuse to comply with the dress code, in other respects they present no discipline problems, however.
   (B) Many students who otherwise present no discipline problems refuse to comply with the dress code.
   (C) Many students refuse to comply with the dress code and present no discipline problems in other respects.
   (D) Although presenting no discipline problems in other respects, many students, however, refuse to comply with the dress code.
   (E) Many of the students which refuse to comply with the dress code present in other respects no discipline problems.

7. Funding for many of the library's renovation projects, including the new children's room and the Skillman wing, donated by private sources.

   (A) donated by
   (B) it was donated by
   (C) it has been donated by
   (D) was donated by
   (E) which was donated by

8. As exempt employees, the Human Resources department remind you that you are not entitled to claim overtime pay on your timesheets.

   (A) As exempt employees, the Human Resources department remind you that you
   (B) As exempt employees, the Human Resources department reminds you that you
   (C) You, as exempt employees, are reminded by the Human Resources department, and you
   (D) The Human Resources department, who remind you that you, as exempt employees,
   (E) The Human Resources department reminds you that as exempt employees, you

9. Beginning her tour of the museum, do not touch the bronze sculptures was the request that Julia made of the group.

   (A) do not touch the bronze sculptures was the request that Julia made of the group
   (B) the bronze sculptures were what Julia requested that her group not touch
   (C) her group was requested by Julia not to touch the bronze sculptures
   (D) the bronze sculptures, requested Julia, were what the group should not touch
   (E) Julia requested that her group not touch the bronze sculptures

10. Maurice reads *The New York Times* more frequently than our other coworkers because of having a subscription.

    (A) coworkers because of having a subscription
    (B) coworkers, this is the result of his having a subscription
    (C) coworkers because he has a subscription
    (D) coworkers as a result of his having a subscription
    (E) coworkers since he is one of its subscribers

GO ON TO THE NEXT PAGE

KAPLAN

11. The love letters that Grace's father wrote to her mother <u>begin by describing his parents' hometown in France and conclude</u> with the news that he is being sent home from the war.

   (A) begin by describing his parents' hometown in France and conclude

   (B) that begin by describing his parents' hometown in France and conclude

   (C) have begun by describing his parents' hometown in France and concluding

   (D) beginning by describing his parents' hometown in France and concluding

   (E) are begun by describing his parents' hometown in France and concluded

12. Javier, the leader of the hiking trip, could not attempt to scale the cliff until he <u>can find a partner who is as skilled as he is</u>.

   (A) can find a partner who is as skilled as he is

   (B) could find a partner who was as skilled as he was

   (C) would be able to find a partner who is as skilled as he is

   (D) can find a partner who had a skill equal to his own skill

   (E) could find a partner who has a skill equal to his own skill

13. Because the editor insists that the *Daily Sun* be virtually free of errors, <u>it is a staff of several proofreaders who carefully review each article before it goes to print</u>.

   (A) it is a staff of several proofreaders who carefully review each article before it goes to print

   (B) a staff of several proofreaders carefully reviews each article before it goes to print

   (C) each article being carefully reviewed before it goes to press by a staff of several proofreaders

   (D) the staff of several proofreaders review, carefully and before it goes to print, each article

   (E) the staff of proofreaders are the ones carefully reviewing each article before it goes to print

14. Outsourcing jobs to a consulting firm in another country is more cost-effective than paying employees locally, but <u>overwhelmingly negative are its effects on customer satisfaction</u>.

   (A) overwhelmingly negative are its effects on customer satisfaction

   (B) it has overwhelmingly negative customer satisfaction effects

   (C) in its customer satisfaction effects it is overwhelmingly negative

   (D) there are the overwhelmingly negative effects in customer satisfaction

   (E) its effects on customer satisfaction are overwhelmingly negative

IF YOU FINISH BEFORE TIME IS CALLED, YOU MAY CHECK YOUR WORK ON THIS SECTION ONLY. DO NOT TURN TO ANY OTHER SECTION IN THE TEST. **STOP**

KAPLAN

Answers and Explanations

SECTION 1

The Essay

This section contains sample essays for the essay topic in Practice Test C. Use these sample essays as benchmarks to help you grade your own essay on the same topic. Does your essay sound more like the grade 6 essay or the grade 4 essay?

Sample Grade 6 Essay

People often complain that our generation is politically apathetic. Just 25 years ago, it was common for students to join in strikes and antiwar protests, but nowadays, the stereotype goes, young people are more likely to be found watching YouTube or shopping at the mall. I certainly was no different. Appallingly ignorant of current events, I never read a paper or watched the news, but I knew all about the personal lives of popular TV and movie stars. Then something happened to change my outlook forever.

In my social studies class, we had an assignment to interview an older person about the changes he or she had witnessed in his or her lifetime. I decided to interview my neighbor, Mrs. Fletcher. Since she had never spoken to me much before, I figured she would have little to say and I could complete the assignment quickly. Instead she started telling me all about life in our town before the civil rights movement. I was astonished to learn that in the 1950s, blacks went to separate schools, rode at the backs of buses, and were prevented from living in white neighborhoods. As Mrs. Fletcher talked about how she and other African Americans helped break the color barrier by insisting on being served at white-only lunch counters, I became filled with shame at my own ignorance. How could I have been so unaware?

From that moment onward, politics and history became my passions. In school we had been taught that there was no society freer than the United States, but that was only part of the story. By reading about the political struggles of minorities, women, blue-collar workers, and others, I learned that freedom is not something you're given, it's something you have to fight for. And once you win it, you have to make sure no one tries to take it away again. I learned so much from Mrs. Fletcher that day, and our conversation transformed me forever. I developed an awareness of the world around me, became less self-absorbed, and took a very important lesson from the past: progress begins with people who choose to stand up for what is right. It was like I'd had a rebirth after talking with Mrs. Fletcher, and that is why I agree with the idea that the most memorable days of our lives are those in which we learn something new about ourselves and experience an awakening.

Grader's comments: This essay is outstanding. Its ideas are well developed, well organized, and supported by appropriate evidence. Furthermore, the writing flows nicely as a result of the varied sentence structure and vocabulary.

Sample Grade 4 Essay

One day I will never forget because I had a major awakening is the day my father got laid off from work. I was about 12 at the time and I selfishly wanted a new bike. When I got home from school, my father was already home. This surprised me for a minute but I plunged on: "Daddy, can I have a new bike? All the other kids have ten-speed mountain bikes and I don't even have a three-speed. Please Daddy?" He looked down at me and I saw there were tears in his eyes. "I'm sorry but we can't afford it. I was just laid off." I didn't understand what that meant yet but over the next few months I would learn. It meant school shopping at thrift shops instead of department stores. It meant no steak, only chicken or spaghetti. It meant no eating out on weekends. And no new bike. I had to learn to accept all these new changes in my life.

But the good thing was it taught me to be more self reliant. My parents couldn't afford to give me my allowence any more so I got a paper route. This was the first time I ever had to work and it taught me the disipline of getting up early, getting a job done, plus saving money and not just spending it all at once. I guess you could say every cloud has a silver lining. My dad got laid off and was out of work for several months and then had to take a much lower paying one. But even though it wasn't a great experience, it still made me have a personal trasformation and because of that one thing for sure: I'll never forget that day.

Grader's comments: This essay demonstrates adequate competence. Although it displays some grammatical errors and some lapses in quality, the essay's overall organization and development are clear, and its ideas are supported with appropriate evidence.

Sample Grade 2 Essay

My life has been filled with alot of good days. For instance, the day I passed my math test was a good day. My life has also been filled with many bad days. Like, the day when I was a kid and I fell down and broke my arm. That was certainly a day you could classify as "bad". Then there are the days I don't remember, which covers most of them because how often is it that something truely memorible happens in a day? Most days you just get up, go to school, come home, do chores or homework, eat dinner, watch a little TV and go to bed so you can get up and do it all over again. But one day I'll never, ever, ever forget is the day I met my best friend Jill. She lived down the street from me but we went to differant schools so we didn't see much of each other. Anyway it was summer vacation so we both happened to be around. I was going to the local swimming pool and my mother said why don't we invite Jill from down the street. So I did. We had such a good time that day, standing on our hands on the bottom of the pool, seeing who could hold their breathe the longest, jumping off the high diving board, etc. We made so much noise the life guard had to tell us to be quiet! I never liked her much, she was always so stuck up. We spent the whole day together. Then I asked my mother if Jill could come over for dinner and she said "YES". She even spent the night! I'd never had a slumber party before. From then on we were inseperable. So that was really I day I won't ever forget, as long as I live I'll remember it because I learned something new about myself. I learned that you never know who youll like and become best friends with, even if you didn't like them at first. Life is just funny that way.

Grader's comments: This essay is flawed. It's poorly organized, tends to ramble, is repetitive, and strays from the assigned topic. Development is thin at best and ideas are not especially well supported. Errors in grammar, diction, and sentence structure are numerous.

The Multiple-Choice Section

Answer Key

Section 2			
1.	B	18.	C
2.	D	19.	C
3.	A	20.	B
4.	E	21.	A
5.	D	22.	B
6.	E	23.	A
7.	E	24.	C
8.	E	25.	D
9.	C	26.	A
10.	D	27.	D
11.	B	28.	E
12.	C	29.	A
13.	C	30.	B
14.	A	31.	E
15.	C	32.	C
16.	D	33.	C
17.	D	34.	B
		35.	A

Section 3	
1.	D
2.	B
3.	E
4.	A
5.	B
6.	B
7.	D
8.	E
9.	E
10.	C
11.	A
12.	B
13.	B
14.	E

Section 2

1. B

The subject of the sentence is *Mary Cassatt*; the noun phrase *an American painter strongly influenced by French impressionism* is an appositive. The pronoun *she* is therefore an extra subject, completely superfluous in (A) and (D). (B) correctly omits this pronoun. (C) and (E) also omit the pronoun, but they change the present-tense verb into a present participle, which can't act as a verb all by itself.

2. D

The original sentence turns the whole first part of the sentence into an elliptical clause. It's awkward, and the chronology becomes muddled. (B), (C), and (E) all start the same, but then diverge after *anthropologist*. (B) implies that Dunham's development of *a distinctive dance method* was part of her training as an anthropologist, but that's not very likely. (C) links so many ideas with *and* that it's hard to tell what goes with what. (E) totally muddies the chronology and other links among various parts of the sentence.

3. A

The original sentence is best. The parallelism of the construction *not only...but also...* goes awry in the revisions.

4. E

If you eliminate all of the clutter, the original sentence boils down to *Because...is why...*, a grammatically and idiomatically unacceptable construction. The original sentence is also wordy and convoluted. (E) is the best available sentence.

5. D

Choices (A) and (E) are comma splices. *Whom* is unnecessary in (B). (C) is a fragment.

6. E

Items in a list joined by *and* or *or* should be grammatically parallel. This sentence lists two noun phrases and an independent clause. (E) provides a third noun phrase.

7. E

John Milton has to be the subject of the sentence. The introductory phrase in this sentence can't modify anything else.

8. E

An introductory modifying phrase must modify the subject of the sentence. Since the introductory phrase isn't underlined, the subject must be changed. It's the *project*, not the *cranes* or the *conservationists*, that was initiated in 1975. (E) gets it right.

9. C

The original sentence is a run-on, in which two independent clauses are improperly coordinated without linking punctuation. (C) corrects this problem by transforming one clause into a dependent clause.

10. D

Items in a list must be parallel. In this sentence, neither of the first two items is underlined. Each is a predicate consisting of a verb and direct object, so the third item must also be a predicate—not a prepositional phrase.

11. B

A semicolon separates two complete, but related, sentences.

12. C

Agreed to and *agreed with* are both perfectly good idioms, but they mean different things. This context calls for *agreed with*.

13. C

Unlike *rise*, *raise* requires a direct object. Prices can't raise by themselves; something or someone has to raise them.

14. A

Even if you didn't know that a past participle can't stand alone, *begun* should still have "sounded" wrong to you.

15. C

The subject isn't *stunts, stars,* or *disasters*, but *death*, a singular noun. Therefore, the verb must be singular. *Was* is correct here.

16. D

Temporarily ignoring the clause *on which it was based*, the phrase *now that* strongly suggests that the disproving has happened recently. The verb should be *have been*: the present perfect, used to represent a present state as the outcome of recent past events, or to express actions occurring in the past and continuing in the present.

17. D

The subject of the clause is *number*, not *firms*. Thus, a singular verb, *increases*, is needed.

18. C

The correct answer is *to play*.

19. C

Who tore down the old buildings? Surely not the *longtime residents.* The antecedent—some group such as *landlords* or *developers*—is missing.

20. B

Neither calls for *nor*.

21. A

Which can't refer to people; *that* or *who* or *whom* should be used instead. This sentence calls for *whom*.

22. B

To see the double negative more easily, remove the intervening words: *None of this…wouldn't have happened.* The correct phrase is *would have.*

23. A

In this sentence, the plural noun *athletes* is modified by the prepositional phrase *with a history of severe asthma.* But the athletes don't have a collective medical history; each athlete has his or her own. The sentence should read either *young athletes with histories of severe asthma* or *a young athlete with a history of severe asthma.* Since the prepositional phrase is underlined, it must be changed.

24. C

The subject of this sentence, *piano*, is singular. Thus, the main verb must also be singular: *is* instead of *are.*

25. D

The ongoing decline in façade building is happening *simultaneously with* (and as a result of) two other ongoing developments. *Soar* should be in the same tense as *die*, because these two trends coincide. Both verbs should be in the present tense, because although these trends are continuing into the future, they're also happening now.

26. A

Urge is the only true subject in this sentence (*as well as* doesn't create a true compound subject). Therefore, *are* should be *is.*

27. D

Elements of comparison should be parallel. *Hiking* is not underlined, so we have to change the infinitive to a gerund to match. *Cruising* is correct.

28. E

This sentence contains no error.

29. A

Their should be singular, since its antecedent is *the typical booking agent*, which is singular.

30. B

The sentence contains a dangling modifier: *my volunteer experience* cannot be modified by a clause beginning *As a student…* (B) fixes this problem by recasting the sentence so that *I* is the subject. Of the wrong choices, only (D) correctly uses *I* as the subject, but (D)'s use of the future tense is inconsistent with the rest of the sentence.

31. E

E corrects the inconsistency in tense and skillfully conveys the sense of contrast between the two clauses with the conjunction *but.* Choice (A) contains a misplaced modifier. The clause *Working at a hamburger joint*, which describes the author, must be followed by *I*, not *it*, and does not convey any idea of contrast. (B), too, contains a misplaced modifier, and its use of *until* changes the original meaning of the sentence. (C) is incorrect in context because of its use of *when*. (D) is also incorrect in context because of its use of *when*; moreover, its use of *Despite* is inappropriate.

32. C

Although it is clear from the context that the author means that one is motivated by something higher than a mere paycheck, in the sentence as written it sounds as though it is the paycheck, not the motivation, that is *something higher*. (C) is the only choice that clearly conveys the correct meaning. (B), (D), and (E) have the same problem in meaning as the original sentence; moreover, (D) is unnecessarily wordy, and (E) is awkward and grammatically incorrect.

33. C

This sentence offers the example of taking care of the elderly to illustrate that students can learn to value nonmaterial things (as expressed in sentence 7).

34. B

Look at the relationship between sentences 8 and 9. They both provide examples in support of sentence 7, so the proper connecting word would show that these are closely related ideas. (B) does this best. The other choices misrepresent the relationship between the sentences.

35. A

Sentence 12 brings up an entirely new idea at the end of the essay and would therefore be best improved if it expanded on this idea, as (A) suggests. As for (B), there is no need for a definition of *low income*, since this is a commonly used term. Including other criticisms would only introduce more new ideas at the last minute, so (C) is no good. (D) fails because the author gives examples of volunteer opportunities elsewhere in the essay. Finally, (E) is out because student opinion is irrelevant.

Section 3

1. D

A correctly written sentence will follow an opening modifying phrase with the subject that is modified. As it's written, this sentence seems to say that the petition learned about the funding cut for the drama department! The correct answer will follow the modifier (learning about the cut) with the person who did the action (the junior class president). (B) and (C) do nothing to correct the problem, but simply rearrange the words in a new, yet still incorrect, order. (D) and (E) both place the subject correctly within the sentence. Of the two, (D) is worded more clearly and avoids unnecessary shifts in verb tense, so it is the correct answer.

2. B

This sentence incorrectly uses a comma to connect two independent clauses. You can rule out (C) immediately because it includes the same error. (B) connects the two clauses correctly and is the most simply worded of the choices, so it is the correct answer. (D) uses the semicolon correctly but introduces an unnecessarily wordy verb, *is often being made*. (E) has no verb in the second clause; *being made* is the modifier form.

3. E

The length and wordiness of this sentence make it difficult to take apart, but an understanding of what's being said will be invaluable in finding the correct choice. Genevieve worked overtime to help the center open on time, but she wouldn't allow two things: to have her name included in the program or to be acknowledged in any other way. (B) is incorrect because it fails to convey that Genevieve refused to be acknowledged. (C) uses varying verb tenses and confuses the meaning of the sentence. (D) also mixes verb tenses. (E) is correct; it keeps verbs in the same tense, expresses the meaning effectively, and maintains a parallel construction.

4. A

Comparison questions often test your ability to decide which choice presents the information in the most straight-forward way. In this case, while each choice presents the same comparison, all but (A) are unnecessarily wordy. (B) and (C) create phrases that are not idiomatic (*of an almost equal talent* and *of the same talent*). (D) comes closest to expressing the comparison correctly, but is still not stated as succinctly as (A). (E) is wordy and, again, creates a non-idiomatic phrase, *almost so talented*. The sentence is correct as it stands.

5. B

This question requires you to choose the most appropriate introductory clause or phrase. (A) and (C) both introduce the fact that the play's conclusion is being discussed, but both are wordy, particularly (C), which uses a passive verb. (B) is the best choice here and effectively expresses the information without adding any confusing phrasing. (D) uses a possessive pronoun, *its*, which has no antecedent in the sentence. (E) is awkwardly worded and confuses the meaning of the phrase.

6. B

The use of the comma to connect two independent thoughts should tip you off immediately that this sentence, as written, is a run-on. (B) is the correct choice here; it corrects the run-on and reorders the sentence in a way that makes sense to readers. (C) lacks the element of contrast presented in the original sentence; the use of *however* tells us that the author is trying to say, "Many students don't comply with the dress code, but they don't present other discipline problems." (D) is redundant, using both *however* and *although* when one of them would suffice. Finally, (E) uses the wrong pronoun (*which* rather than *who*) and is awkwardly phrased.

7. D

The sentence is a fragment containing no verb. (D) corrects this. (B) needlessly adds the pronoun *it*, which doesn't have a clear antecedent. (C) repeats that error and changes the verb tense. (E), introduced by *which*, is another subordinate clause.

8. E

As exempt employees needs to be followed by the thing it's modifying: not *the Human Resources department*, but *you*. Additionally, the subject and verb don't agree. (E) corrects both problems. (B) corrects the verb agreement but doesn't address the modifier problem. (C) uses an unnecessary passive verb. (D) is a fragment.

9. E

The modifier *Beginning her tour of the museum* needs to be followed by the subject of the sentence: Julia. Only (E) does this. (B) and (C) would imply that the sculptures were beginning a tour. (D) introduces an unnecessary passive verb.

10. C

Because of having is not idiomatic, and the verb tense is incorrect. (C) is the best choice, since it states the answer clearly and with no extra words. Why does he read the *Times* more frequently than his coworkers? Because he has a subscription. (B) is a run-on sentence. (D) and (E) are unnecessarily wordy.

11. A

Because the sentence does not express a shift in time, both verbs should be in the same tense. (A) is the only choice that maintains a consistent tense. (B) and (D) create fragments. (C) and (E) introduce an incorrect shift in tense.

12. B

The verb tense in the answer choice should be consistent with the tense in the rest of the sentence. He *could not* attempt to scale the cliff, so the correct choice will also use *could*. (The past tense would also be correct.) (C) and (D) use incorrect verb forms and keep the tense from being consistent within the sentence. (E) is wordy and incorrectly uses the present tense.

13. B

The *it is...who* construction here is wordy and serves no purpose in the sentence. (B) removes the construction without altering the wording of the sentence. (C) creates a fragment and also uses an unnecessary passive verb. (D) misplaces the modifiers in the sentence. (E) simply replaces one wordy construction with another (*are the ones*).

14. E

The subject and action are in the wrong order in this sentence. (E) corrects the unnecessary reversal. (B) does nothing to solve the problem. (C) creates the awkward phrase *customer satisfaction effects*. (D) unnecessarily introduces the phrase *there are the* and uses *in* where *on* is correct.

Compute Your Score

Your Writing score report will reflect three different scores: an essay subscore, a multiple-choice subscore, and an overall score, the most important of the three. Here are step-by-step instructions for calculating subscores and overall scores for the Practice Tests in this book.

These scores are intended to give you an approximate idea of your performance. There is no way to determine your exact score for the following reasons:

- Various statistical factors and formulas are taken into account on the real test.
- For each grade, the scaled score range changes from year to year.
- There is no way to accurately grade your essay on these Practice Tests. Additionally, there will be two graders reading your essay on the real test.

The official score range for each section of the SAT will be 200–800. Taken together, the perfect total score becomes 2400.

STEP 1: CALCULATE YOUR ESSAY SUBSCORE

Read through your essay carefully and use the Essay Grading Criteria to assign a 1–6 score to it. Better still, have a parent, older sibling, or trusted teacher read the essay and assign a score. Note your essay score for each Practice Test in the boxes on page 258.

Essay Grading Criteria

6 Outstanding Essay—convincingly and insightfully fulfills the writing assignment; ideas are well developed, clearly presented, and logically organized; superior command of vocabulary, grammar, style, and accepted conventions of writing; a few minor flaws may occur.

5 Solid Essay—convincingly fulfills the writing assignment; ideas are adequately developed, clearly presented, and logically organized; strong command of vocabulary, grammar, style, and accepted conventions of writing; some minor flaws may occur.

4 Adequate Essay—fulfills the writing assignment; ideas are adequately developed, presented, and organized; satisfactory command of vocabulary, grammar, style, and accepted conventions of writing; some flaws may occur.

3 Limited Essay—doesn't adequately fulfill the writing assignment; ideas aren't adequately developed, clearly presented, or logically organized; unsatisfactory command of vocabulary, grammar, style, and accepted conventions of writing; contains many flaws.

2 Flawed Essay—doesn't fulfill the writing assignment; ideas are vague, poorly presented, and not logically organized; poor command of vocabulary, grammar, style, and accepted conventions of writing; contains numerous serious flaws.

1 Deficient Essay—doesn't fulfill the writing assignment; ideas are extremely vague, very poorly presented, and not logically organized; extremely poor command of vocabulary, grammar, style, and accepted conventions of writing; is so seriously flawed that basic meaning is obscured.

Essay Score

Test A: ☐

Test B: ☐

Test C: ☐

STEP 2: FIND YOUR MULTIPLE-CHOICE SUBSCORE

Refer to your Practice Test answer sheet for the number of questions you answered right and the number you answered wrong. You can use the chart below as a guide to calculate your raw score. Multiply the number wrong by .25, and subtract the result from the number right. Round your raw score to the nearest whole number. This is your multiple-choice raw score.

PRACTICE TEST A

	Number Right	Number Wrong	Raw Score
Section 2:	☐	− (.25 × ☐)	= ☐
Section 3:	☐	− (.25 × ☐)	= ☐

Raw Score = ☐
(rounded up)

PRACTICE TEST B

	Number Right	Number Wrong	Raw Score
Section 2:	☐	− (.25 × ☐)	= ☐
Section 3:	☐	− (.25 × ☐)	= ☐

Raw Score = ☐
(rounded up)

PRACTICE TEST C

	Number Right	Number Wrong	Raw Score
Section 2:	☐	− (.25 × ☐)	= ☐
Section 3:	☐	− (.25 × ☐)	= ☐
		Raw Score =	☐
		(rounded up)	

STEP 3: CONVERT YOUR RAW SCORE TO A SCALED SCORE

SCALED						
Essay 0	Essay 1	Essay 2	Essay 3	Essay 4	Essay 5	Essay 6
670	700	720	740	780	790	800
660	680	700	730	760	780	790
650	670	690	720	750	770	780
640	660	680	710	740	750	770
630	650	670	700	740	750	770
620	640	660	690	730	750	760
600	630	650	680	710	740	750
600	620	640	670	700	730	750
590	610	630	660	690	730	740
580	600	620	650	690	720	740
570	590	610	640	680	710	740
560	590	610	630	670	700	730
550	580	600	630	660	690	720
540	570	590	620	650	680	710
540	560	580	610	640	680	710
530	550	570	600	640	670	700
520	540	560	590	630	660	690
510	540	560	580	620	650	680
500	530	550	580	610	640	670
490	520	540	570	600	630	660
490	510	530	560	590	630	650
480	500	520	550	590	620	640
470	490	510	540	580	610	640
460	490	500	530	570	600	630
450	480	500	520	560	590	620

440	470	490	510	550	580	610
430	460	480	510	540	570	600
430	450	470	500	530	570	590
430	450	470	500	530	570	590
420	440	460	490	520	560	580
410	430	450	480	520	550	570
400	420	440	470	510	540	570
390	420	430	460	500	530	560
380	410	430	450	490	520	550
370	400	420	450	480	510	540
360	390	410	440	470	500	530
360	380	400	430	460	500	520
340	370	390	420	450	490	510
340	360	380	410	450	480	510
330	350	370	400	440	470	500
320	350	360	390	430	460	490
310	340	360	390	420	450	480
300	330	350	380	410	440	470
290	320	340	370	400	430	460
290	310	330	360	390	430	450
280	300	320	350	390	420	450
270	290	310	340	380	410	440
260	280	300	330	370	400	430
250	270	290	320	340	380	410
250	260	280	310	340	370	400
240	260	270	290	320	360	380
230	250	260	270	310	340	370
220	240	250	260	300	330	360
220	230	240	250	290	320	350
200	220	230	240	280	310	340
200	210	220	240	280	310	340
200	210	220	230	270	300	330
200	210	220	230	270	300	330
200	210	220	230	270	300	330
200	210	220	230	270	300	330